D0908487

the Question:

the five
Books
of
blood

Greg Rucka
Writer

"The Lesson of Deceit" . . . . Art by Tom Mandrake

"The Lesson of Lust" . . . . Art by Jesus Saiz

"The Lesson of Greed" . . . . Art by Matthew Clark

"The Lesson of Murder" . . . . Art by Diego Olmos

"The Parable of The Faceless"
Art by Manuel Garcia (with Jimmy Palmiotti)

Book of Blood chapter page art & design by
Steve Lieber & Eric Trautmann

David Baron, Santi Arcas, Javier Mena
Colorists

Steve Wands, Rob Leigh
Letterers

John Van Fleet
Original Covers

the Question:

the five Books of blood

Dan DiDio Senior VP-Executive Editor **Michael Siglain** Editor-original series **Harvey Richards** Assistant Editor-original series **Anton Kawasaki** Editor-collected edition
Robbin Brosterman Senior Art Director **Paul Levitz** President & Publisher **Georg Brewer** VP-Design & DC Direct Creative **Richard Bruning** Senior VP-Creative Director
Patrick Caldon Executive VP-Finance & Operations **Chris Caramalis** VP-Finance **John Cunningham** VP-Marketing **Terri Cunningham** VP-Managing Editor
Alison Gill VP-Manufacturing **David Hyde** VP-Publicity **Hank Kanalz** VP-General Manager, WildStorm **Jim Lee** Editorial Director-WildStorm
Paula Lowitt Senior VP-Business & Legal Affairs **MaryEllen McLaughlin** VP-Advertising & Custom Publishing **John Nee** Senior VP-Business Development
Gregory Noveck Senior VP-Creative Affairs **Sue Pohja** VP-Book Trade Sales **Steve Rotterdam** Senior VP-Sales & Marketing **Cheryl Rubin** Senior VP-Brand Management
Jeff Trojan VP-Business Development, DC Direct **Bob Wayne** VP-Sales

Cover by **John Van Fleet**

 Printed in USA. First Printing. ISBN: 978-1-4012-1799-0

The First Book of Blood
Chapter 8, Verses 16–27

¹⁶ Then to the host assembled the Caitiff raised the stone high, so that all might gaze upon it, and see the stain he had placed upon it.

¹⁷ Thus spake the Caitiff, Behold! The Red Rock, anointed by the blood of my brother; for in my hand I hold Murder, and thus hold Murder over all who walk this Earth.

¹⁸ And believing this, the foolish host did as commanded, and did fall upon knee, and so granted much power to him.

¹⁹ Then to the Defile the Caitiff descended, where he went amongst them; and all the host hid their eyes in darkness from him as the Caitiff passed, and thus he took from them what service he pleased; and their screaming and sobbing did fill the very depths of the heavens.

²⁰ So it was that to the Defile came the First in His wanderings, and bearing witness to the Caitiff's blasphemy, found Himself much amused by the villainy seen there.

²¹ And His laughter echoed through all the gorge, and even the gathered host were much disturbed at His merriment, and turned from fear of one to fear another themselves; and they did raise countenance to behold Him.

²² And it was the Caitiff, so devoted in his deception, gazed upon Him, but did not see; and enraged, he confronted the First, saying, Wanderer, thou makest mock of Murder, and would demand its reckoning upon you.

²³ Then the First did reveal His palm to the Caitiff and all his followers; and showing in it the Stain, spake thus, saying, By Deceit ye have freed yourself from the illusion of truth, and thus do I name this the First Lesson of Blood.

²⁴ But ye have also fallen as its prey, and in all the glories of Deceit, there can be but one sin; make not your deception become your truth, and thus make a slavery of it.

²⁵ And then the First brought forth the shard of Red Rock from His palm, and it shone with the blood of His brother; and laughing, He did bury it deep in the sinister eye of the Caitiff.

²⁷ Then the following host did panic, and seek to flee the Defile of Sem for their kind.

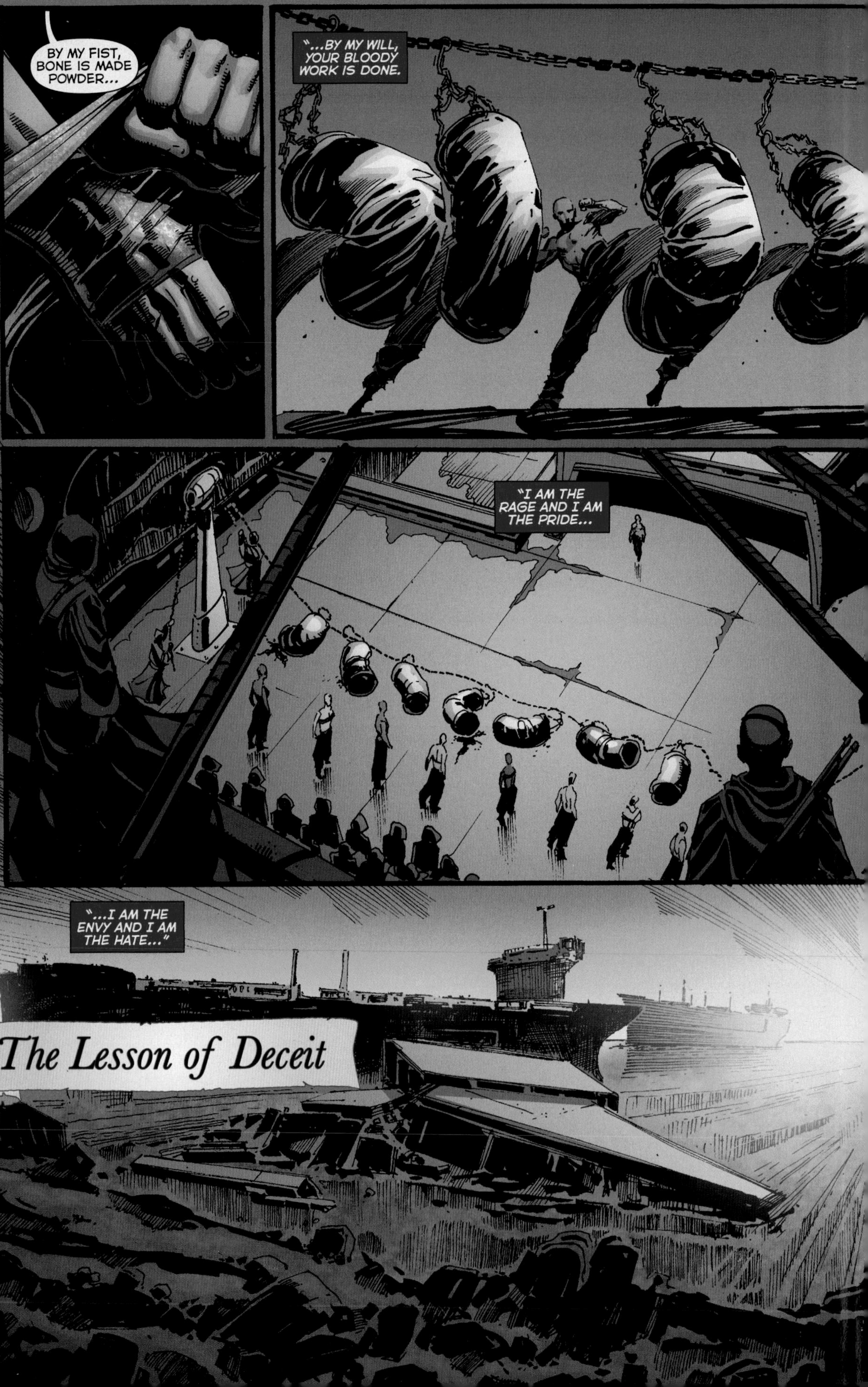
BY MY FIST, BONE IS MADE POWDER...
"...BY MY WILL, YOUR BLOODY WORK IS DONE.
"I AM THE RAGE AND I AM THE PRIDE...
"...I AM THE ENVY AND I AM THE HATE..."
The Lesson of Deceit

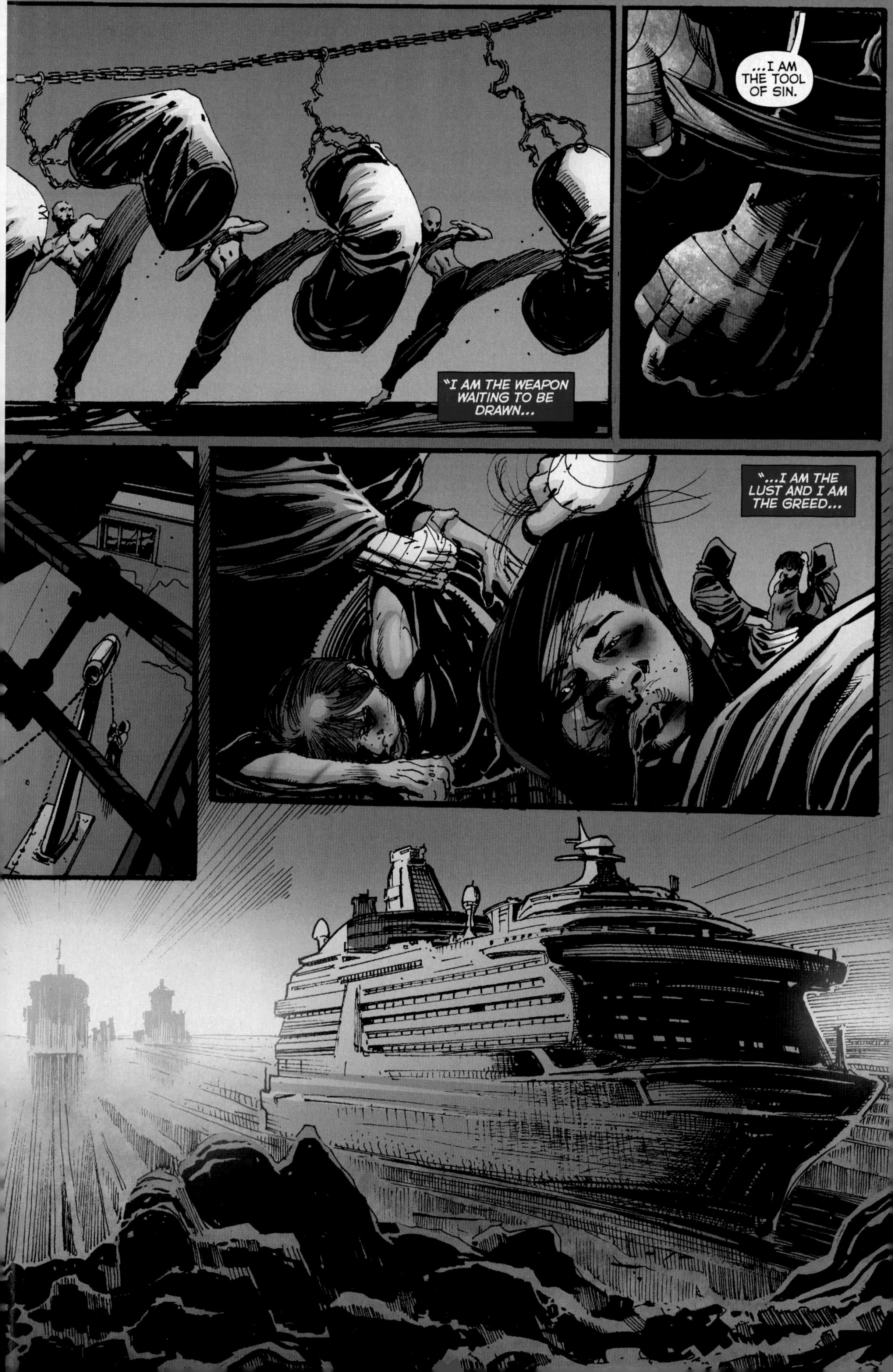
"I AM THE WEAPON WAITING TO BE DRAWN...
...I AM THE TOOL OF SIN.
"...I AM THE LUST AND I AM THE GREED...

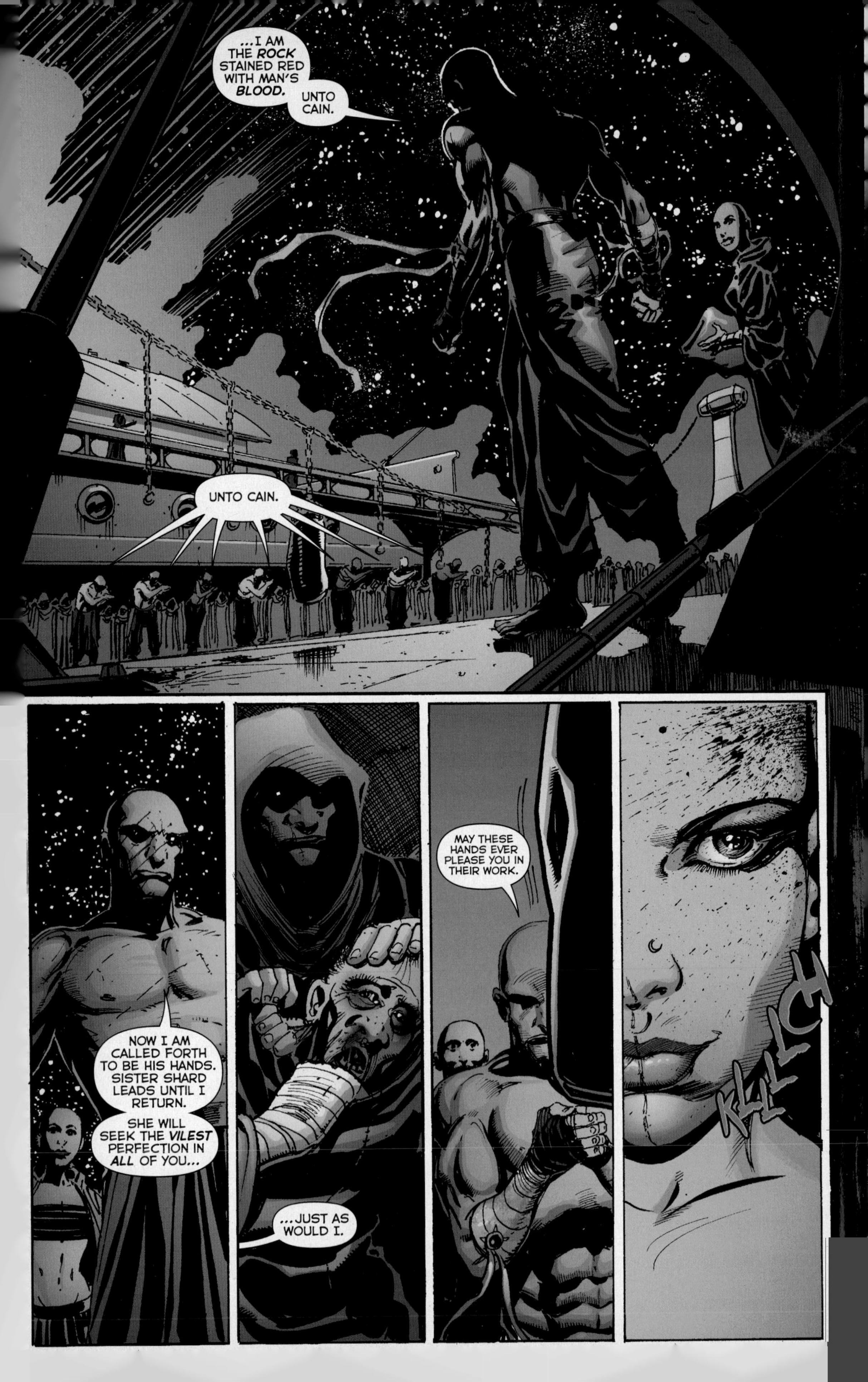
...I AM THE *ROCK* STAINED RED WITH MAN'S *BLOOD.*
UNTO CAIN.
UNTO CAIN.
NOW I AM CALLED FORTH TO BE HIS HANDS. SISTER SHARD LEADS UNTIL I RETURN.
SHE WILL SEEK THE *VILEST* PERFECTION IN *ALL* OF YOU...
...JUST AS WOULD I.
MAY THESE HANDS EVER PLEASE YOU IN THEIR WORK.
KLLLCH

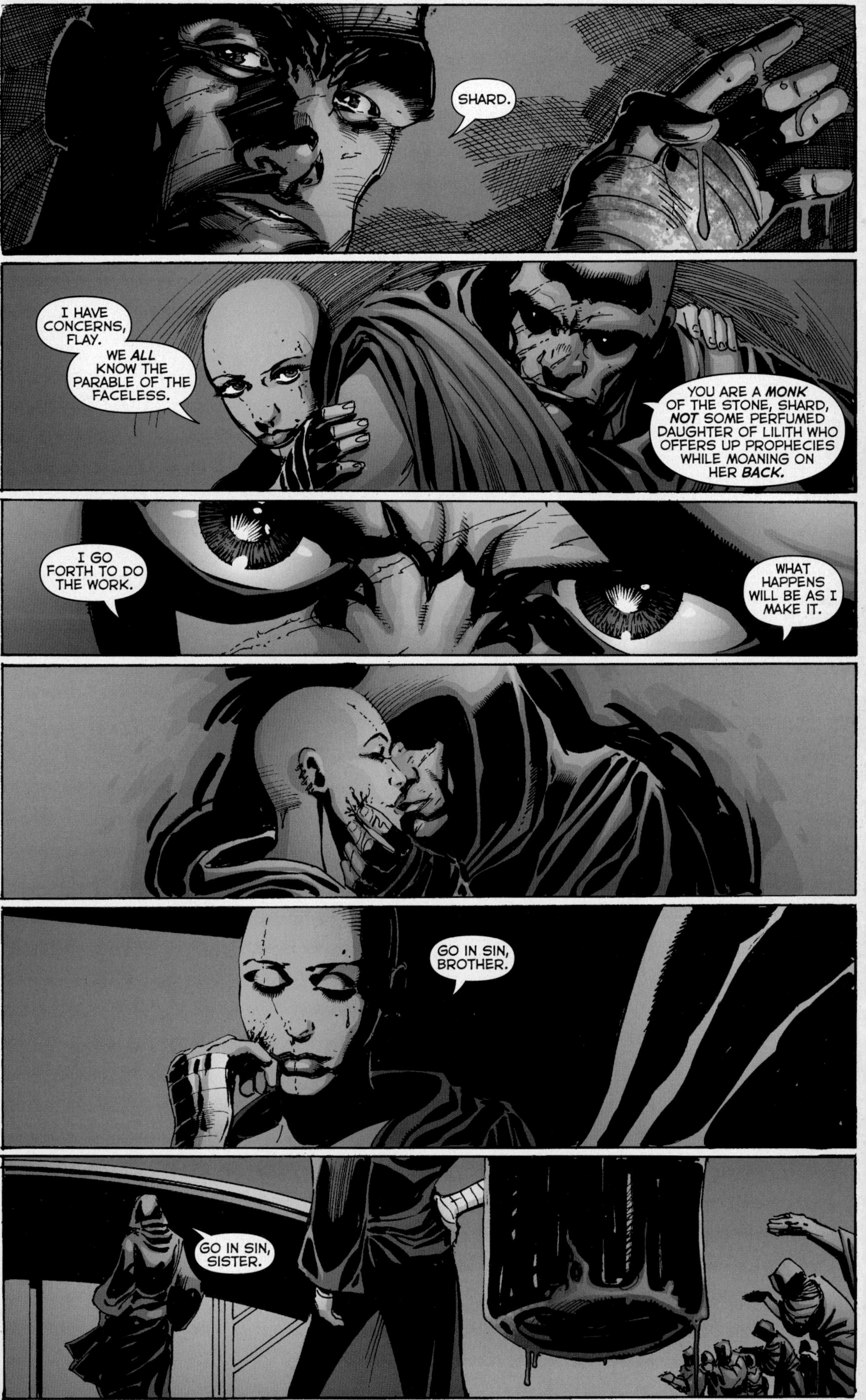
SHARD.
I HAVE CONCERNS, FLAY.
WE ALL KNOW THE PARABLE OF THE FACELESS.
YOU ARE A MONK OF THE STONE, SHARD, NOT SOME PERFUMED DAUGHTER OF LILITH WHO OFFERS UP PROPHECIES WHILE MOANING ON HER BACK.
I GO FORTH TO DO THE WORK.
WHAT HAPPENS WILL BE AS I MAKE IT.
GO IN SIN, BROTHER.
GO IN SIN, SISTER.

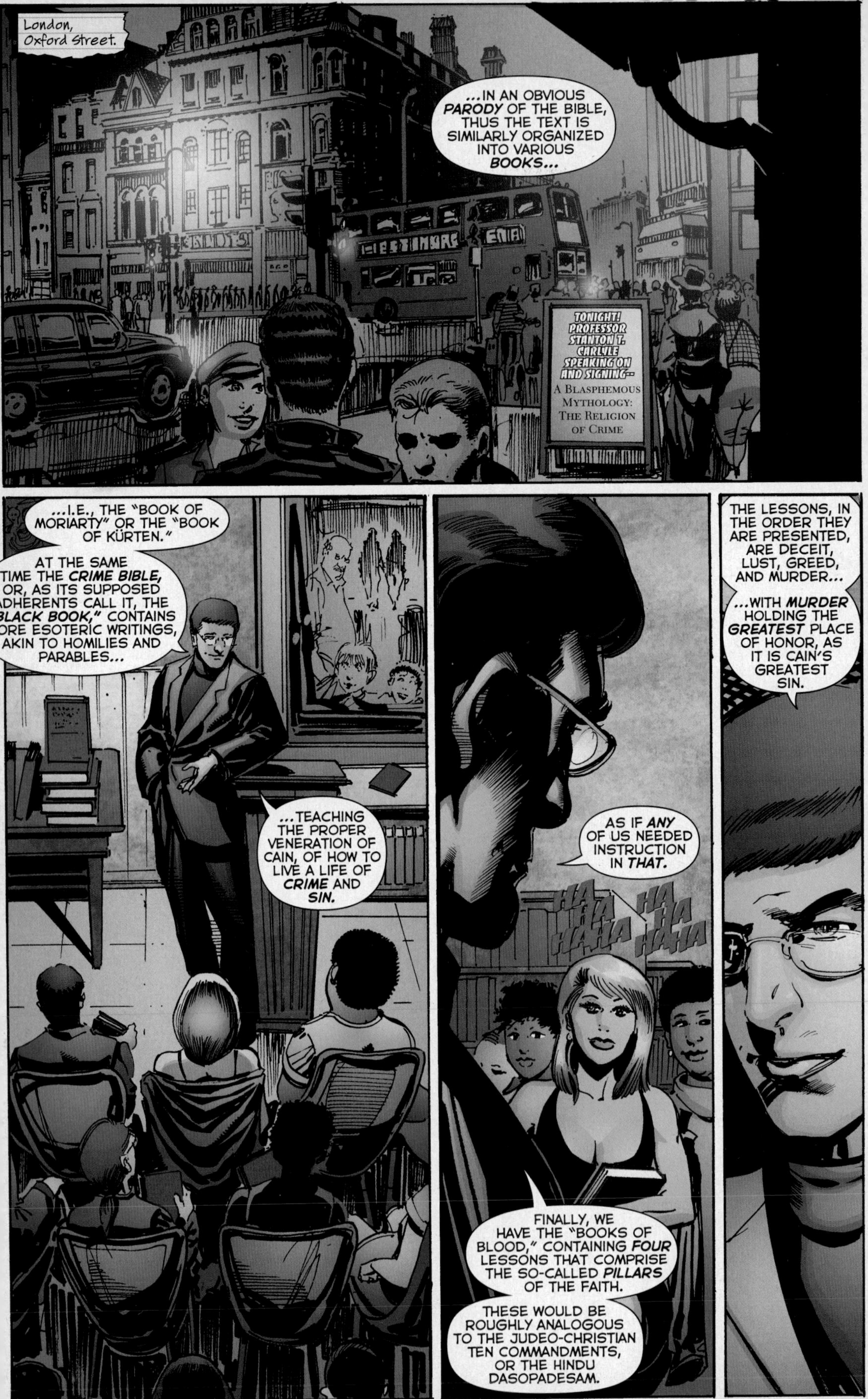
London, Oxford Street.
...IN AN OBVIOUS PARODY OF THE BIBLE, THUS THE TEXT IS SIMILARLY ORGANIZED INTO VARIOUS BOOKS...
TONIGHT! PROFESSOR STANTON T. CARLYLE SPEAKING ON AND SIGNING--
A BLASPHEMOUS MYTHOLOGY: THE RELIGION OF CRIME
...I.E., THE "BOOK OF MORIARTY" OR THE "BOOK OF KÜRTEN."
AT THE SAME TIME THE CRIME BIBLE, OR, AS ITS SUPPOSED ADHERENTS CALL IT, THE "BLACK BOOK," CONTAINS ORE ESOTERIC WRITINGS, AKIN TO HOMILIES AND PARABLES...
...TEACHING THE PROPER VENERATION OF CAIN, OF HOW TO LIVE A LIFE OF CRIME AND SIN.
AS IF ANY OF US NEEDED INSTRUCTION IN THAT.
HA HA HAHA HA HA HAHA
FINALLY, WE HAVE THE "BOOKS OF BLOOD," CONTAINING FOUR LESSONS THAT COMPRISE THE SO-CALLED PILLARS OF THE FAITH.
THESE WOULD BE ROUGHLY ANALOGOUS TO THE JUDEO-CHRISTIAN TEN COMMANDMENTS, OR THE HINDU DASOPADESAM.
THE LESSONS, IN THE ORDER THEY ARE PRESENTED, ARE DECEIT, LUST, GREED, AND MURDER...
...WITH MURDER HOLDING THE GREATEST PLACE OF HONOR, AS IT IS CAIN'S GREATEST SIN.

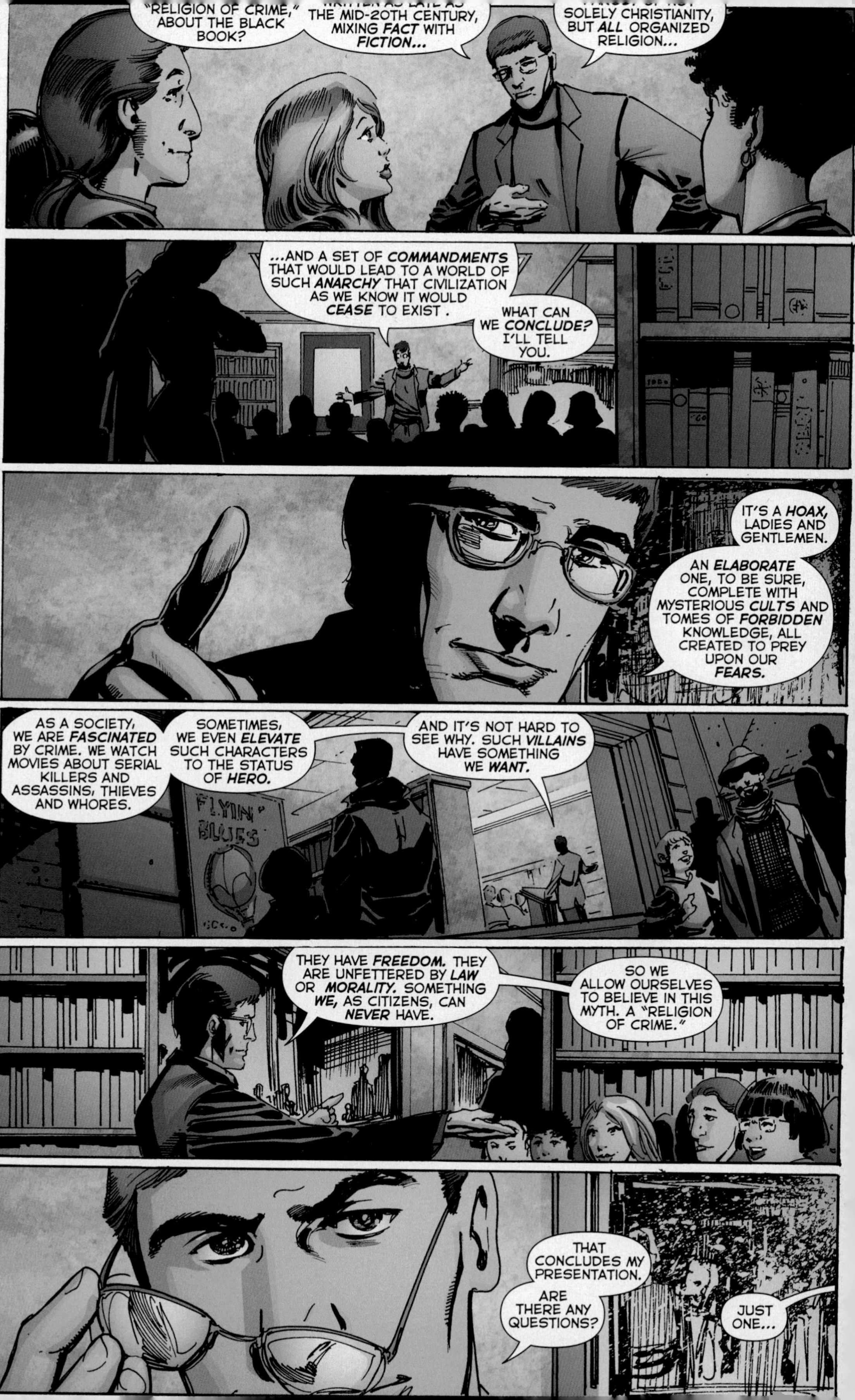
"RELIGION OF CRIME," ABOUT THE BLACK BOOK?
THE MID-20TH CENTURY, MIXING FACT WITH FICTION...
SOLELY CHRISTIANITY, BUT ALL ORGANIZED RELIGION...
...AND A SET OF COMMANDMENTS THAT WOULD LEAD TO A WORLD OF SUCH ANARCHY THAT CIVILIZATION AS WE KNOW IT WOULD CEASE TO EXIST .
WHAT CAN WE CONCLUDE? I'LL TELL YOU.
IT'S A HOAX, LADIES AND GENTLEMEN.
AN ELABORATE ONE, TO BE SURE, COMPLETE WITH MYSTERIOUS CULTS AND TOMES OF FORBIDDEN KNOWLEDGE, ALL CREATED TO PREY UPON OUR FEARS.
AS A SOCIETY, WE ARE FASCINATED BY CRIME. WE WATCH MOVIES ABOUT SERIAL KILLERS AND ASSASSINS, THIEVES AND WHORES.
SOMETIMES, WE EVEN ELEVATE SUCH CHARACTERS TO THE STATUS OF HERO.
AND IT'S NOT HARD TO SEE WHY. SUCH VILLAINS HAVE SOMETHING WE WANT.
FLYIN' BLUES
THEY HAVE FREEDOM. THEY ARE UNFETTERED BY LAW OR MORALITY. SOMETHING WE, AS CITIZENS, CAN NEVER HAVE.
SO WE ALLOW OURSELVES TO BELIEVE IN THIS MYTH. A "RELIGION OF CRIME."
THAT CONCLUDES MY PRESENTATION.
ARE THERE ANY QUESTIONS?
JUST ONE...

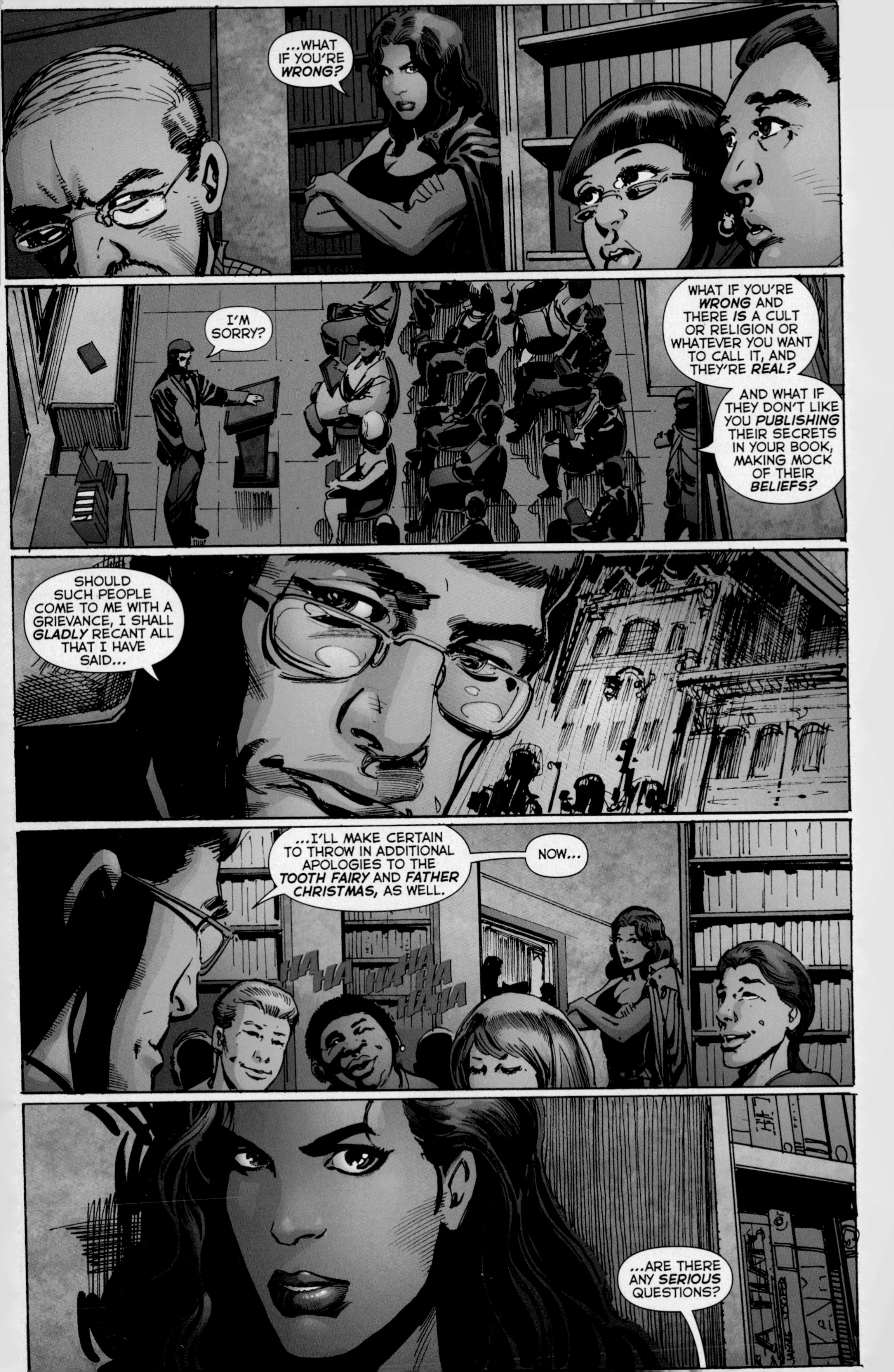
...WHAT IF YOU'RE *WRONG?*
I'M SORRY?
WHAT IF YOU'RE *WRONG* AND THERE *IS* A CULT OR RELIGION OR WHATEVER YOU WANT TO CALL IT, AND THEY'RE *REAL?*
AND WHAT IF THEY DON'T LIKE YOU *PUBLISHING* THEIR SECRETS IN YOUR BOOK, MAKING MOCK OF THEIR *BELIEFS?*
SHOULD SUCH PEOPLE COME TO ME WITH A GRIEVANCE, I SHALL *GLADLY* RECANT ALL THAT I HAVE SAID...
...I'LL MAKE CERTAIN TO THROW IN ADDITIONAL APOLOGIES TO THE *TOOTH FAIRY* AND *FATHER CHRISTMAS,* AS WELL.
NOW...
HA HA HA HA HA HA HA
...ARE THERE ANY *SERIOUS* QUESTIONS?

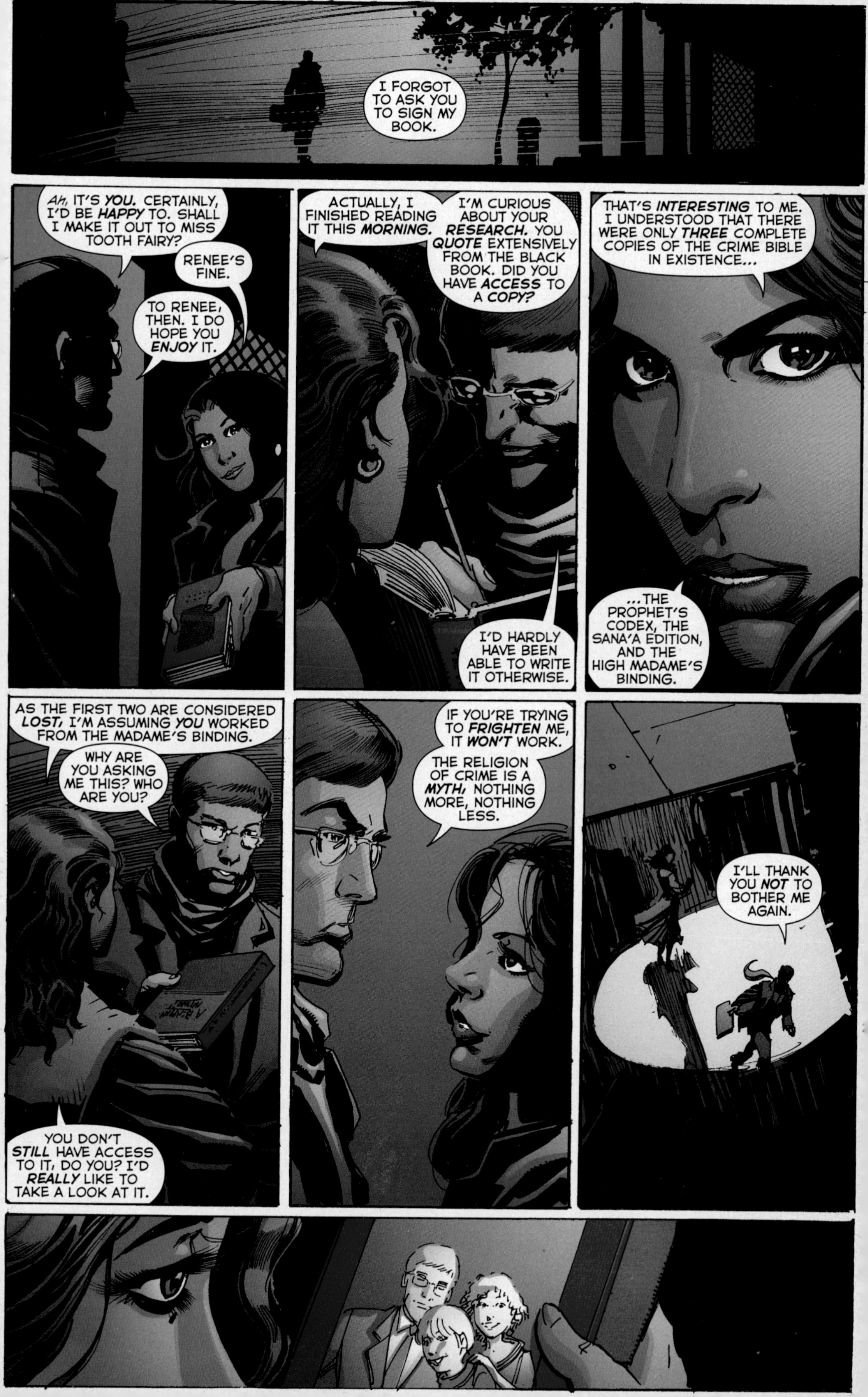
I FORGOT TO ASK YOU TO SIGN MY BOOK.
Ah, IT'S YOU. CERTAINLY, I'D BE HAPPY TO. SHALL I MAKE IT OUT TO MISS TOOTH FAIRY?
RENEE'S FINE.
TO RENEE, THEN. I DO HOPE YOU ENJOY IT.
ACTUALLY, I FINISHED READING IT THIS MORNING.
I'M CURIOUS ABOUT YOUR RESEARCH. YOU QUOTE EXTENSIVELY FROM THE BLACK BOOK. DID YOU HAVE ACCESS TO A COPY?
I'D HARDLY HAVE BEEN ABLE TO WRITE IT OTHERWISE.
THAT'S INTERESTING TO ME. I UNDERSTOOD THAT THERE WERE ONLY THREE COMPLETE COPIES OF THE CRIME BIBLE IN EXISTENCE...
...THE PROPHET'S CODEX, THE SANA'A EDITION, AND THE HIGH MADAME'S BINDING.
AS THE FIRST TWO ARE CONSIDERED LOST, I'M ASSUMING YOU WORKED FROM THE MADAME'S BINDING.
WHY ARE YOU ASKING ME THIS? WHO ARE YOU?
YOU DON'T STILL HAVE ACCESS TO IT, DO YOU? I'D REALLY LIKE TO TAKE A LOOK AT IT.
IF YOU'RE TRYING TO FRIGHTEN ME, IT WON'T WORK.
THE RELIGION OF CRIME IS A MYTH, NOTHING MORE, NOTHING LESS.
I'LL THANK YOU NOT TO BOTHER ME AGAIN.

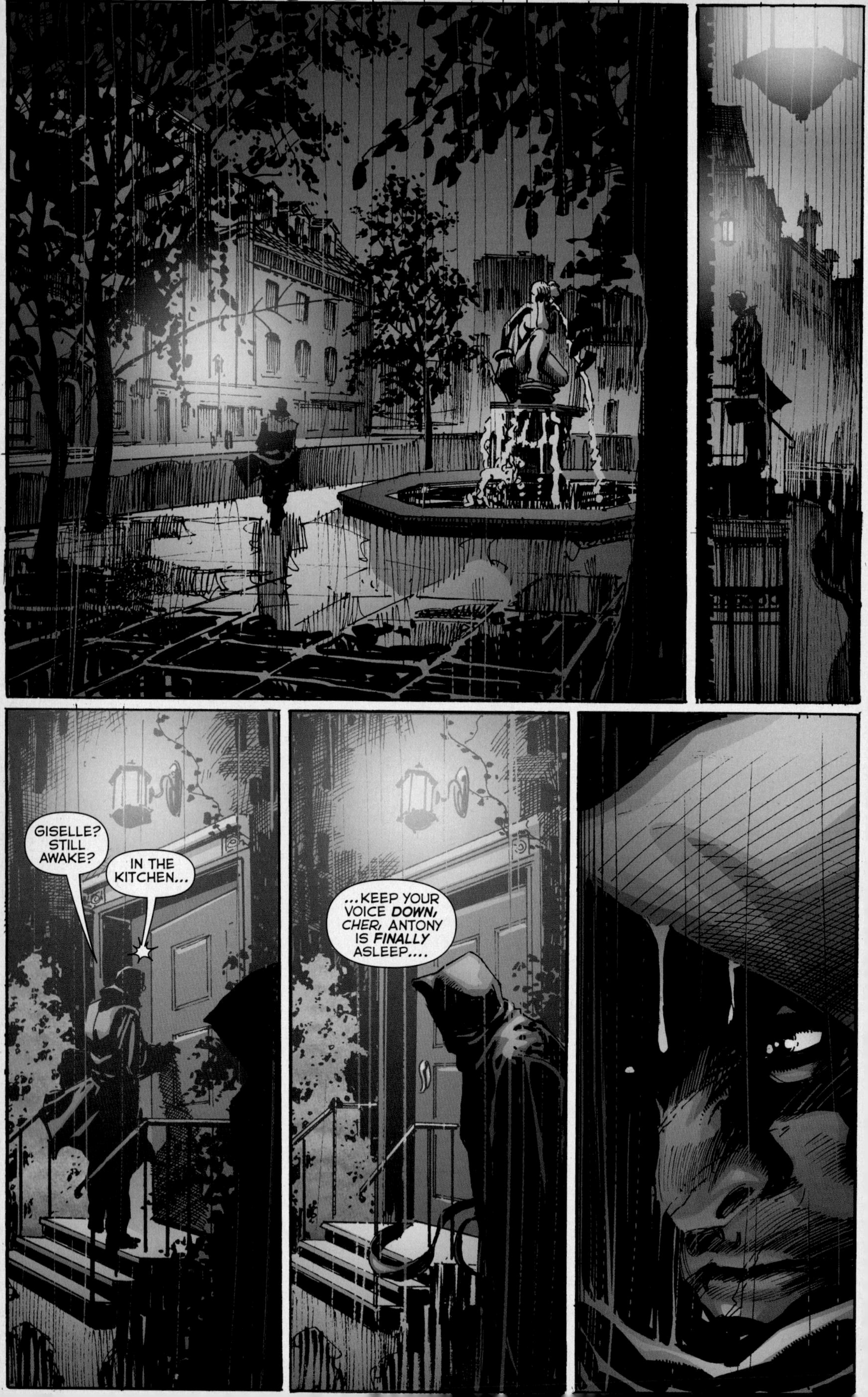
GISELLE? STILL AWAKE?
IN THE KITCHEN...
...KEEP YOUR VOICE DOWN, CHER, ANTONY IS FINALLY ASLEEP....

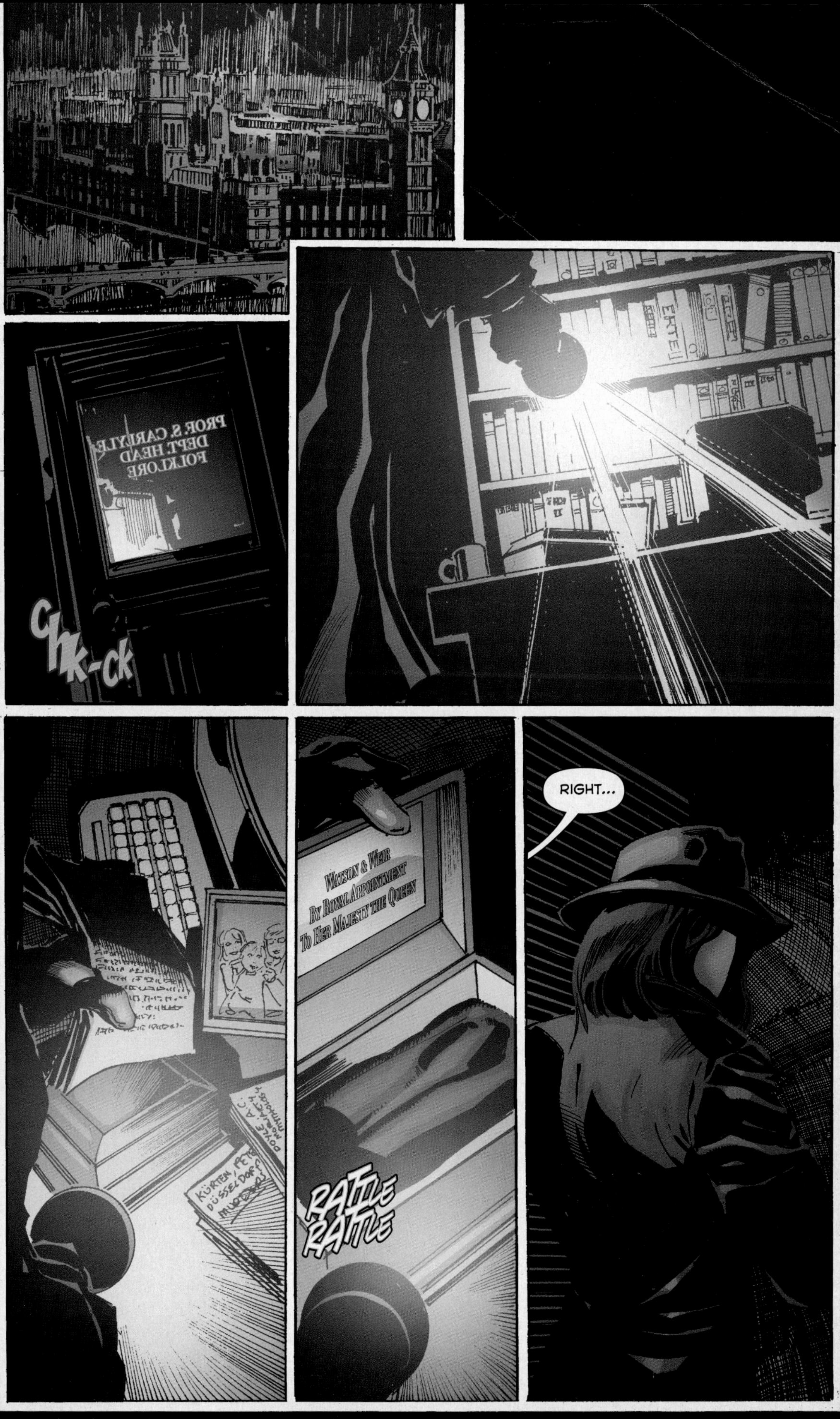
PROF. S. CARLYLE
DEPT. HEAD
FOLKLORE
CHK-CK
KÜRTEN, PETER
DÜSSELDORF
WATSON & WEIR
BY ROYAL APPOINTMENT
TO HER MAJESTY THE QUEEN
RATTLE
RATTLE
RIGHT...

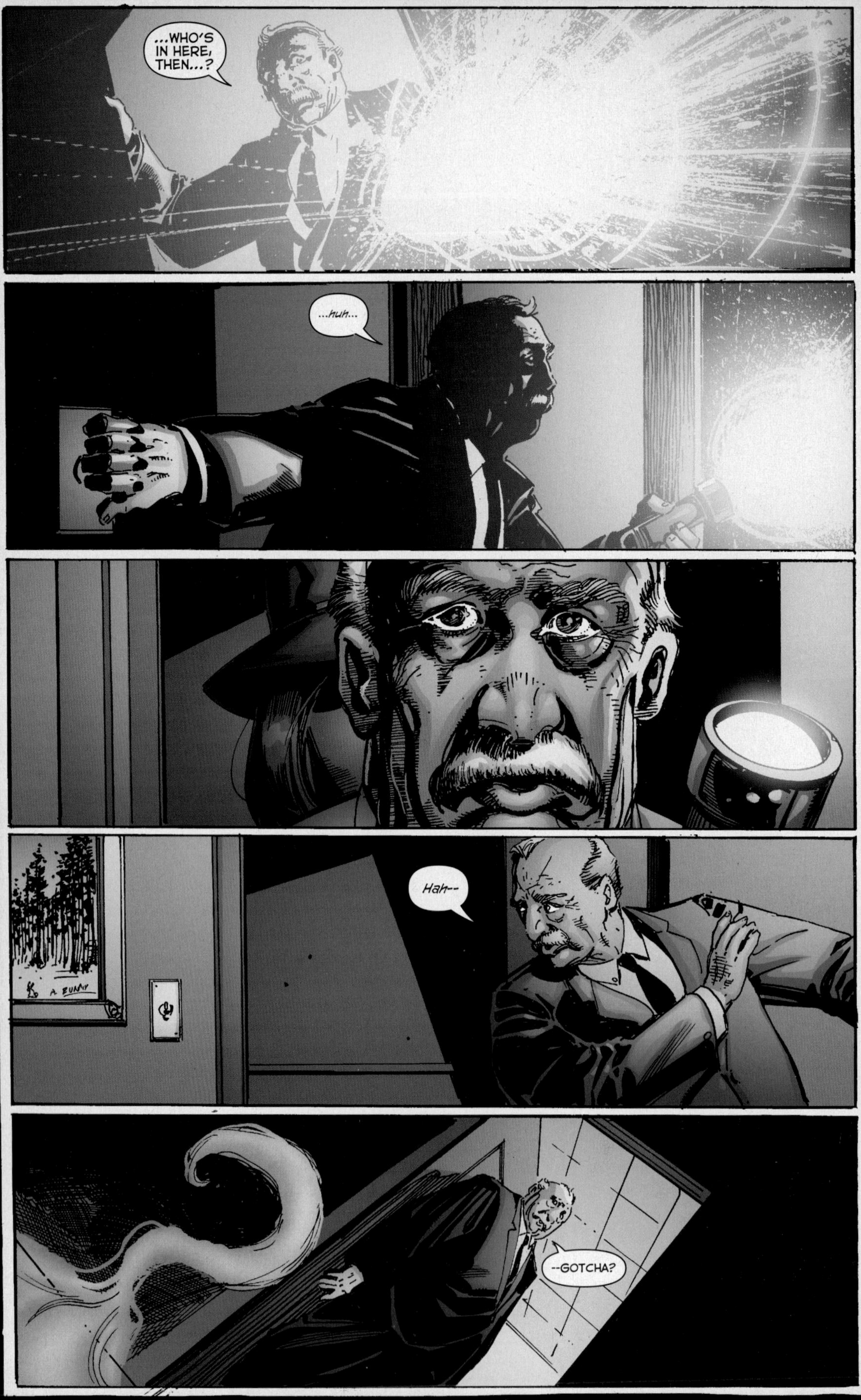
...WHO'S IN HERE, THEN...?
...huh...
Hah--
--GOTCHA?

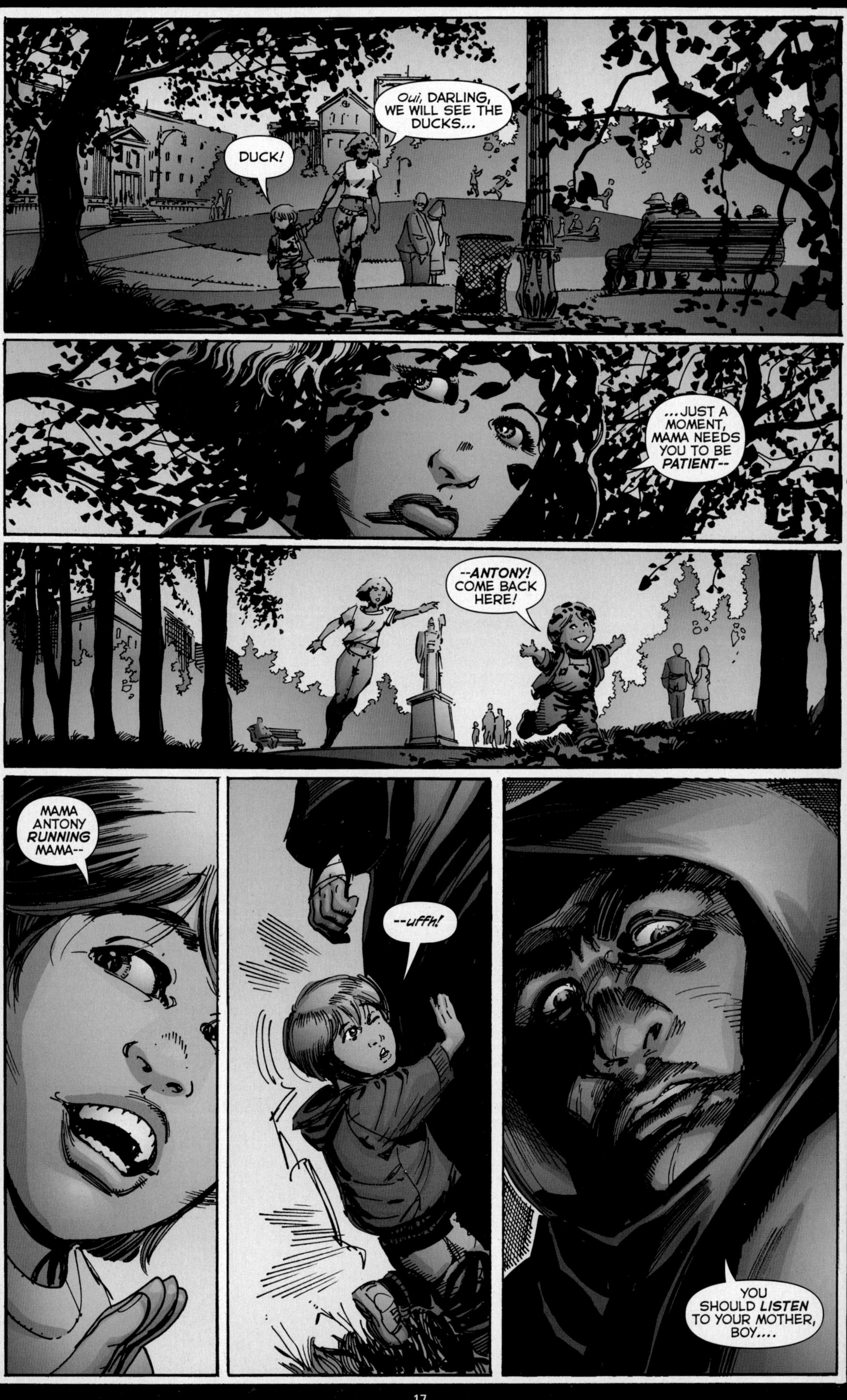
Oui, DARLING, WE WILL SEE THE DUCKS...
DUCK!
...JUST A MOMENT, MAMA NEEDS YOU TO BE *PATIENT*--
--*ANTONY!* COME BACK HERE!
MAMA ANTONY *RUNNING* MAMA--
--*uffh!*
YOU SHOULD *LISTEN* TO YOUR MOTHER, BOY....

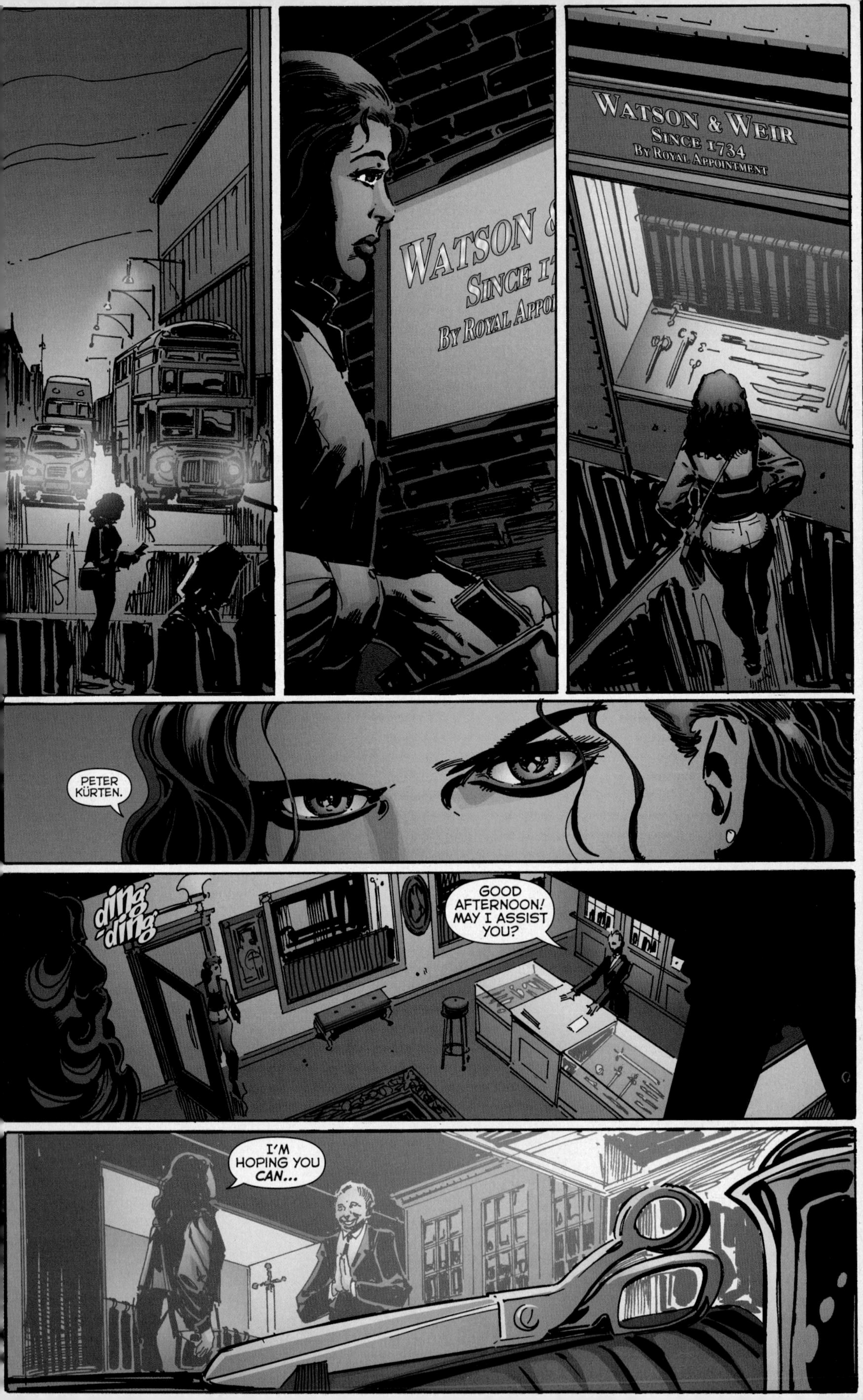
WATSON &
SINCE 17
BY ROYAL APPOI
WATSON & WEIR
SINCE 1734
BY ROYAL APPOINTMENT
PETER KÜRTEN.
DING DING
GOOD AFTERNOON! MAY I ASSIST YOU?
I'M HOPING YOU *CAN*...

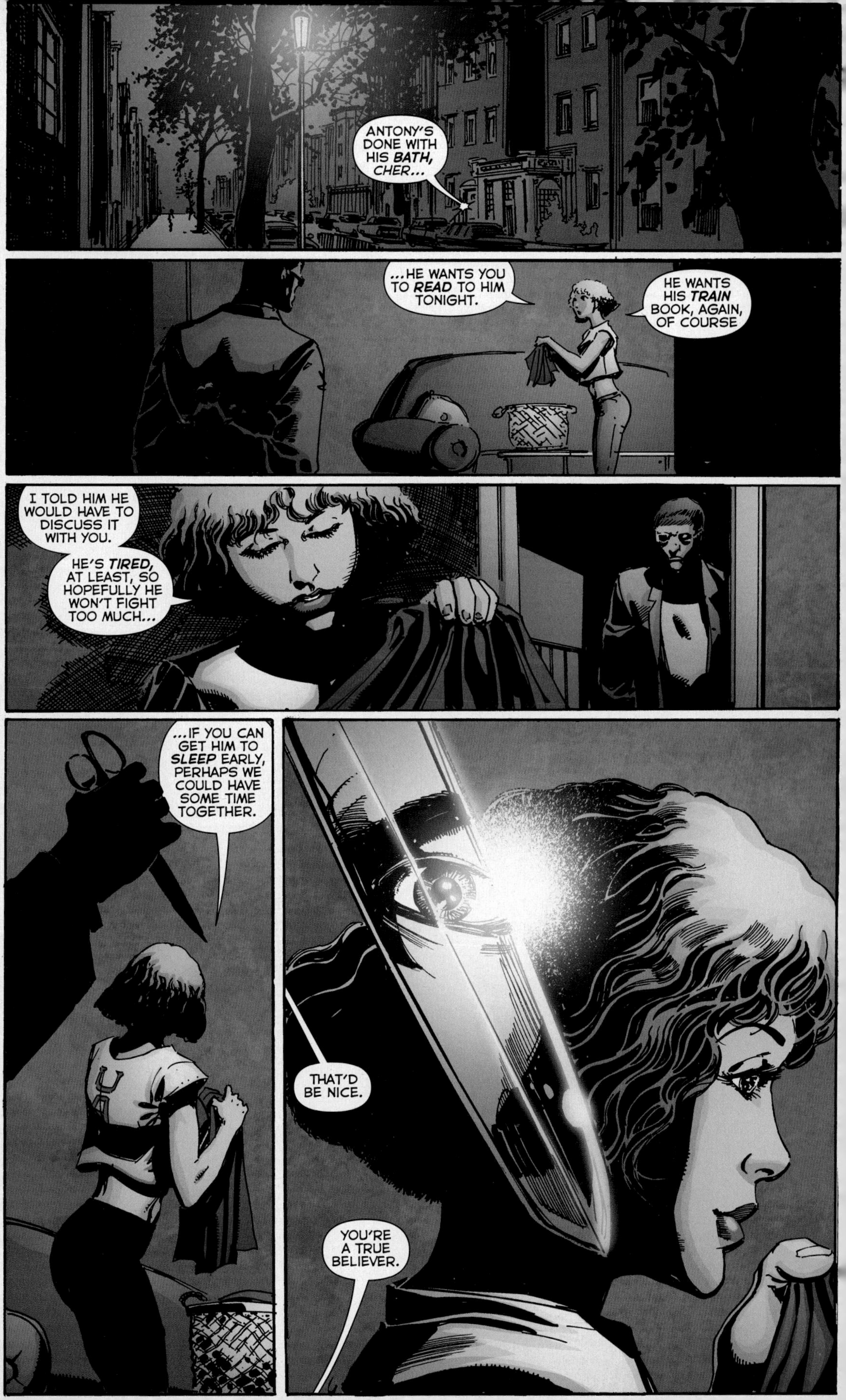

ANTONY'S DONE WITH HIS BATH, CHER...
...HE WANTS YOU TO READ TO HIM TONIGHT.
HE WANTS HIS TRAIN BOOK, AGAIN, OF COURSE
I TOLD HIM HE WOULD HAVE TO DISCUSS IT WITH YOU.
HE'S TIRED, AT LEAST, SO HOPEFULLY HE WON'T FIGHT TOO MUCH...
...IF YOU CAN GET HIM TO SLEEP EARLY, PERHAPS WE COULD HAVE SOME TIME TOGETHER.
THAT'D BE NICE.
YOU'RE A TRUE BELIEVER.

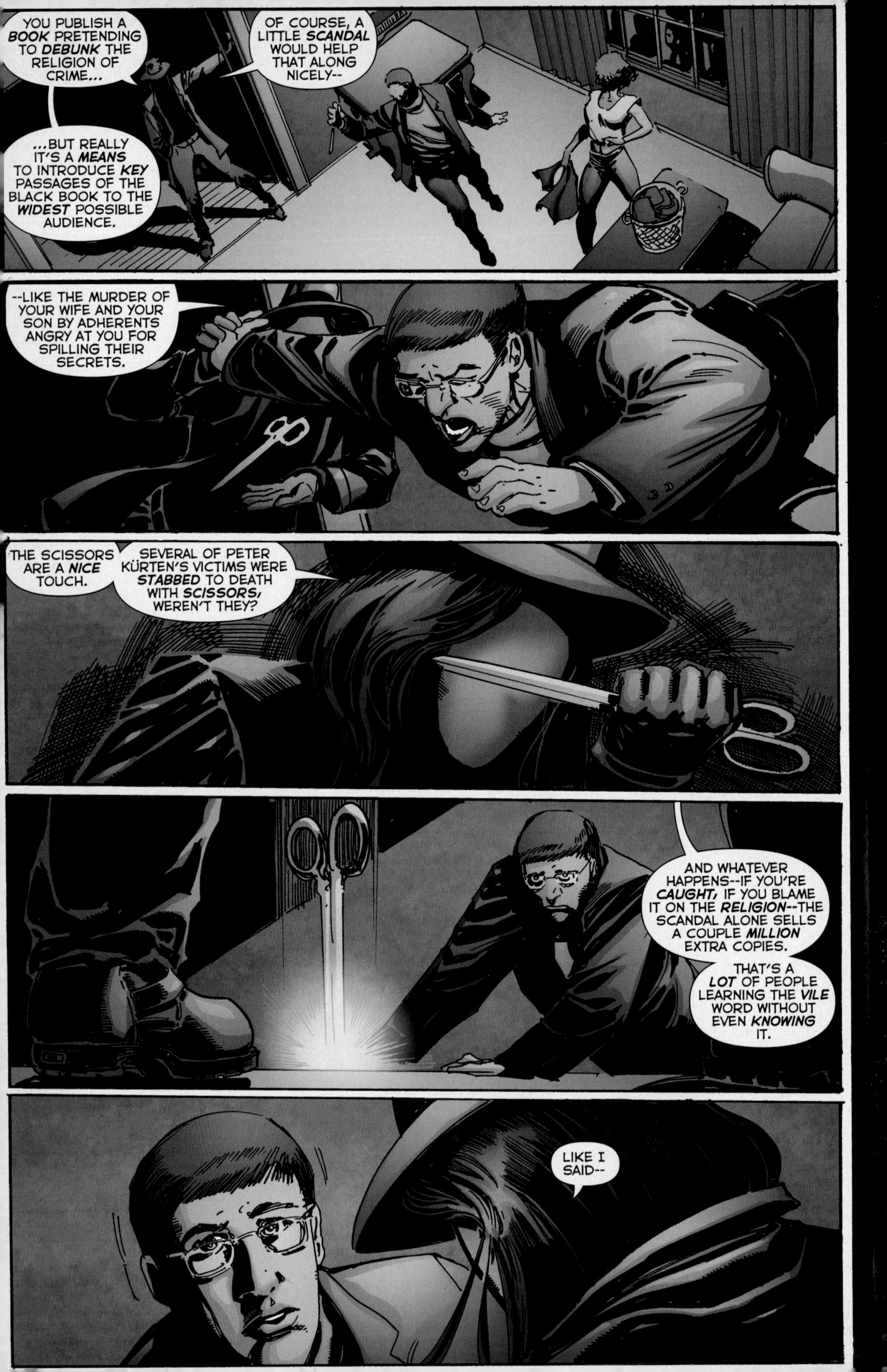
YOU PUBLISH A BOOK PRETENDING TO DEBUNK THE RELIGION OF CRIME...
...BUT REALLY IT'S A MEANS TO INTRODUCE KEY PASSAGES OF THE BLACK BOOK TO THE WIDEST POSSIBLE AUDIENCE.
OF COURSE, A LITTLE SCANDAL WOULD HELP THAT ALONG NICELY--
--LIKE THE MURDER OF YOUR WIFE AND YOUR SON BY ADHERENTS ANGRY AT YOU FOR SPILLING THEIR SECRETS.
THE SCISSORS ARE A NICE TOUCH.
SEVERAL OF PETER KÜRTEN'S VICTIMS WERE STABBED TO DEATH WITH SCISSORS, WEREN'T THEY?
AND WHATEVER HAPPENS--IF YOU'RE CAUGHT, IF YOU BLAME IT ON THE RELIGION--THE SCANDAL ALONE SELLS A COUPLE MILLION EXTRA COPIES.
THAT'S A LOT OF PEOPLE LEARNING THE VILE WORD WITHOUT EVEN KNOWING IT.
LIKE I SAID--

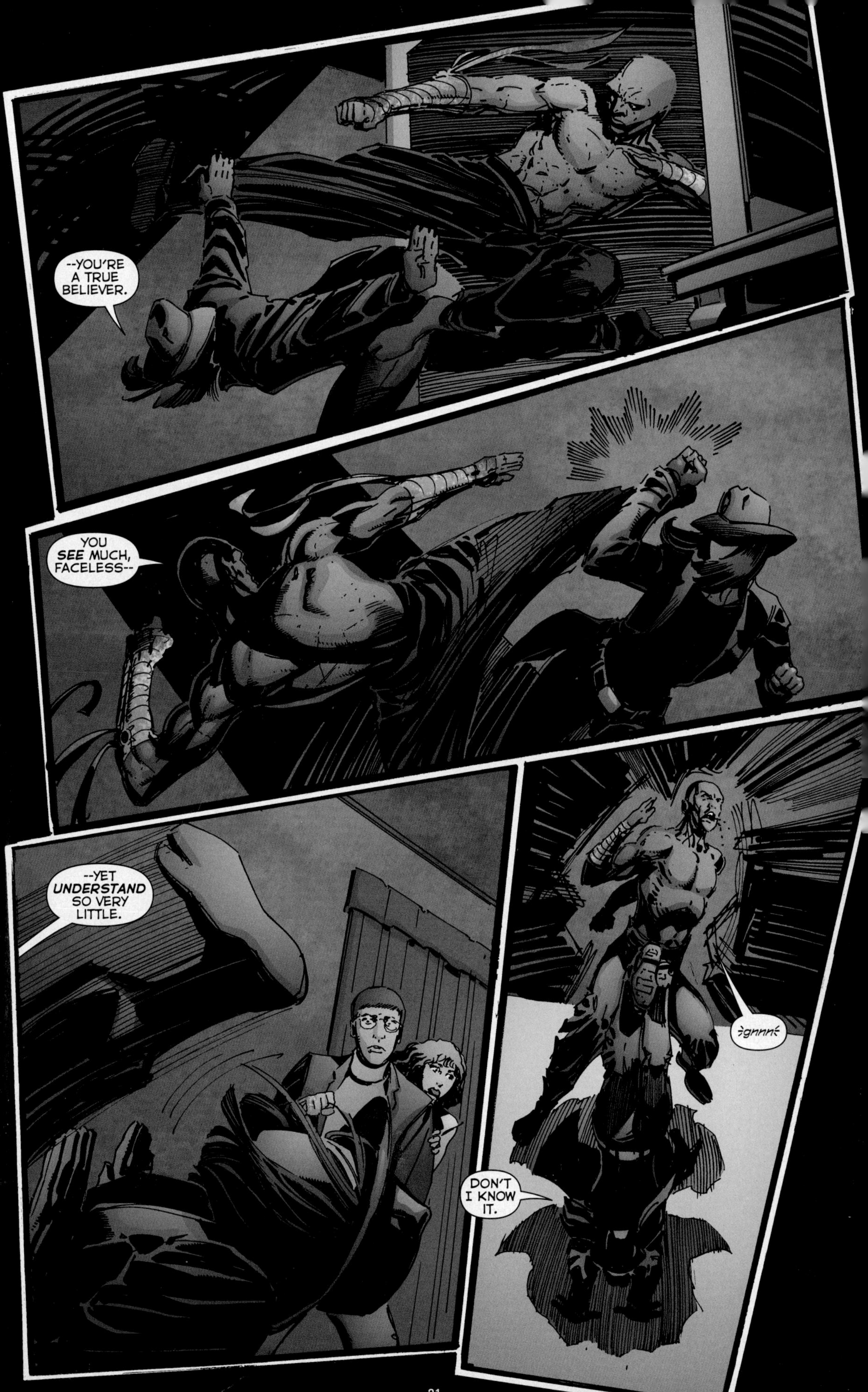
--YOU'RE A TRUE BELIEVER.
YOU SEE MUCH, FACELESS--
--YET UNDERSTAND SO VERY LITTLE.
gnnn
DON'T I KNOW IT.

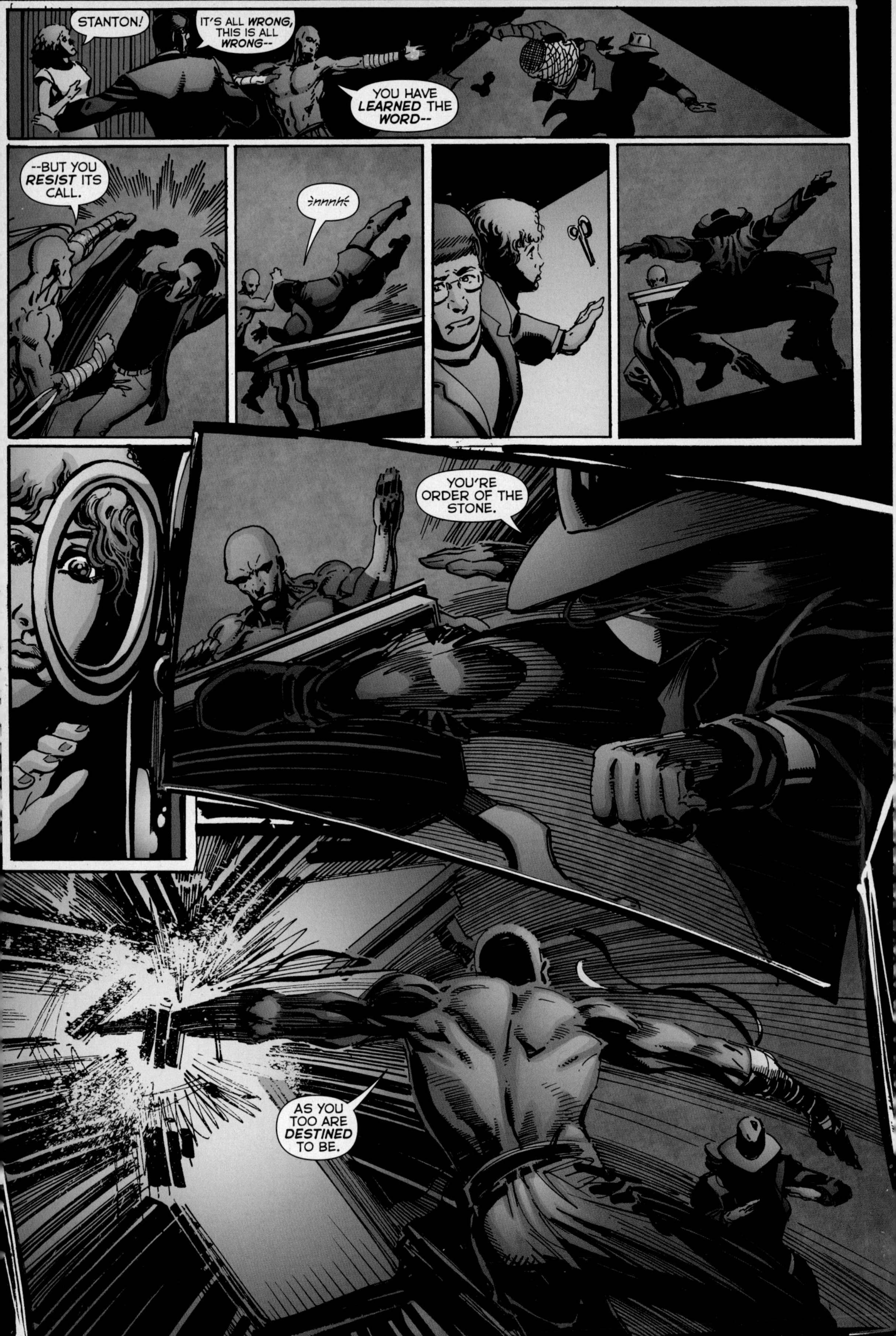
STANTON!
IT'S ALL WRONG, THIS IS ALL WRONG--
YOU HAVE LEARNED THE WORD--
--BUT YOU RESIST ITS CALL.
≥nnnh≤
YOU'RE ORDER OF THE STONE.
AS YOU TOO ARE DESTINED TO BE.

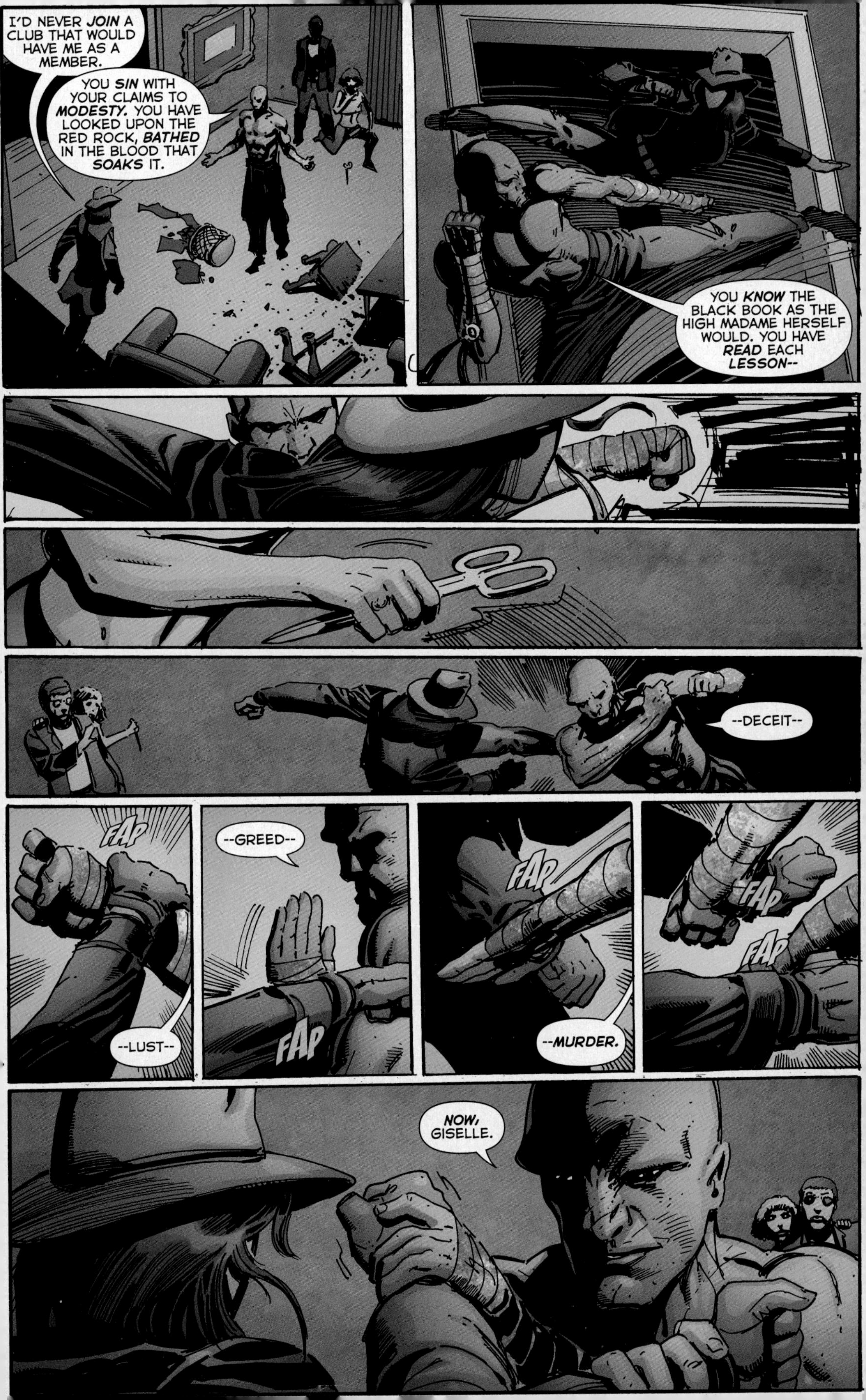
I'D NEVER JOIN A CLUB THAT WOULD HAVE ME AS A MEMBER.
YOU SIN WITH YOUR CLAIMS TO MODESTY. YOU HAVE LOOKED UPON THE RED ROCK, BATHED IN THE BLOOD THAT SOAKS IT.
YOU KNOW THE BLACK BOOK AS THE HIGH MADAME HERSELF WOULD. YOU HAVE READ EACH LESSON--
--DECEIT--
FAP
--LUST--
--GREED--
FAP
FAP
--MURDER.
FAP
FAP
NOW, GISELLE.

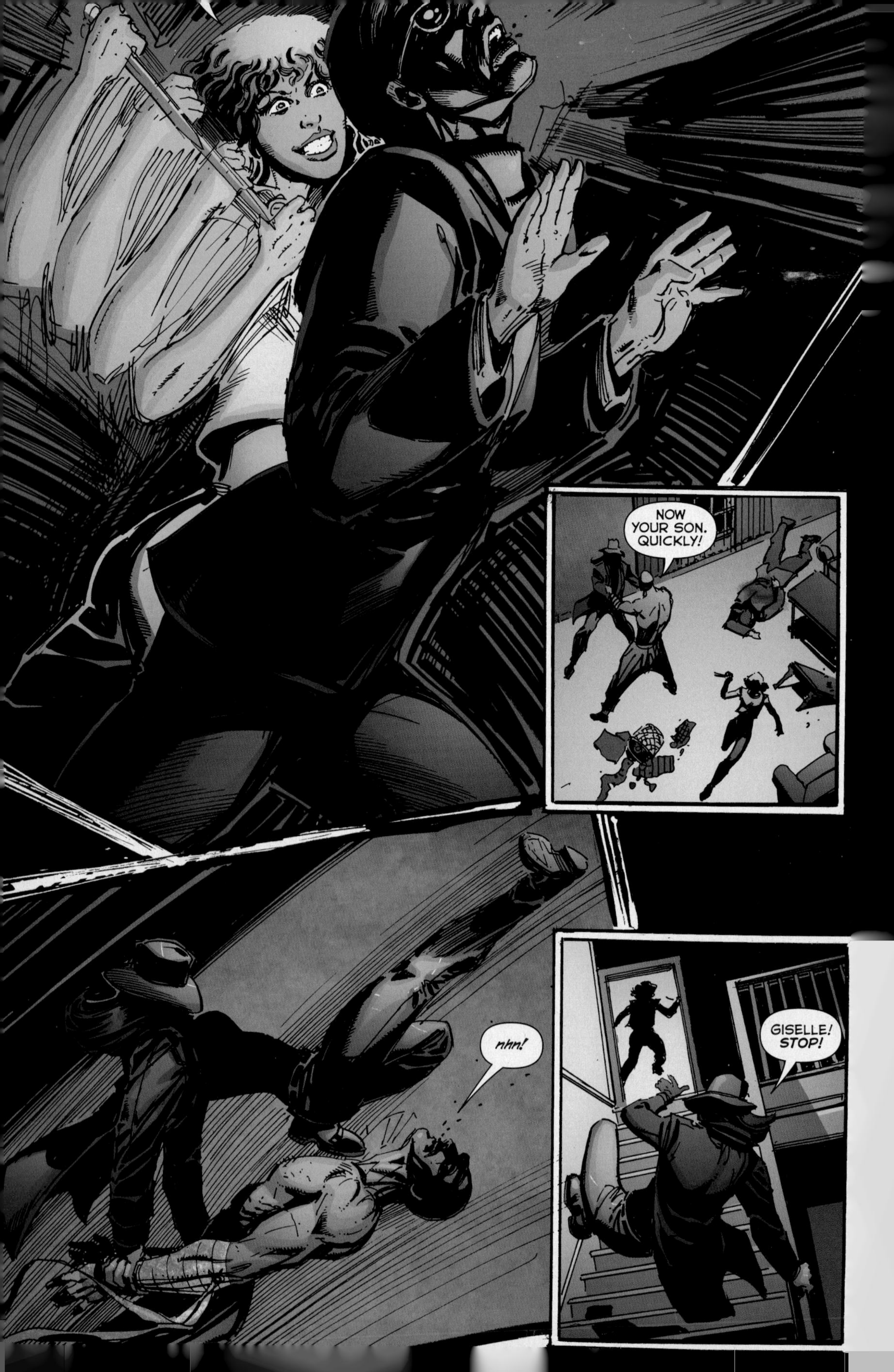
NOW YOUR SON. QUICKLY!
nhn!
GISELLE! STOP!

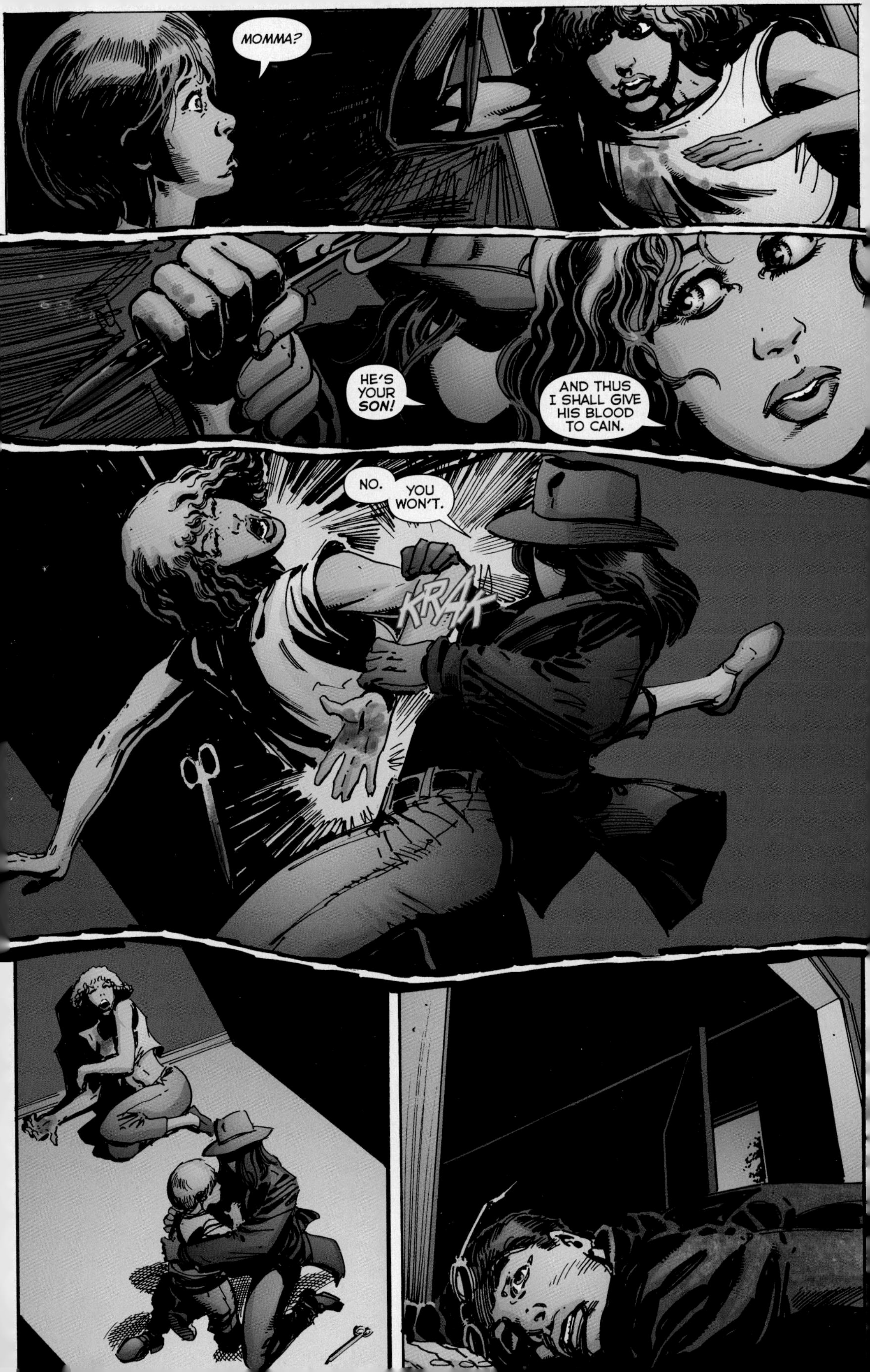

MOMMA?
HE'S YOUR SON!
AND THUS I SHALL GIVE HIS BLOOD TO CAIN.
NO.
YOU WON'T.
KRAK

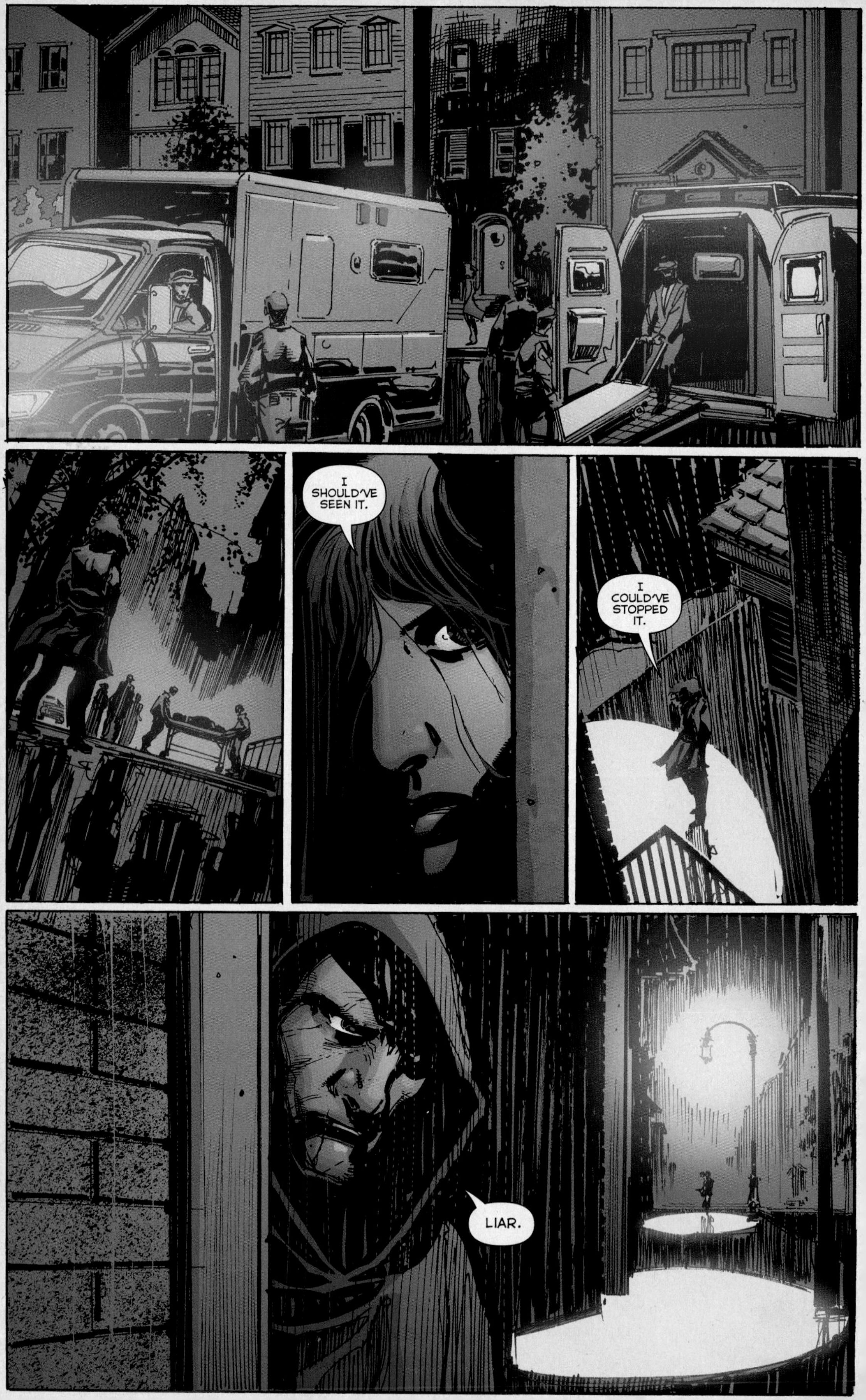
I SHOULD'VE SEEN IT.
I COULD'VE STOPPED IT.
LIAR.

The Second Book of Blood

Chapter 40, Verses 31–40

31 And the fire of it came upon Him; He was as the stallion snorting in want, as the swine rutting in the sty, as the bitches in heat in the allies, and all this He thought made Him cursed, and He thought it a vile burden upon His soul, and thought it His lot to endure such iniquity in His heart.

32 And still desire for her continued to grow, and so He was much agonized by Lust, so much she filled His mind, not a thought was free, and in this way the First didst know He was still a slave.

33 Then did the First practise all manner of things to slake it; with all manner and work did He try, and thus did fornicate with many a beauty, but naught were as drink to his thirst, only didst they feed it, and still the First shook and wept, so hungry was He for her.

34 Thus was His shame when Lilith camst upon Him again, and saw at once what she had wrought, and laughed she did at His great misery.

35 And Lilith asked, What hath put you in such way, my lord, to cause a prophet as mighty as thee to tremble and shake so at the site of a madame such as I? What hath laid you so low and made you so weak?

36 But the First spake not, so consumed was He then at the wanting of her, for so close was her flesh that the Lust screamed in him, and did cloud his mind; and He didst look away in his shame.

37 Then it was Lilith raised Him up, and setting His hands upon her, spake with breath hot on His neck.

38 What ye name virtue, I call weakness, for ye Lust heartily, but have not strength nor courage enough to slake it; if thou canst not take what ye want, then ye shall ne'er command it.

39 Then did Lilith turn away, with mock of Him; and this the First knew as counsel to be praised, and so was writ the Second Lesson of Blood.

40 So it was He took her there, until her laughter turned to all manner of cries and moaning, and both were changed, and stronger for it.

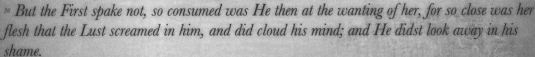

Lesson of Lust

HIS NAME IS COLONEL DOMINIC G. *CASUCCI*.

HE'S BEEN VISITING THE *CONVENT* HERE ONCE A WEEK FOR THE LAST MONTH, SINCE HE ASSUMED HIS POSTING AT THE PENTAGON.

HE'S GOT QUITE A KINK ABOUT WOMEN IN UNIFORM, AS YOU CAN SEE. IT'S AN ITCH WE'RE HAPPY TO HELP HIM SCRATCH.

BECAUSE OF *OUR* ...ORTS, *CAIN'S* NAME ...ISPERED IN PRAISE ... THE TREASURY TO ... WHITE HOUSE.

I WON'T HAVE SOME *UNWASHED* MONK OF THE *STONE*--NOT EVEN THE *HEAD* OF THEIR *ORDER*-- THREATENING OUR WORK.

WE SERVE THE *SAME* MASTER, MOTHER SUPERIOR...

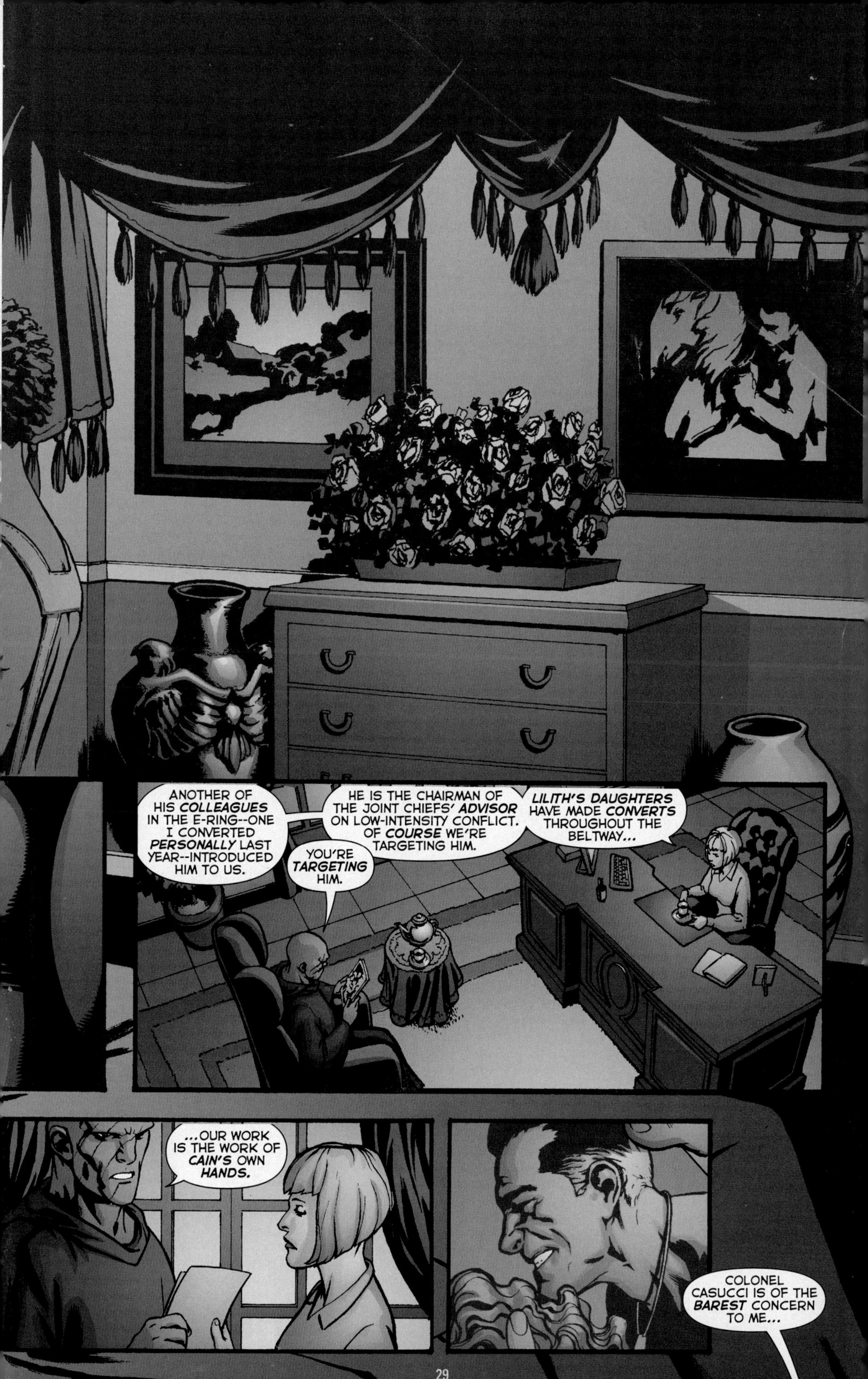
ANOTHER OF HIS COLLEAGUES IN THE E-RING--ONE I CONVERTED PERSONALLY LAST YEAR--INTRODUCED HIM TO US.
YOU'RE TARGETING HIM.
HE IS THE CHAIRMAN OF THE JOINT CHIEFS' ADVISOR ON LOW-INTENSITY CONFLICT. OF COURSE WE'RE TARGETING HIM.
LILITH'S DAUGHTERS HAVE MADE CONVERTS THROUGHOUT THE BELTWAY...
...OUR WORK IS THE WORK OF CAIN'S OWN HANDS.
COLONEL CASUCCI IS OF THE BAREST CONCERN TO ME...

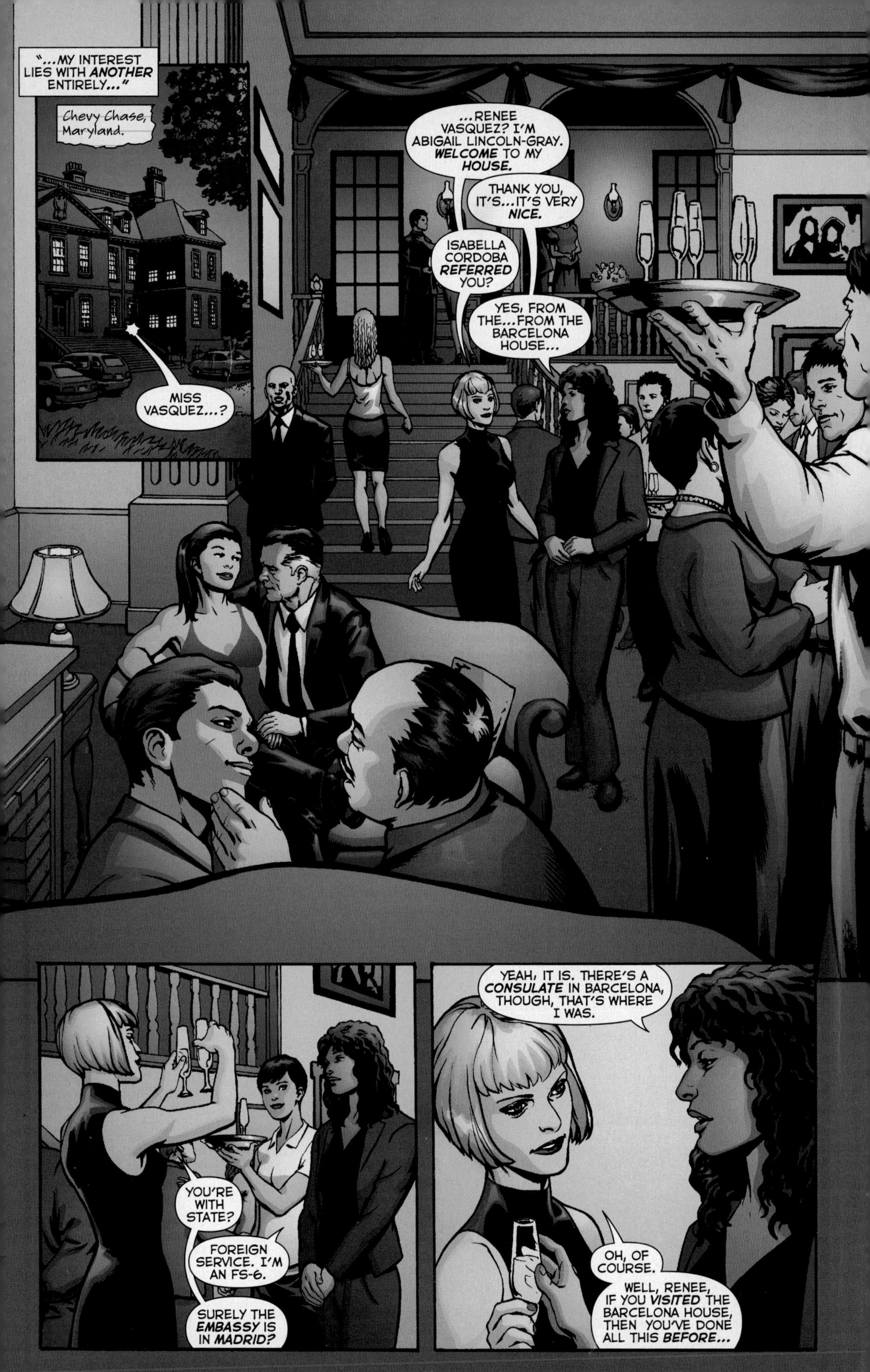
"...MY INTEREST LIES WITH ANOTHER ENTIRELY..."
Chevy Chase, Maryland.
MISS VASQUEZ...?
...RENEE VASQUEZ? I'M ABIGAIL LINCOLN-GRAY. WELCOME TO MY HOUSE.
THANK YOU, IT'S...IT'S VERY NICE.
ISABELLA CORDOBA REFERRED YOU?
YES, FROM THE...FROM THE BARCELONA HOUSE...
YOU'RE WITH STATE?
FOREIGN SERVICE. I'M AN FS-6.
SURELY THE EMBASSY IS IN MADRID?
YEAH, IT IS. THERE'S A CONSULATE IN BARCELONA, THOUGH, THAT'S WHERE I WAS.
OH, OF COURSE.
WELL, RENEE, IF YOU VISITED THE BARCELONA HOUSE, THEN YOU'VE DONE ALL THIS BEFORE...

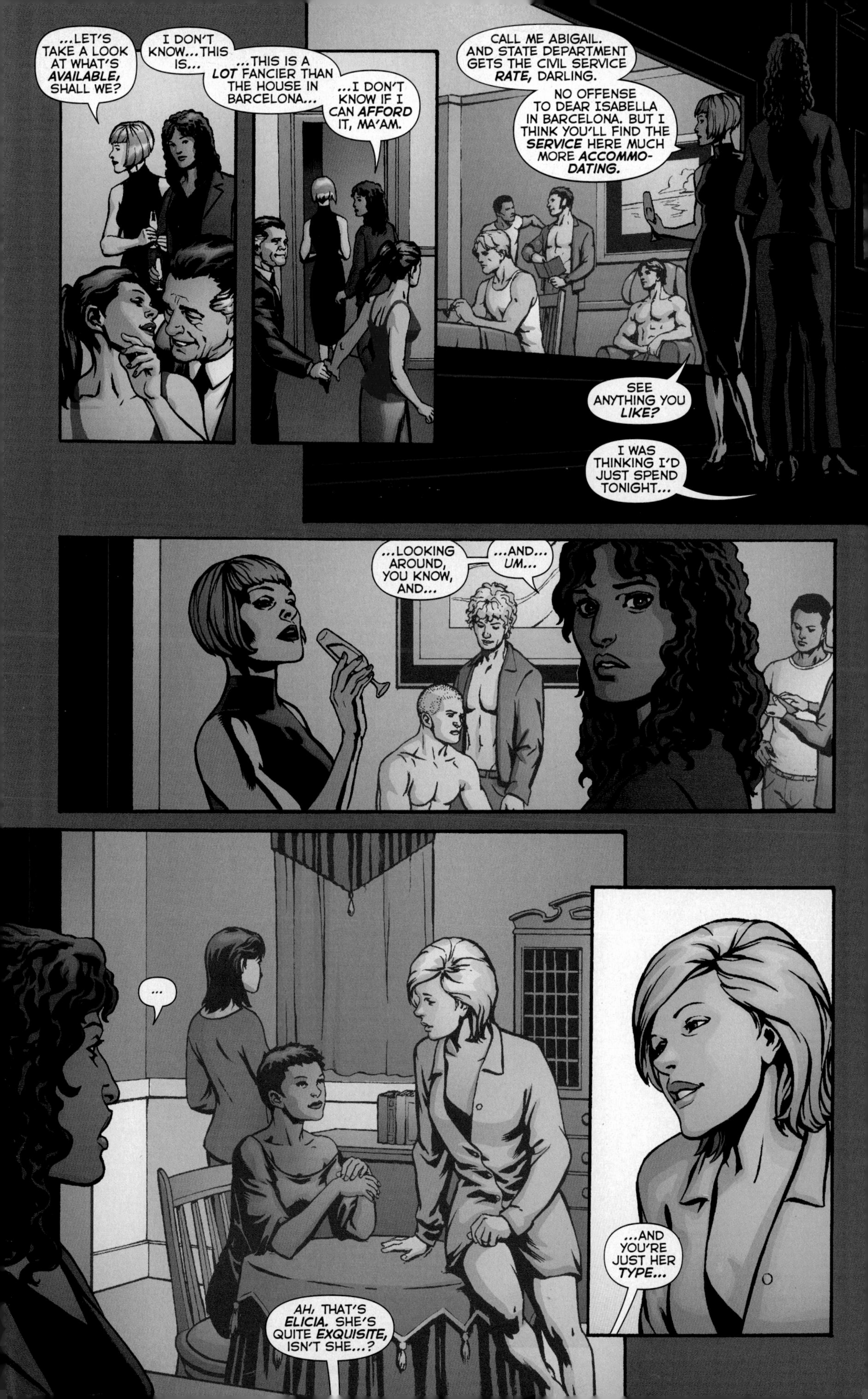

...LET'S TAKE A LOOK AT WHAT'S AVAILABLE, SHALL WE?
I DON'T KNOW...THIS IS...
...THIS IS A LOT FANCIER THAN THE HOUSE IN BARCELONA...
...I DON'T KNOW IF I CAN AFFORD IT, MA'AM.
CALL ME ABIGAIL. AND STATE DEPARTMENT GETS THE CIVIL SERVICE RATE, DARLING.
NO OFFENSE TO DEAR ISABELLA IN BARCELONA. BUT I THINK YOU'LL FIND THE SERVICE HERE MUCH MORE ACCOMMO-DATING.
SEE ANYTHING YOU LIKE?
I WAS THINKING I'D JUST SPEND TONIGHT...
...LOOKING AROUND, YOU KNOW, AND...
...AND... UM...
...
AH, THAT'S ELICIA. SHE'S QUITE EXQUISITE, ISN'T SHE...?
...AND YOU'RE JUST HER TYPE...

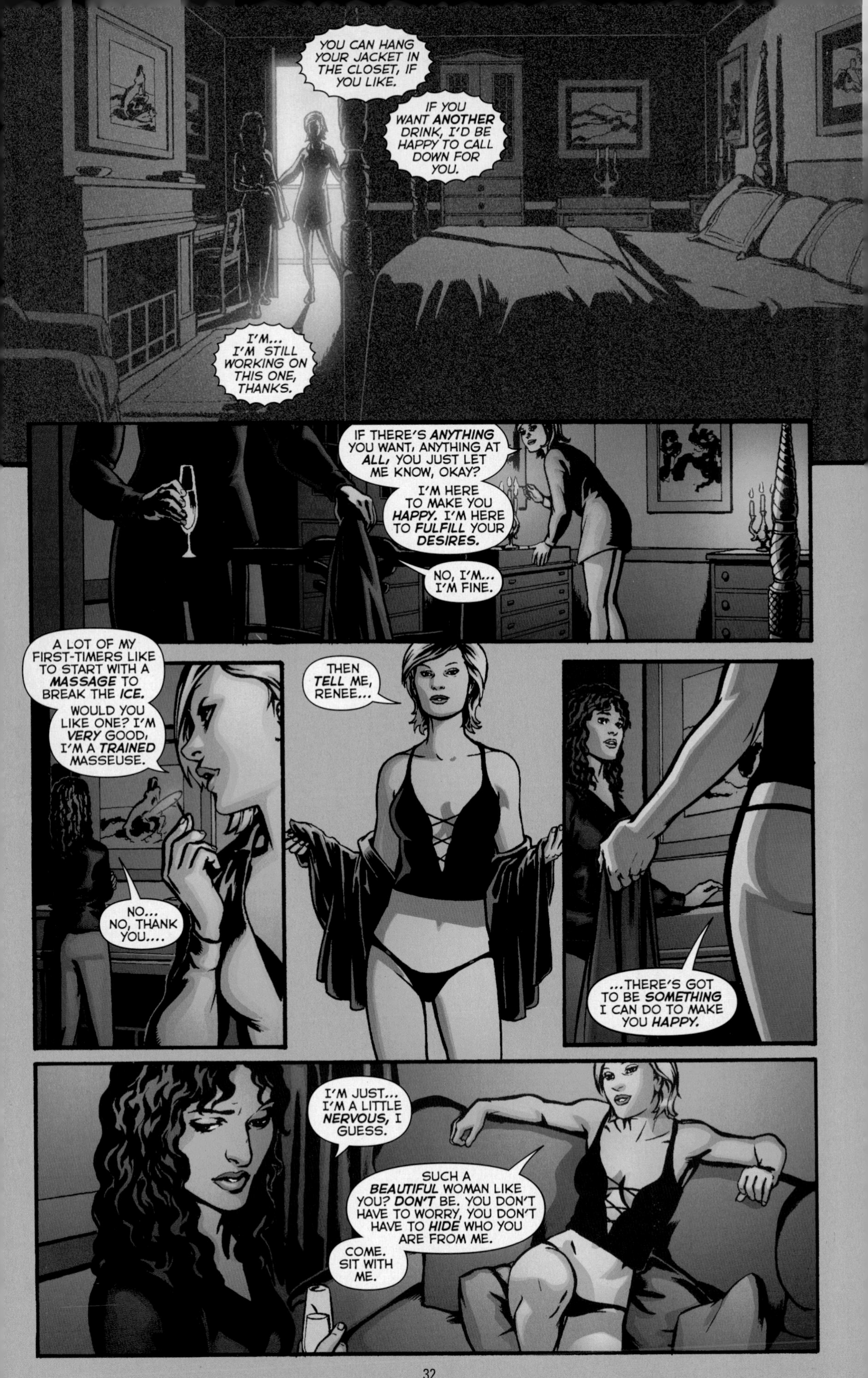
YOU CAN HANG YOUR JACKET IN THE CLOSET, IF YOU LIKE.
IF YOU WANT ANOTHER DRINK, I'D BE HAPPY TO CALL DOWN FOR YOU.
I'M... I'M STILL WORKING ON THIS ONE, THANKS.
IF THERE'S ANYTHING YOU WANT, ANYTHING AT ALL, YOU JUST LET ME KNOW, OKAY?
I'M HERE TO MAKE YOU HAPPY. I'M HERE TO FULFILL YOUR DESIRES.
NO, I'M... I'M FINE.
A LOT OF MY FIRST-TIMERS LIKE TO START WITH A MASSAGE TO BREAK THE ICE.
WOULD YOU LIKE ONE? I'M VERY GOOD, I'M A TRAINED MASSEUSE.
NO... NO, THANK YOU....
THEN TELL ME, RENEE...
...THERE'S GOT TO BE SOMETHING I CAN DO TO MAKE YOU HAPPY.
I'M JUST... I'M A LITTLE NERVOUS, I GUESS.
SUCH A BEAUTIFUL WOMAN LIKE YOU? DON'T BE. YOU DON'T HAVE TO WORRY, YOU DON'T HAVE TO HIDE WHO YOU ARE FROM ME.
COME. SIT WITH ME.

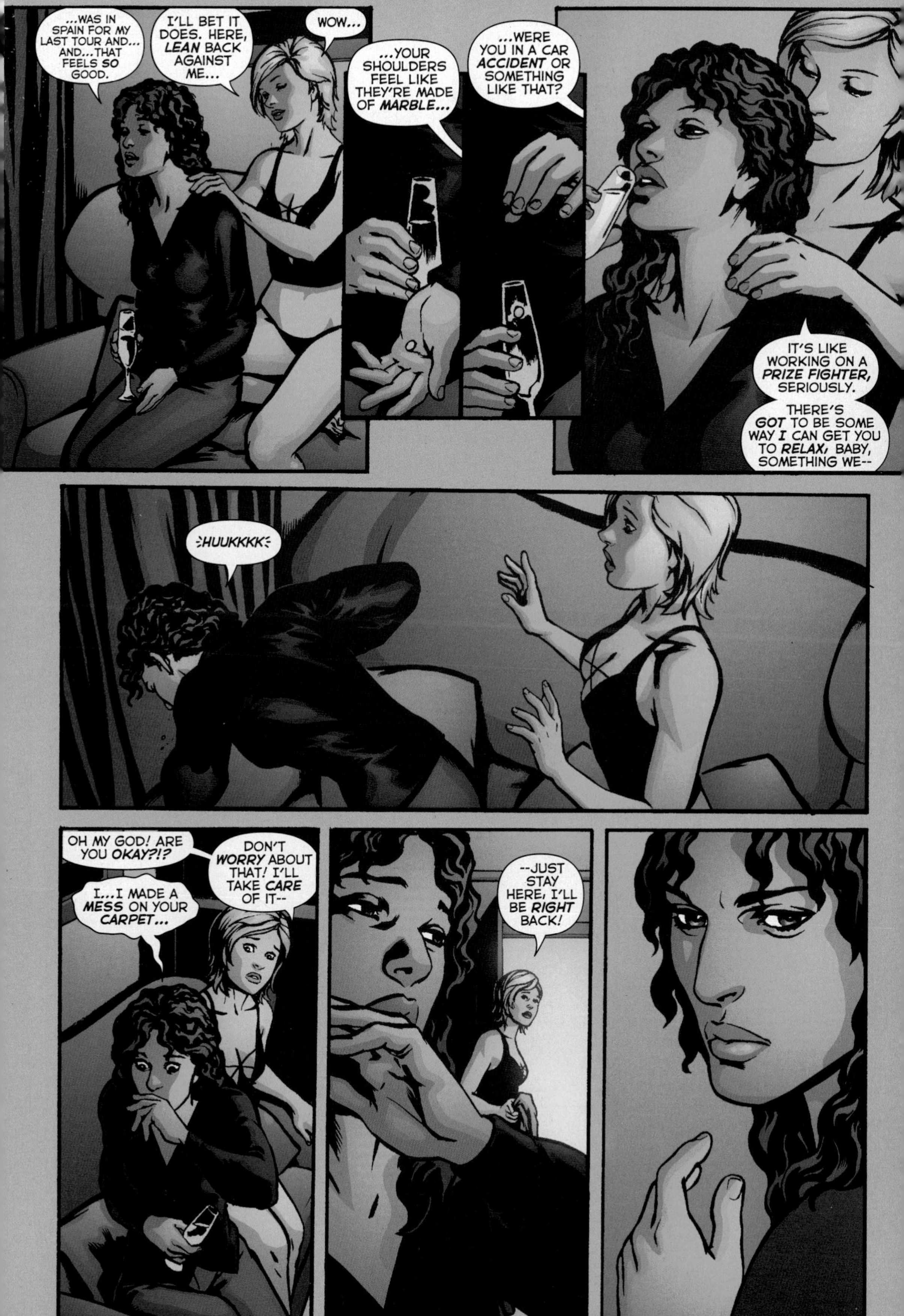
...WAS IN SPAIN FOR MY LAST TOUR AND... AND...THAT FEELS SO GOOD.
I'LL BET IT DOES. HERE, LEAN BACK AGAINST ME...
WOW...
...YOUR SHOULDERS FEEL LIKE THEY'RE MADE OF MARBLE...
...WERE YOU IN A CAR ACCIDENT OR SOMETHING LIKE THAT?
IT'S LIKE WORKING ON A PRIZE FIGHTER, SERIOUSLY.
THERE'S GOT TO BE SOME WAY I CAN GET YOU TO RELAX, BABY, SOMETHING WE--
HUUKKKK
OH MY GOD! ARE YOU OKAY?!?
DON'T WORRY ABOUT THAT! I'LL TAKE CARE OF IT--
I...I MADE A MESS ON YOUR CARPET...
--JUST STAY HERE, I'LL BE RIGHT BACK!

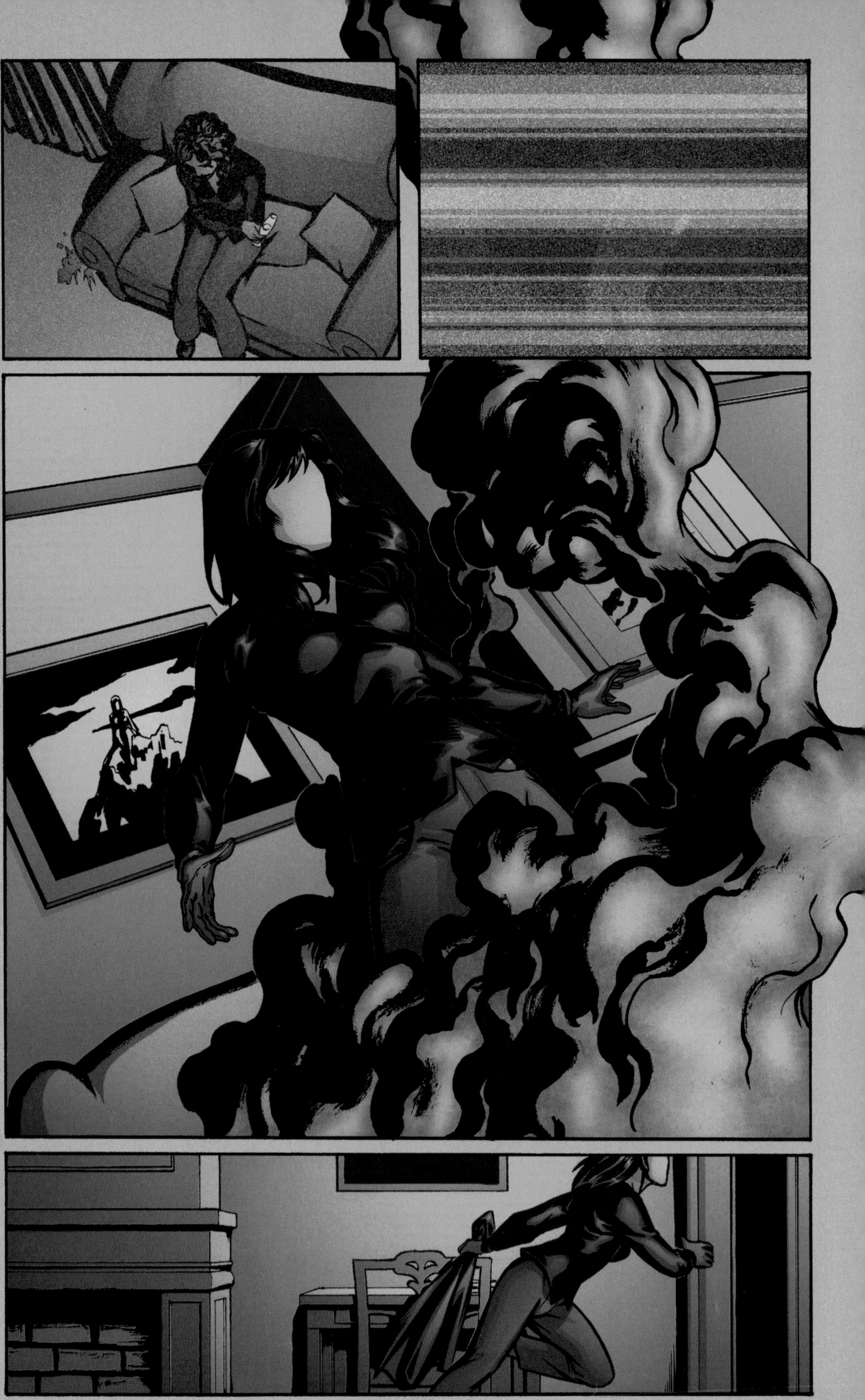

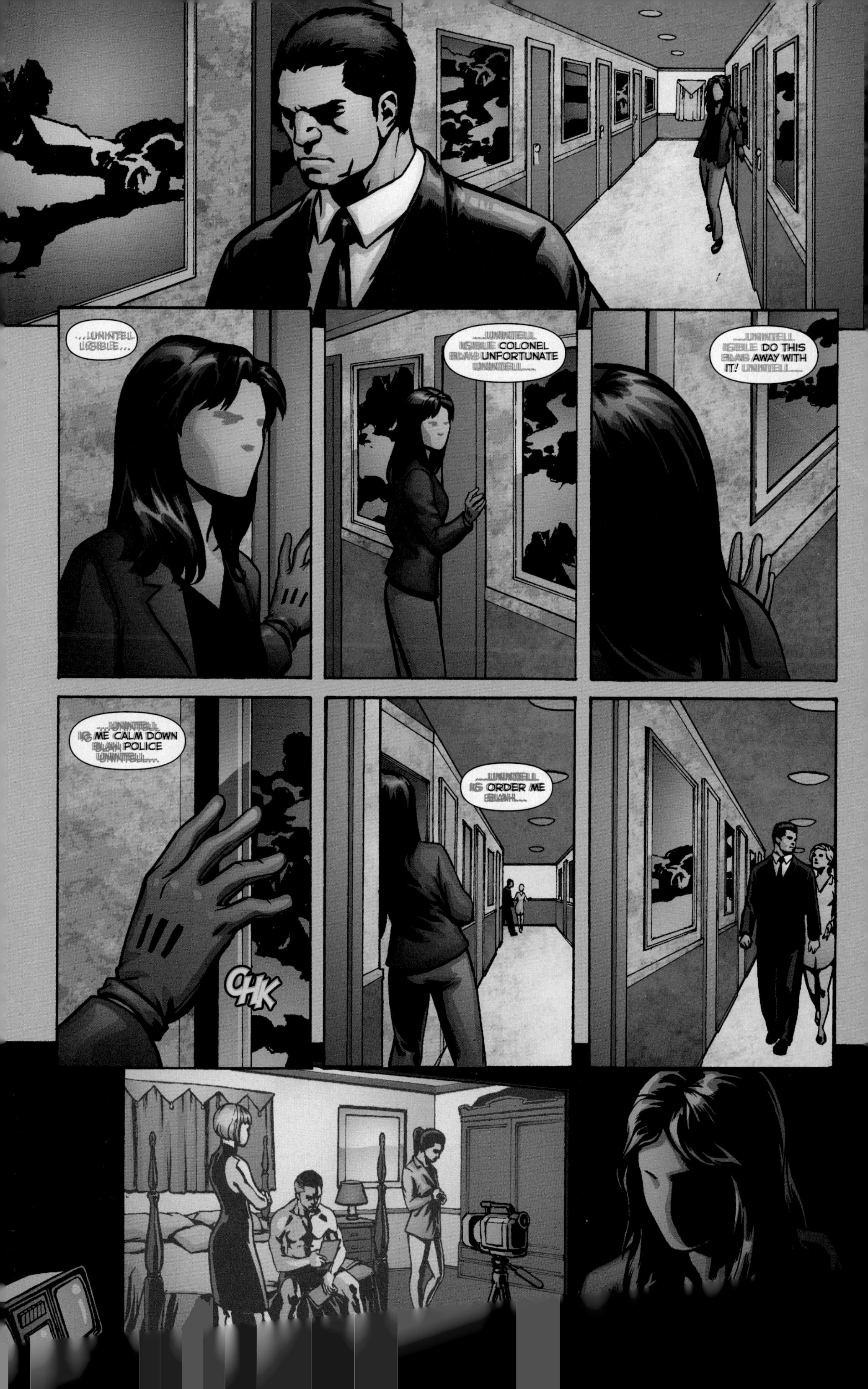
...UNINTELL IGIBLE...
...UNINTELL IGIBLE COLONEL UNFORTUNATE UNINTELL...
...UNINTELL IGIBLE DO THIS AWAY WITH IT! UNINTELL...
...UNINTELL IG ME CALM DOWN POLICE UNINTELL...
CHK
...UNINTELL IG ORDER ME

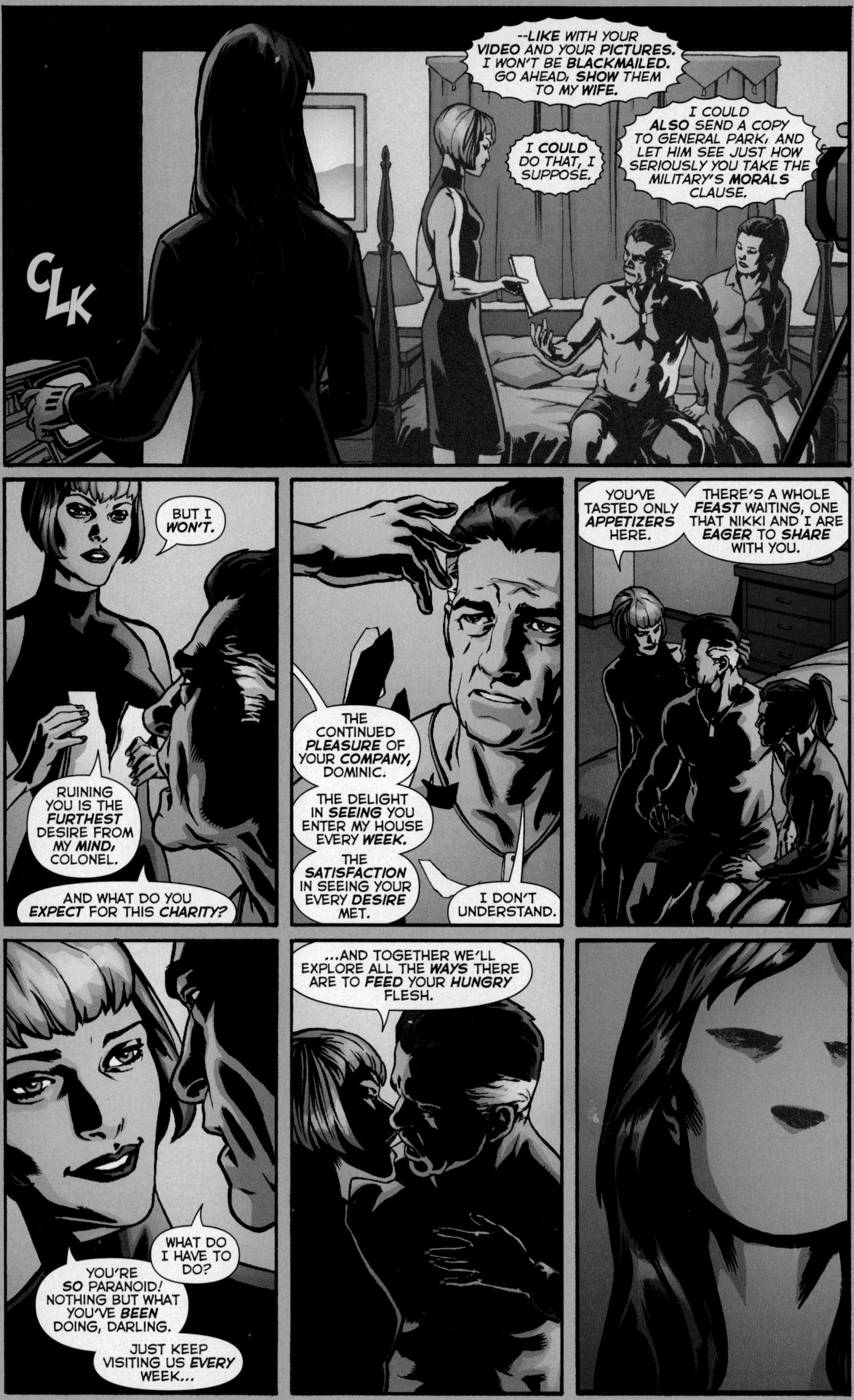

CLK
--LIKE WITH YOUR VIDEO AND YOUR PICTURES. I WON'T BE BLACKMAILED. GO AHEAD, SHOW THEM TO MY WIFE.
I COULD DO THAT, I SUPPOSE.
I COULD ALSO SEND A COPY TO GENERAL PARK, AND LET HIM SEE JUST HOW SERIOUSLY YOU TAKE THE MILITARY'S MORALS CLAUSE.
BUT I WON'T.
RUINING YOU IS THE FURTHEST DESIRE FROM MY MIND, COLONEL.
AND WHAT DO YOU EXPECT FOR THIS CHARITY?
THE CONTINUED PLEASURE OF YOUR COMPANY, DOMINIC.
THE DELIGHT IN SEEING YOU ENTER MY HOUSE EVERY WEEK.
THE SATISFACTION IN SEEING YOUR EVERY DESIRE MET.
I DON'T UNDERSTAND.
YOU'VE TASTED ONLY APPETIZERS HERE.
THERE'S A WHOLE FEAST WAITING, ONE THAT NIKKI AND I ARE EAGER TO SHARE WITH YOU.
WHAT DO I HAVE TO DO?
YOU'RE SO PARANOID! NOTHING BUT WHAT YOU'VE BEEN DOING, DARLING.
JUST KEEP VISITING US EVERY WEEK...
...AND TOGETHER WE'LL EXPLORE ALL THE WAYS THERE ARE TO FEED YOUR HUNGRY FLESH.

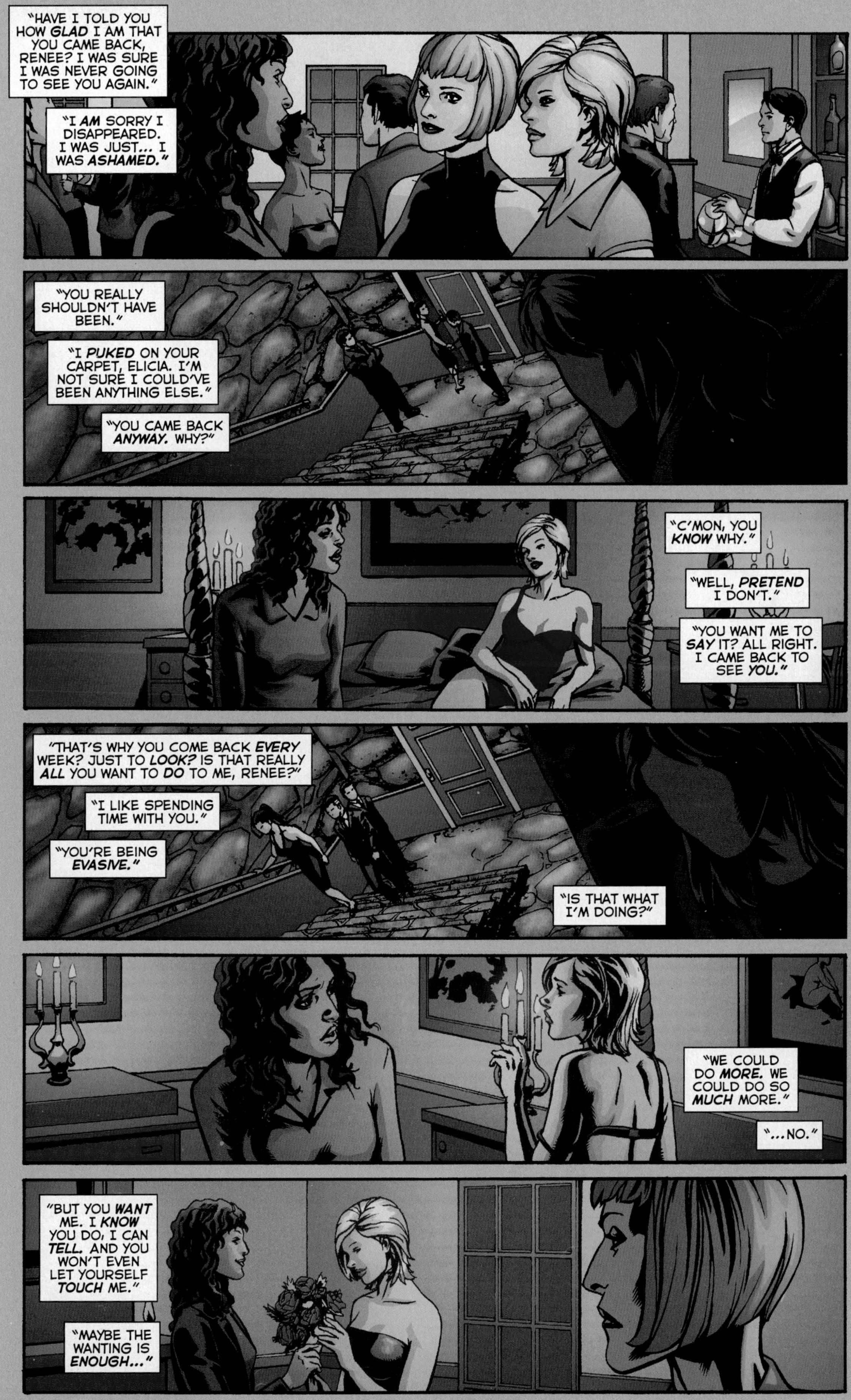
"HAVE I TOLD YOU HOW GLAD I AM THAT YOU CAME BACK, RENEE? I WAS SURE I WAS NEVER GOING TO SEE YOU AGAIN."
"I AM SORRY I DISAPPEARED. I WAS JUST... I WAS ASHAMED."
"YOU REALLY SHOULDN'T HAVE BEEN."
"I PUKED ON YOUR CARPET, ELICIA. I'M NOT SURE I COULD'VE BEEN ANYTHING ELSE."
"YOU CAME BACK ANYWAY. WHY?"
"C'MON, YOU KNOW WHY."
"WELL, PRETEND I DON'T."
"YOU WANT ME TO SAY IT? ALL RIGHT. I CAME BACK TO SEE YOU."
"THAT'S WHY YOU COME BACK EVERY WEEK? JUST TO LOOK? IS THAT REALLY ALL YOU WANT TO DO TO ME, RENEE?"
"I LIKE SPENDING TIME WITH YOU."
"YOU'RE BEING EVASIVE."
"IS THAT WHAT I'M DOING?"
"WE COULD DO MORE. WE COULD DO SO MUCH MORE."
"...NO."
"BUT YOU WANT ME. I KNOW YOU DO, I CAN TELL. AND YOU WON'T EVEN LET YOURSELF TOUCH ME."
"MAYBE THE WANTING IS ENOUGH..."

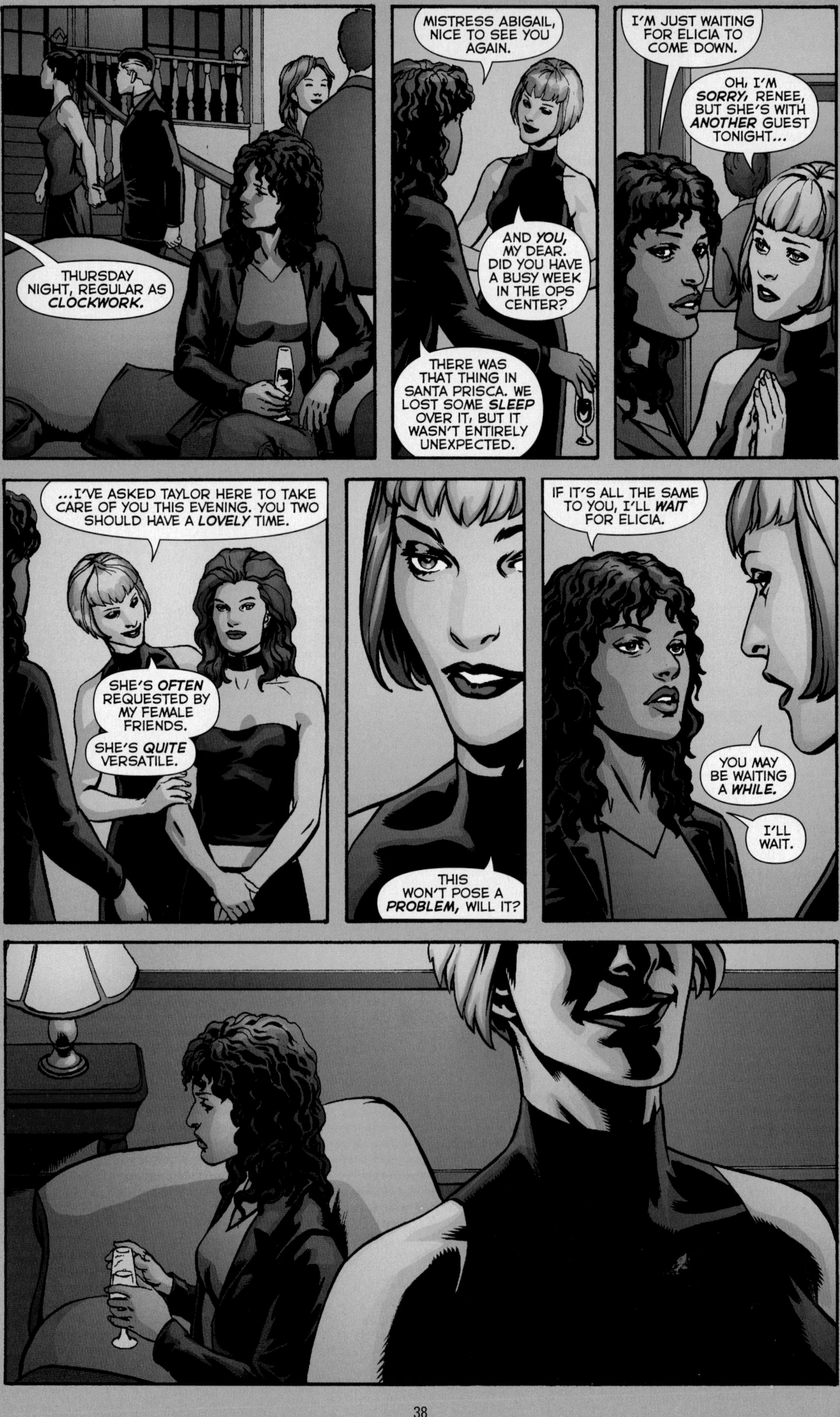
THURSDAY NIGHT, REGULAR AS CLOCKWORK.
MISTRESS ABIGAIL, NICE TO SEE YOU AGAIN.
AND YOU, MY DEAR. DID YOU HAVE A BUSY WEEK IN THE OPS CENTER?
THERE WAS THAT THING IN SANTA PRISCA. WE LOST SOME SLEEP OVER IT, BUT IT WASN'T ENTIRELY UNEXPECTED.
I'M JUST WAITING FOR ELICIA TO COME DOWN.
OH, I'M SORRY, RENEE, BUT SHE'S WITH ANOTHER GUEST TONIGHT...
...I'VE ASKED TAYLOR HERE TO TAKE CARE OF YOU THIS EVENING. YOU TWO SHOULD HAVE A LOVELY TIME.
SHE'S OFTEN REQUESTED BY MY FEMALE FRIENDS.
SHE'S QUITE VERSATILE.
THIS WON'T POSE A PROBLEM, WILL IT?
IF IT'S ALL THE SAME TO YOU, I'LL WAIT FOR ELICIA.
YOU MAY BE WAITING A WHILE.
I'LL WAIT.

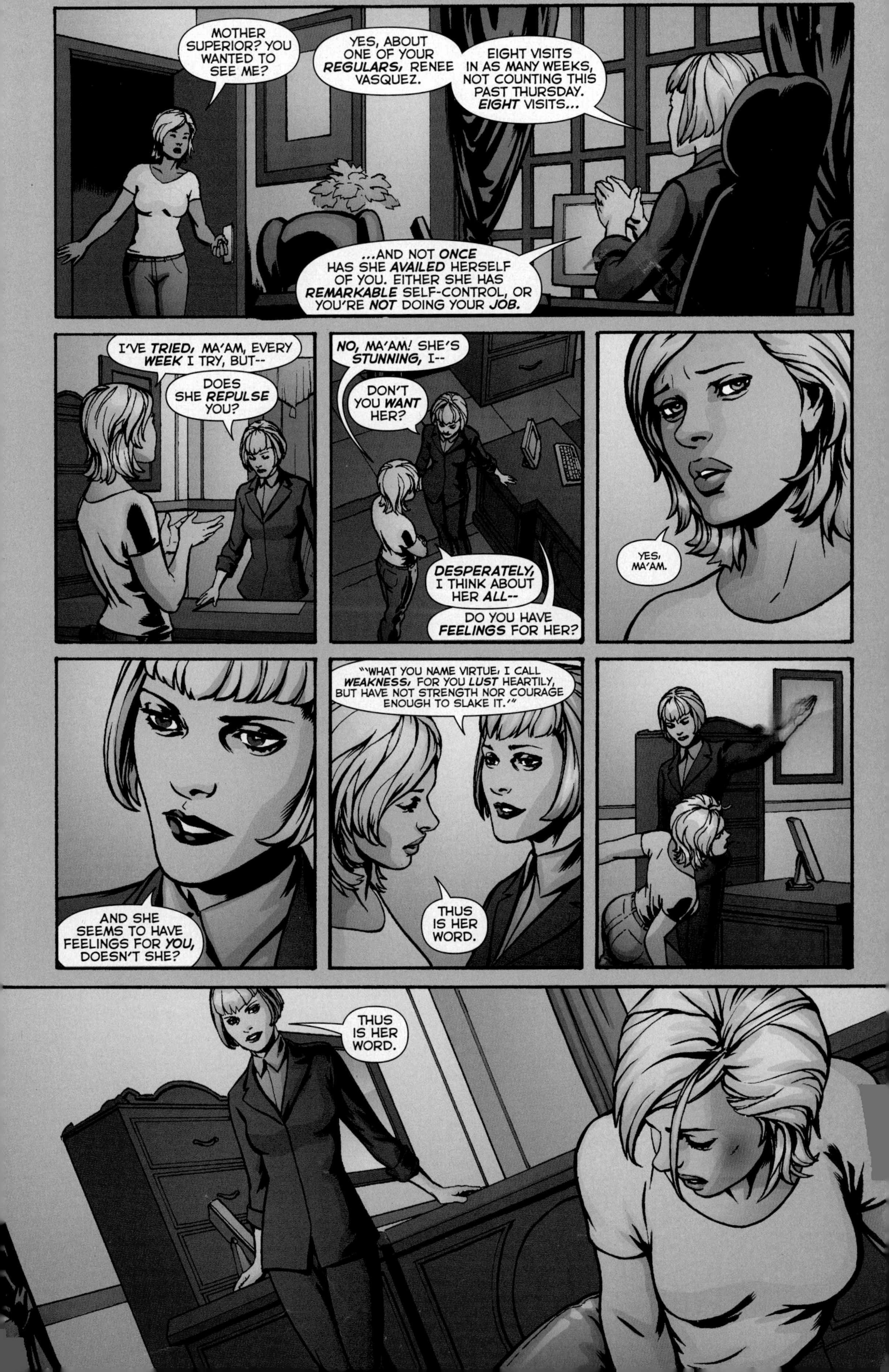
MOTHER SUPERIOR? YOU WANTED TO SEE ME?
YES, ABOUT ONE OF YOUR *REGULARS,* RENEE VASQUEZ.
EIGHT VISITS IN AS MANY WEEKS, NOT COUNTING THIS PAST THURSDAY. *EIGHT* VISITS...
...AND NOT *ONCE* HAS SHE *AVAILED* HERSELF OF YOU. EITHER SHE HAS *REMARKABLE* SELF-CONTROL, OR YOU'RE *NOT* DOING YOUR *JOB.*
I'VE *TRIED,* MA'AM, EVERY *WEEK* I TRY, BUT--
DOES SHE *REPULSE* YOU?
NO, MA'AM! SHE'S *STUNNING,* I--
DON'T YOU *WANT* HER?
DESPERATELY, I THINK ABOUT HER *ALL*--
DO YOU HAVE *FEELINGS* FOR HER?
YES, MA'AM.
AND SHE SEEMS TO HAVE FEELINGS FOR *YOU,* DOESN'T SHE?
"'WHAT YOU NAME VIRTUE, I CALL *WEAKNESS,* FOR YOU *LUST* HEARTILY, BUT HAVE NOT STRENGTH NOR COURAGE ENOUGH TO SLAKE IT.'"
THUS IS HER WORD.
THUS IS HER WORD.

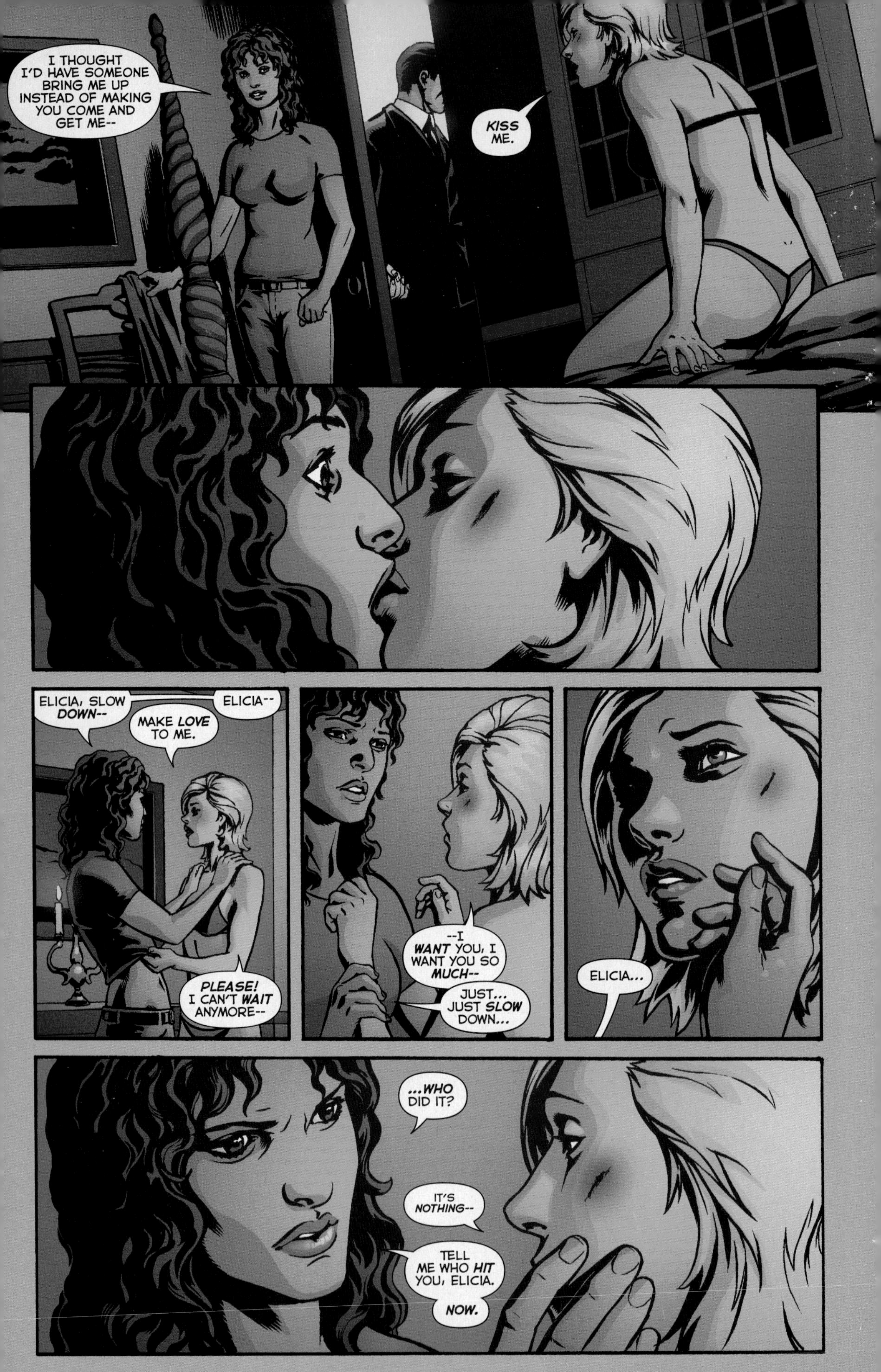
I THOUGHT I'D HAVE SOMEONE BRING ME UP INSTEAD OF MAKING YOU COME AND GET ME--
KISS ME.
ELICIA, SLOW DOWN--
ELICIA--
MAKE LOVE TO ME.
PLEASE! I CAN'T WAIT ANYMORE--
--I WANT YOU, I WANT YOU SO MUCH--
JUST... JUST SLOW DOWN...
ELICIA...
...WHO DID IT?
IT'S NOTHING--
TELL ME WHO HIT YOU, ELICIA.
NOW.

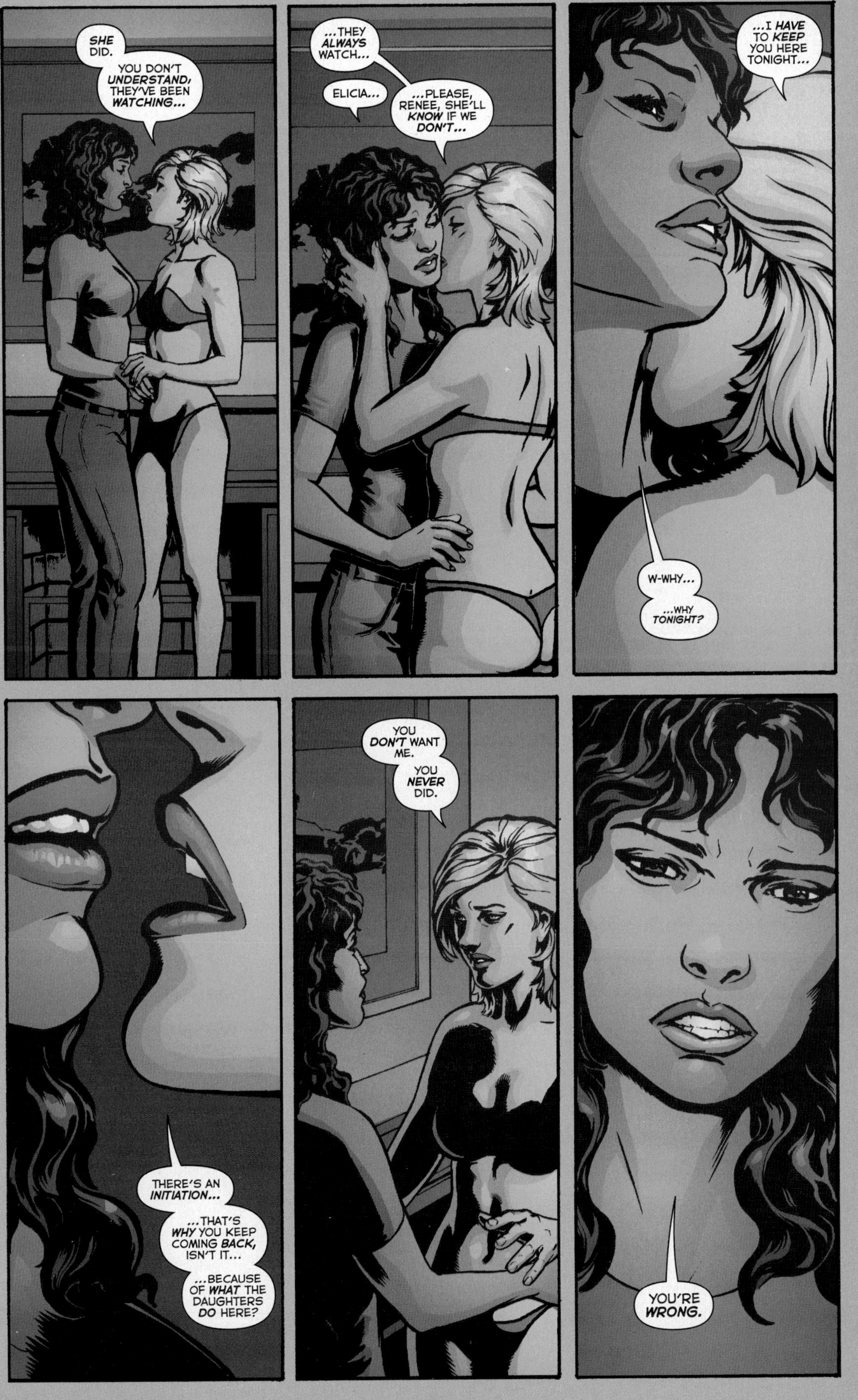
SHE DID.
YOU DON'T UNDERSTAND, THEY'VE BEEN WATCHING...
...THEY ALWAYS WATCH...
ELICIA...
...PLEASE, RENEE, SHE'LL KNOW IF WE DON'T...
...I HAVE TO KEEP YOU HERE TONIGHT...
W-WHY...
...WHY TONIGHT?
THERE'S AN INITIATION...
...THAT'S WHY YOU KEEP COMING BACK, ISN'T IT...
...BECAUSE OF WHAT THE DAUGHTERS DO HERE?
YOU DON'T WANT ME.
YOU NEVER DID.
YOU'RE WRONG.

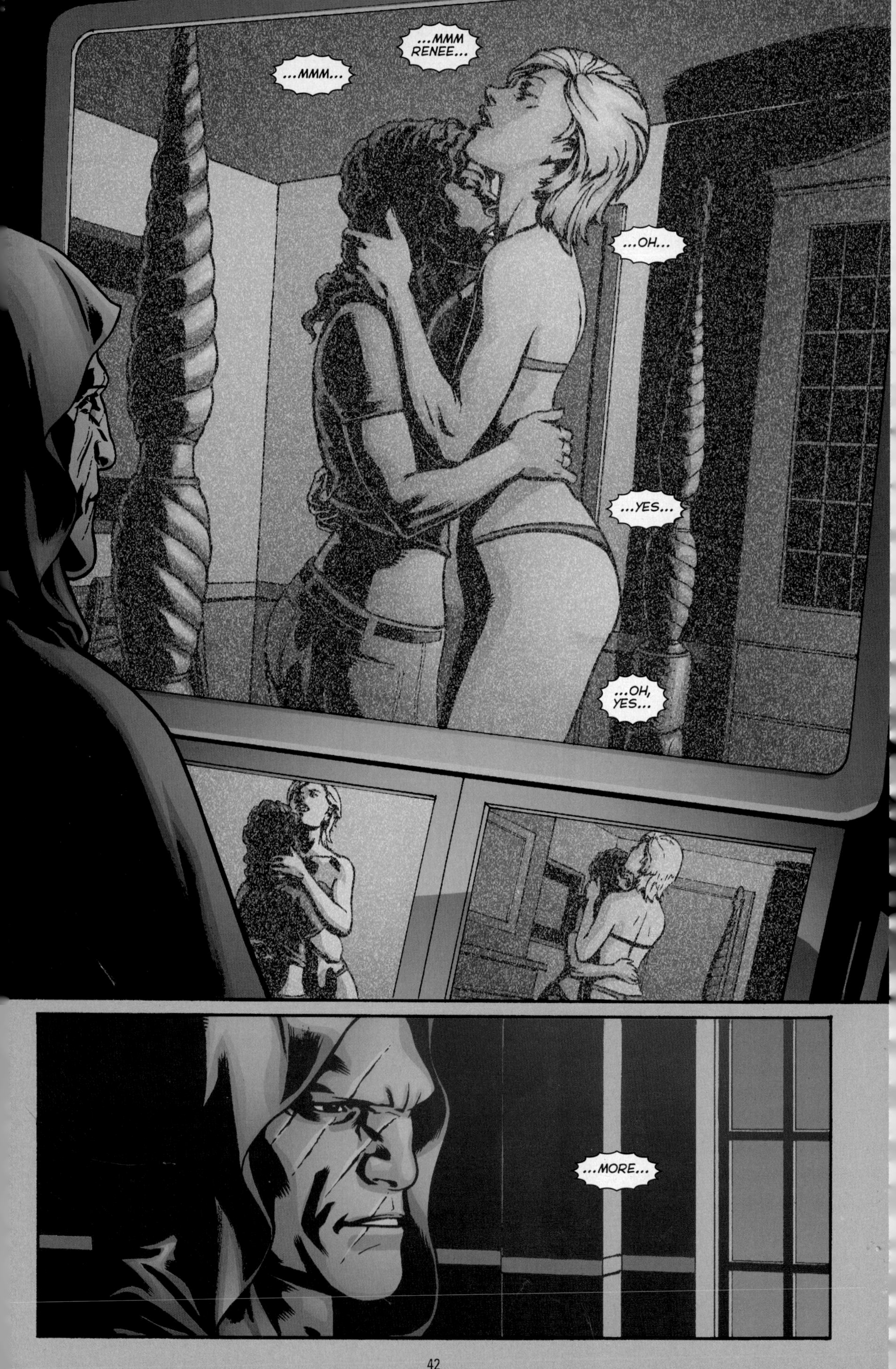
...MMM...
...MMM RENEE...
...OH...
...YES...
...OH, YES...
...MORE...

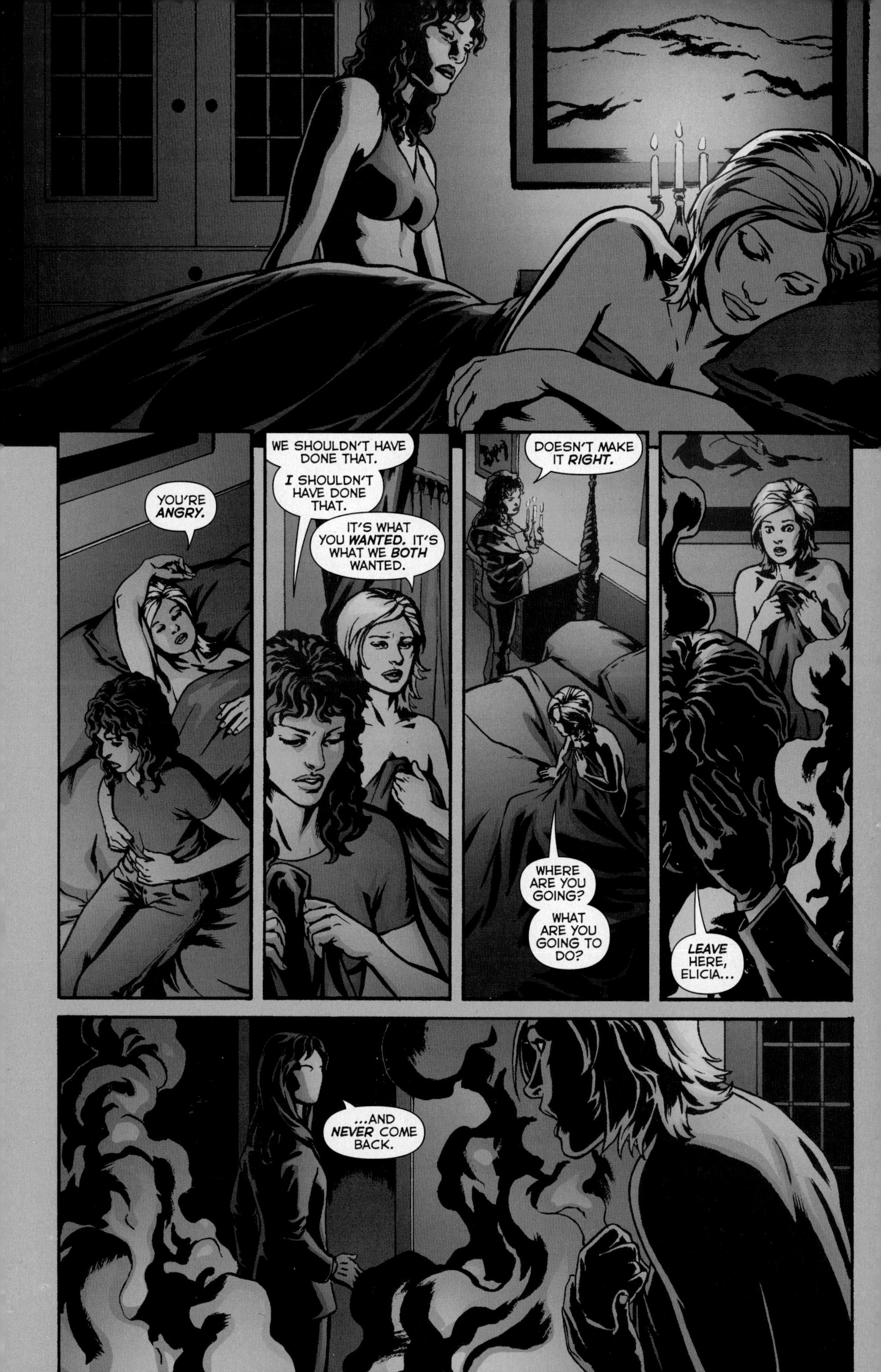
YOU'RE ANGRY.
WE SHOULDN'T HAVE DONE THAT.
I SHOULDN'T HAVE DONE THAT.
IT'S WHAT YOU WANTED. IT'S WHAT WE BOTH WANTED.
DOESN'T MAKE IT RIGHT.
WHERE ARE YOU GOING?
WHAT ARE YOU GOING TO DO?
LEAVE HERE, ELICIA...
...AND NEVER COME BACK.

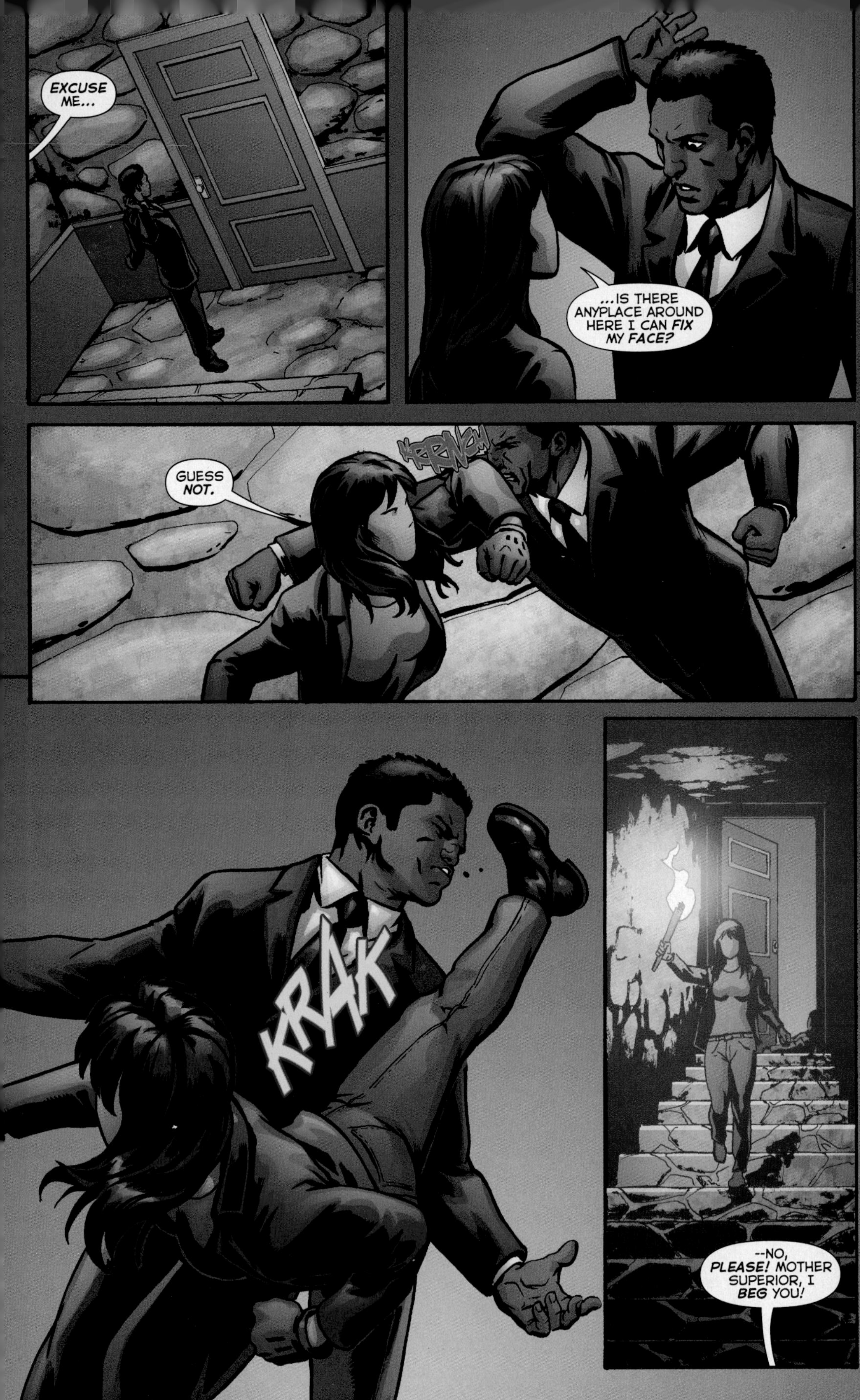
EXCUSE ME...
...IS THERE ANYPLACE AROUND HERE I CAN *FIX* MY *FACE?*
GUESS *NOT.*
KRAK
--NO, *PLEASE!* MOTHER SUPERIOR, I *BEG* YOU!

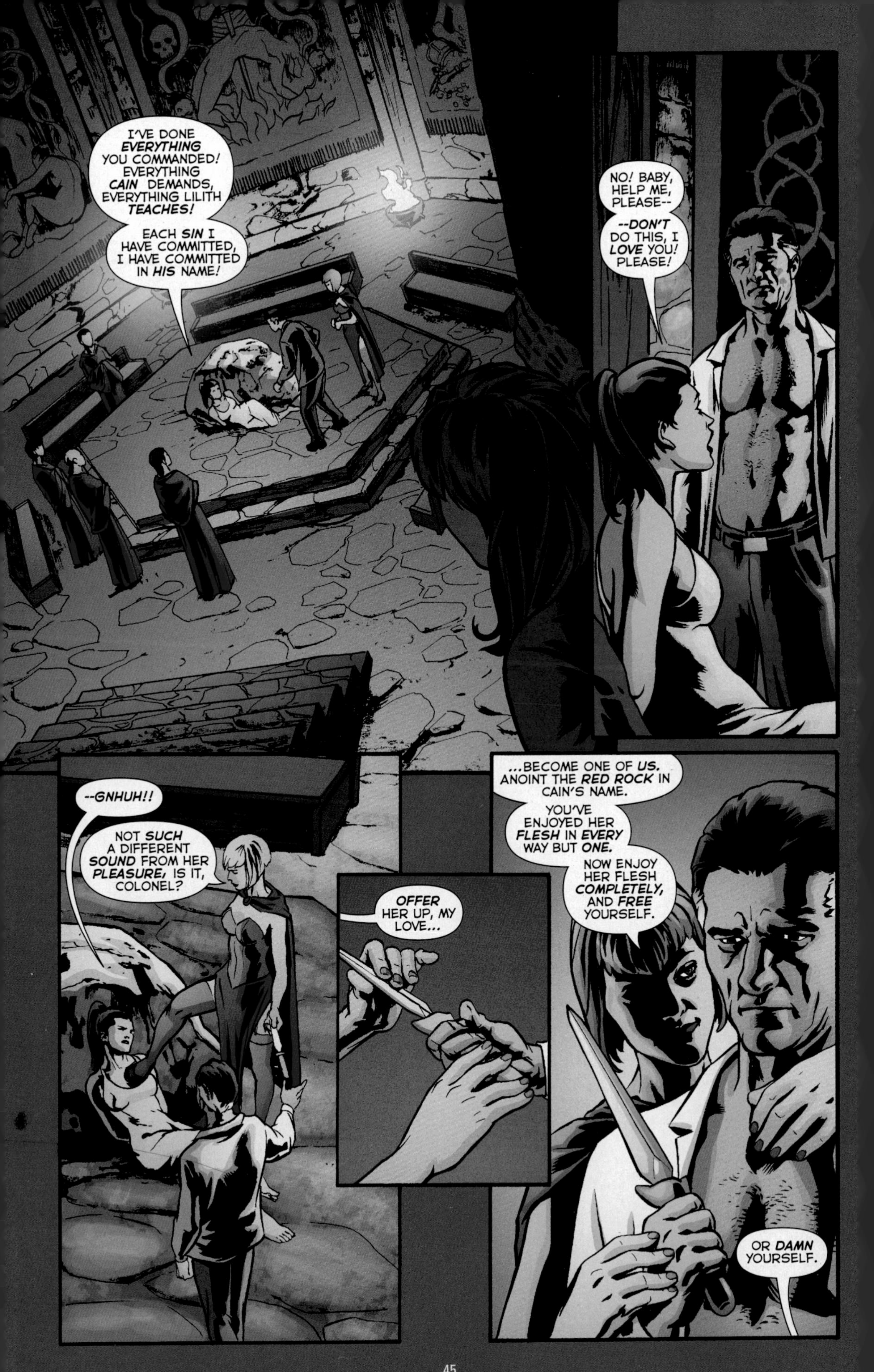
I'VE DONE EVERYTHING YOU COMMANDED! EVERYTHING CAIN DEMANDS, EVERYTHING LILITH TEACHES!
EACH SIN I HAVE COMMITTED, I HAVE COMMITTED IN HIS NAME!
NO! BABY, HELP ME, PLEASE--
--DON'T DO THIS, I LOVE YOU! PLEASE!
--GNHUH!!
NOT SUCH A DIFFERENT SOUND FROM HER PLEASURE, IS IT, COLONEL?
OFFER HER UP, MY LOVE...
...BECOME ONE OF US. ANOINT THE RED ROCK IN CAIN'S NAME.
YOU'VE ENJOYED HER FLESH IN EVERY WAY BUT ONE.
NOW ENJOY HER FLESH COMPLETELY, AND FREE YOURSELF.
OR DAMN YOURSELF.

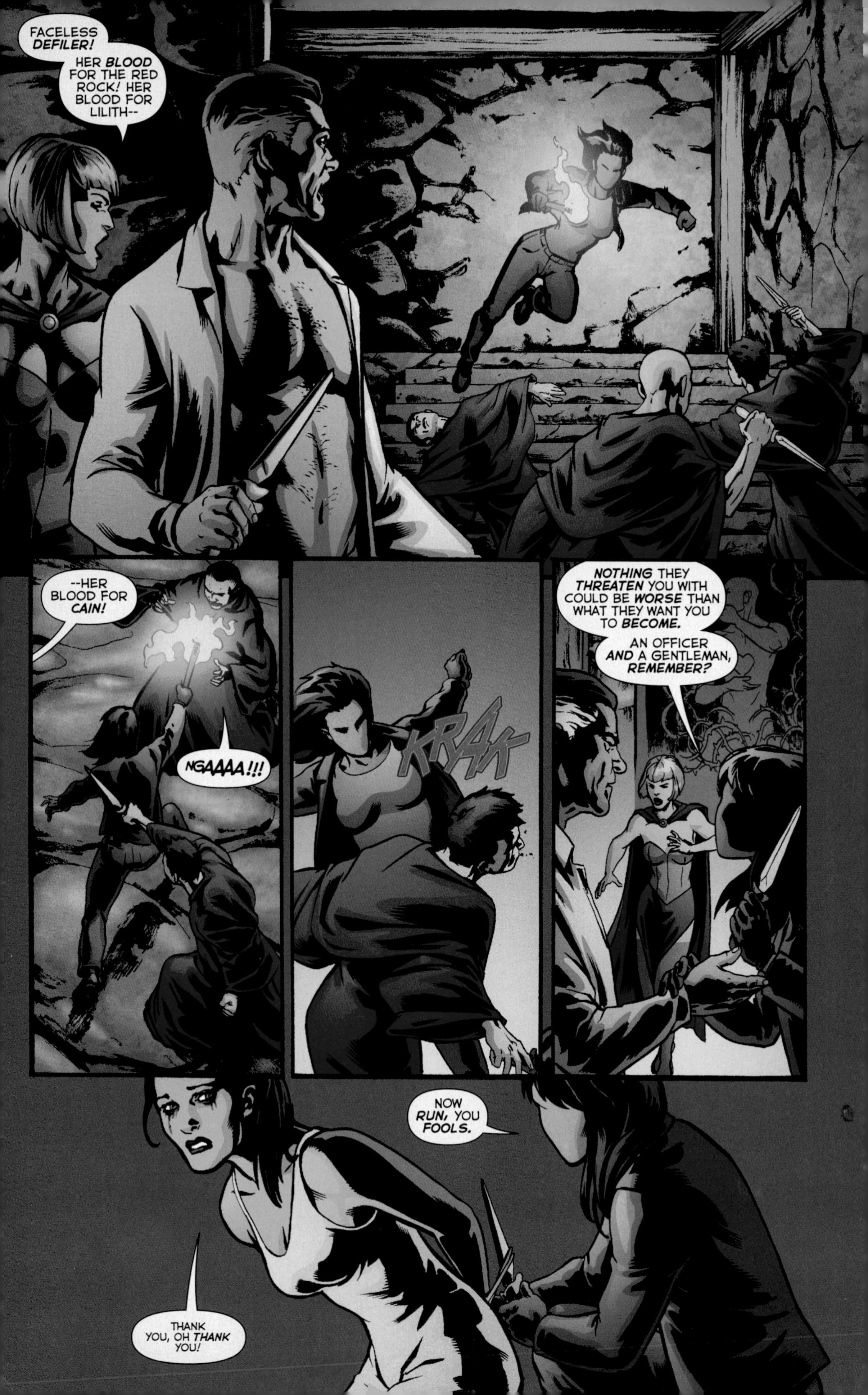
FACELESS DEFILER!
HER BLOOD FOR THE RED ROCK! HER BLOOD FOR LILITH--
--HER BLOOD FOR CAIN!
NGAAAA!!!
KRAK
NOTHING THEY THREATEN YOU WITH COULD BE WORSE THAN WHAT THEY WANT YOU TO BECOME.
AN OFFICER AND A GENTLEMAN, REMEMBER?
NOW RUN, YOU FOOLS.
THANK YOU, OH THANK YOU!

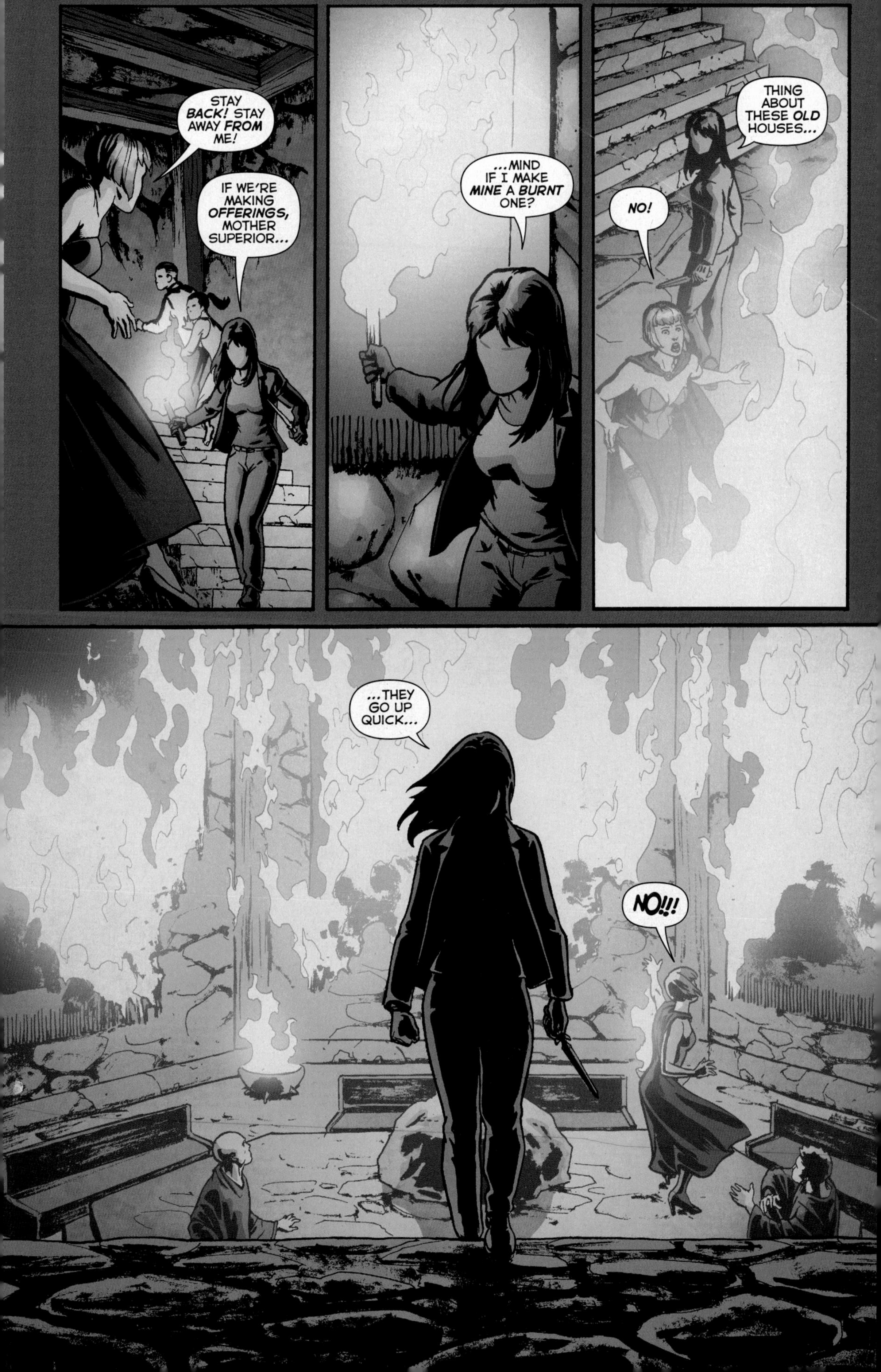
STAY BACK! STAY AWAY FROM ME!
IF WE'RE MAKING OFFERINGS, MOTHER SUPERIOR...
...MIND IF I MAKE MINE A BURNT ONE?
THING ABOUT THESE OLD HOUSES...
NO!
...THEY GO UP QUICK...
NO!!!

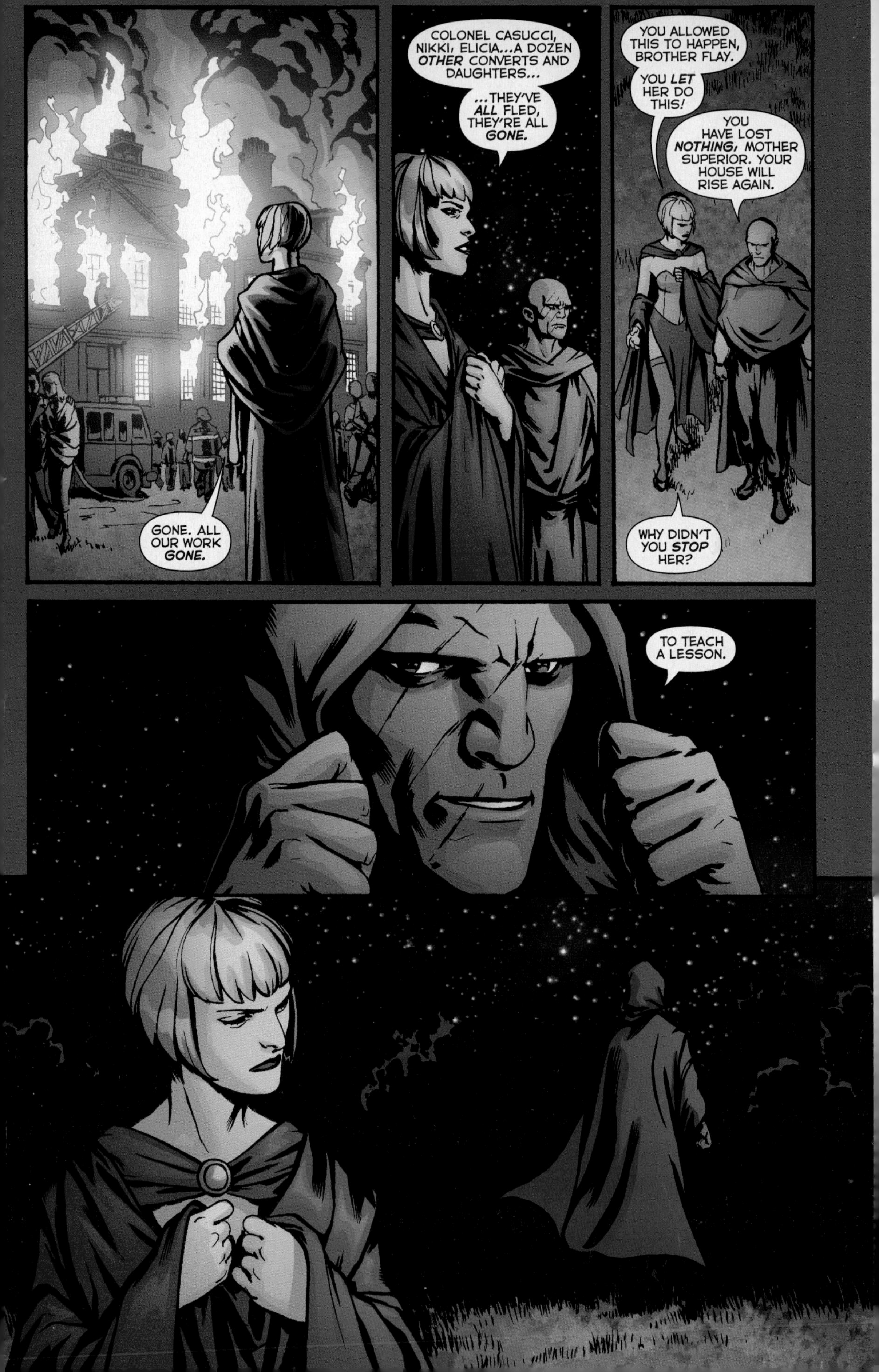
GONE. ALL OUR WORK GONE.
COLONEL CASUCCI, NIKKI, ELICIA...A DOZEN OTHER CONVERTS AND DAUGHTERS...
...THEY'VE ALL FLED, THEY'RE ALL GONE.
YOU ALLOWED THIS TO HAPPEN, BROTHER FLAY.
YOU LET HER DO THIS!
WHY DIDN'T YOU STOP HER?
YOU HAVE LOST NOTHING, MOTHER SUPERIOR. YOUR HOUSE WILL RISE AGAIN.
TO TEACH A LESSON.

The Third Book of Blood

Chapter 19, Verses 4-13

⁴ Much afraid of the shard and the teachings was the Grande, and it was whispered, even, that between the First and Lilith, more than flesh alone had been shared; and that their power was great, and nothing hidden from them would not be divined.

⁵ Thus the Grande sent forth his herald to the gates of the city, to gift the First one thousand pieces of gold; and the messenger did bow, and say with most fine deceit, From my master, in tribute and respect, that ye will leave in peace.

⁶ And the First took up the thousand pieces; then to the herald, he said, Tell thy master I would have entry to Har-Mammon.

⁷ Then was the Grande much disturbed that the First remained, and so did send the herald a second time, with a gift of ten thousand pieces of gold, and the messenger did bow, and say with fine deceit, From my master, who would call ye person of his equal.

⁸ And the First took up the ten thousand pieces; then to the herald, he said, Tell thy master his equal would have entry to Har-Mammon.

⁹ Now it was the Grande came to the gates, and ascending the old wall, did gaze down and there saw the First all wrapped in dust and rags as a beggar; and saw he too the blood dried upon the strips so stained that did encircle His fists.

¹⁰ And to the First, the Grande did offer precious stones, wine, and oils, and slaves of fine feature and bone, devoid of markings, all chained and pleasing to the eye; and four stallions, too, as black as cold apocalypse; and having made such gifts, the Grande did entreat the First to leave Har-Mammon for a far shore, and to not return.

¹¹ And it was that the First looked upon the bounty His coming had brought, and saw still the shining wealth of the Grande and Har-Mammon, and knew He then clear the Third Lesson of Blood, and spake to the Grande thus,

¹² To your gates I came thirsty, and with water would have left contented; but ye have shown me Greed, and this I shall name the Third Lesson; and ye have shown me the sign that thou art its slave, and not its master.

¹³ And the First did bring forth from His palm the shard of the Red Rock, and with it did lead entry unto Har-Mammon, and did take all that His eye did cast upon for Himself.

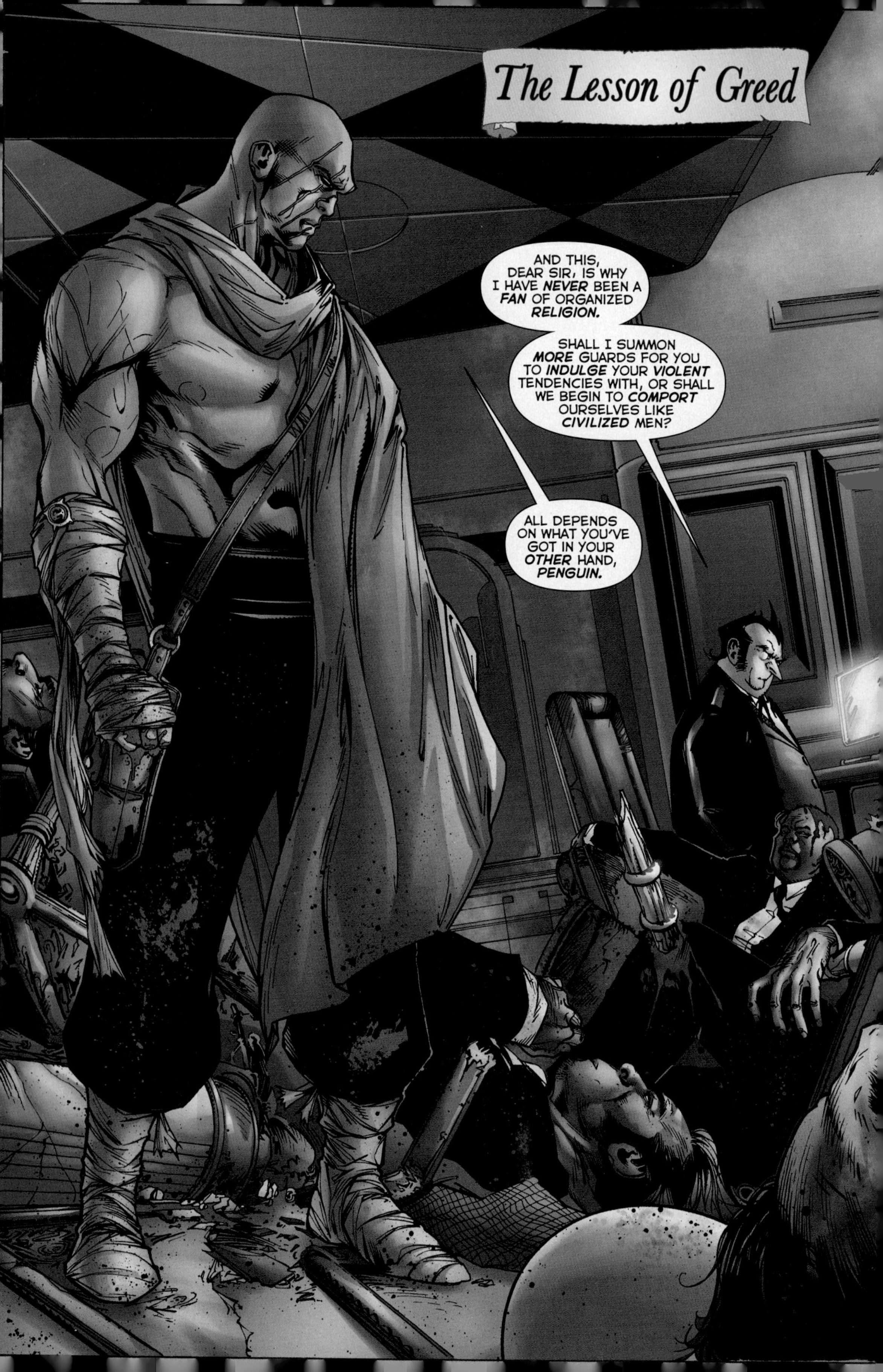
The Lesson of Greed
AND THIS, DEAR SIR, IS WHY I HAVE NEVER BEEN A FAN OF ORGANIZED RELIGION.
SHALL I SUMMON MORE GUARDS FOR YOU TO INDULGE YOUR VIOLENT TENDENCIES WITH, OR SHALL WE BEGIN TO COMPORT OURSELVES LIKE CIVILIZED MEN?
ALL DEPENDS ON WHAT YOU'VE GOT IN YOUR OTHER HAND, PENGUIN.

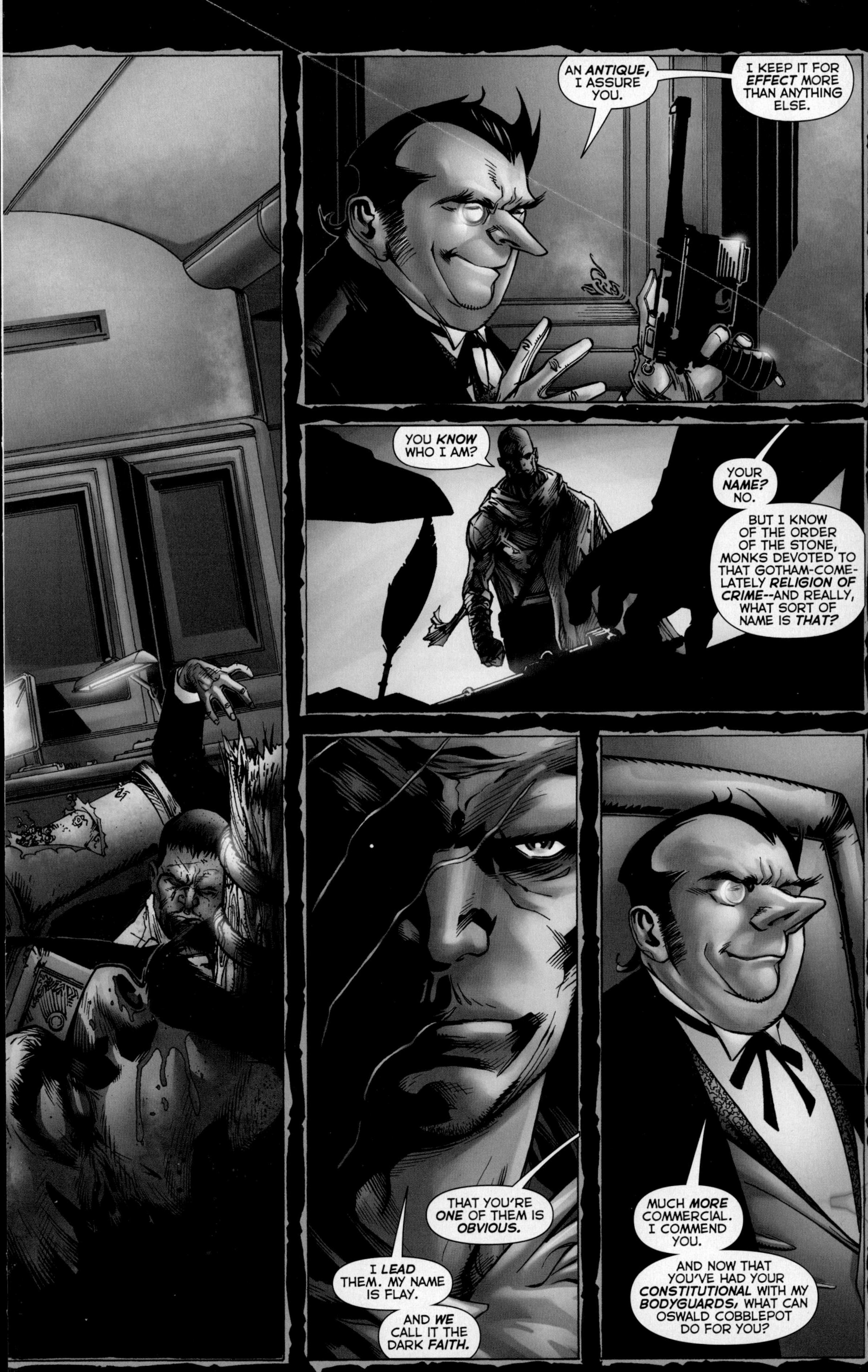
AN ANTIQUE, I ASSURE YOU.
I KEEP IT FOR EFFECT MORE THAN ANYTHING ELSE.
YOU KNOW WHO I AM?
YOUR NAME? NO.
BUT I KNOW OF THE ORDER OF THE STONE, MONKS DEVOTED TO THAT GOTHAM-COME-LATELY RELIGION OF CRIME--AND REALLY, WHAT SORT OF NAME IS THAT?
THAT YOU'RE ONE OF THEM IS OBVIOUS.
I LEAD THEM. MY NAME IS FLAY.
AND WE CALL IT THE DARK FAITH.
MUCH MORE COMMERCIAL. I COMMEND YOU.
AND NOW THAT YOU'VE HAD YOUR CONSTITUTIONAL WITH MY BODYGUARDS, WHAT CAN OSWALD COBBLEPOT DO FOR YOU?

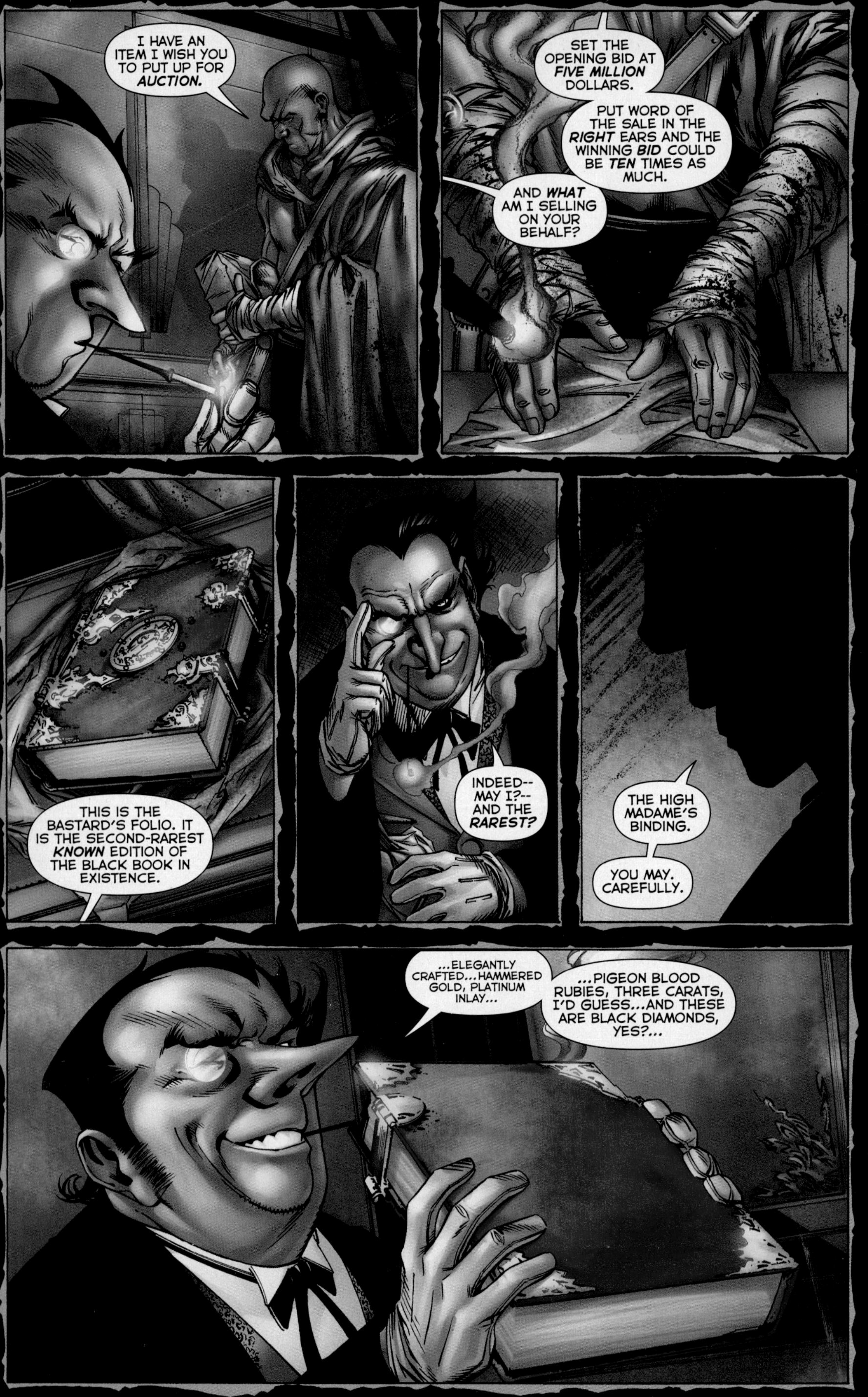
I HAVE AN ITEM I WISH YOU TO PUT UP FOR AUCTION.
SET THE OPENING BID AT FIVE MILLION DOLLARS.
PUT WORD OF THE SALE IN THE RIGHT EARS AND THE WINNING BID COULD BE TEN TIMES AS MUCH.
AND WHAT AM I SELLING ON YOUR BEHALF?
THIS IS THE BASTARD'S FOLIO. IT IS THE SECOND-RAREST KNOWN EDITION OF THE BLACK BOOK IN EXISTENCE.
INDEED-- MAY I?-- AND THE RAREST?
THE HIGH MADAME'S BINDING.
YOU MAY. CAREFULLY.
...ELEGANTLY CRAFTED...HAMMERED GOLD, PLATINUM INLAY...
...PIGEON BLOOD RUBIES, THREE CARATS, I'D GUESS...AND THESE ARE BLACK DIAMONDS, YES?...

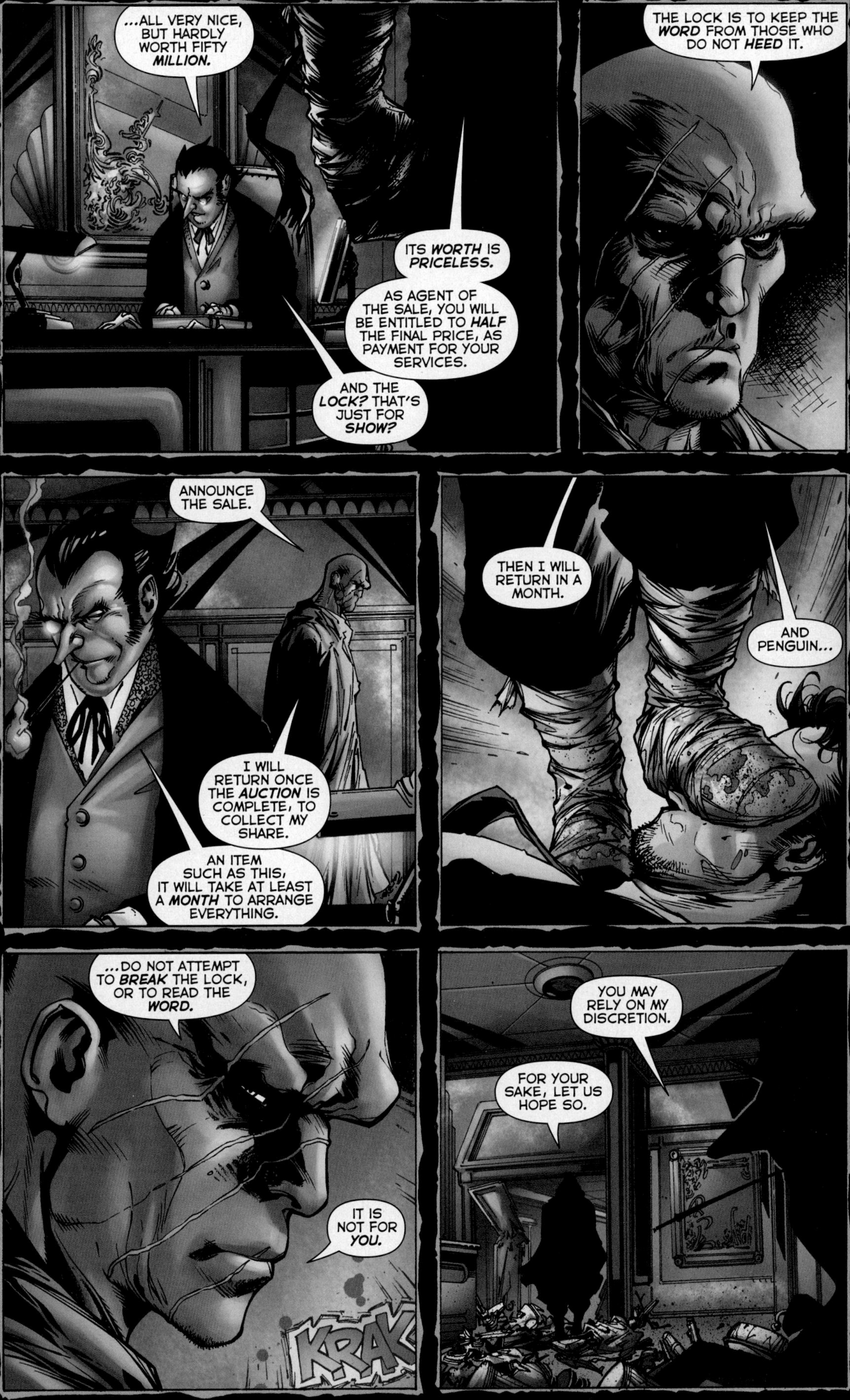
...ALL VERY NICE, BUT HARDLY WORTH FIFTY MILLION.
ITS WORTH IS PRICELESS.
AS AGENT OF THE SALE, YOU WILL BE ENTITLED TO HALF THE FINAL PRICE, AS PAYMENT FOR YOUR SERVICES.
AND THE LOCK? THAT'S JUST FOR SHOW?
THE LOCK IS TO KEEP THE WORD FROM THOSE WHO DO NOT HEED IT.
ANNOUNCE THE SALE.
I WILL RETURN ONCE THE AUCTION IS COMPLETE, TO COLLECT MY SHARE.
AN ITEM SUCH AS THIS, IT WILL TAKE AT LEAST A MONTH TO ARRANGE EVERYTHING.
THEN I WILL RETURN IN A MONTH.
AND PENGUIN...
...DO NOT ATTEMPT TO BREAK THE LOCK, OR TO READ THE WORD.
IT IS NOT FOR YOU.
KRAK
YOU MAY RELY ON MY DISCRETION.
FOR YOUR SAKE, LET US HOPE SO.

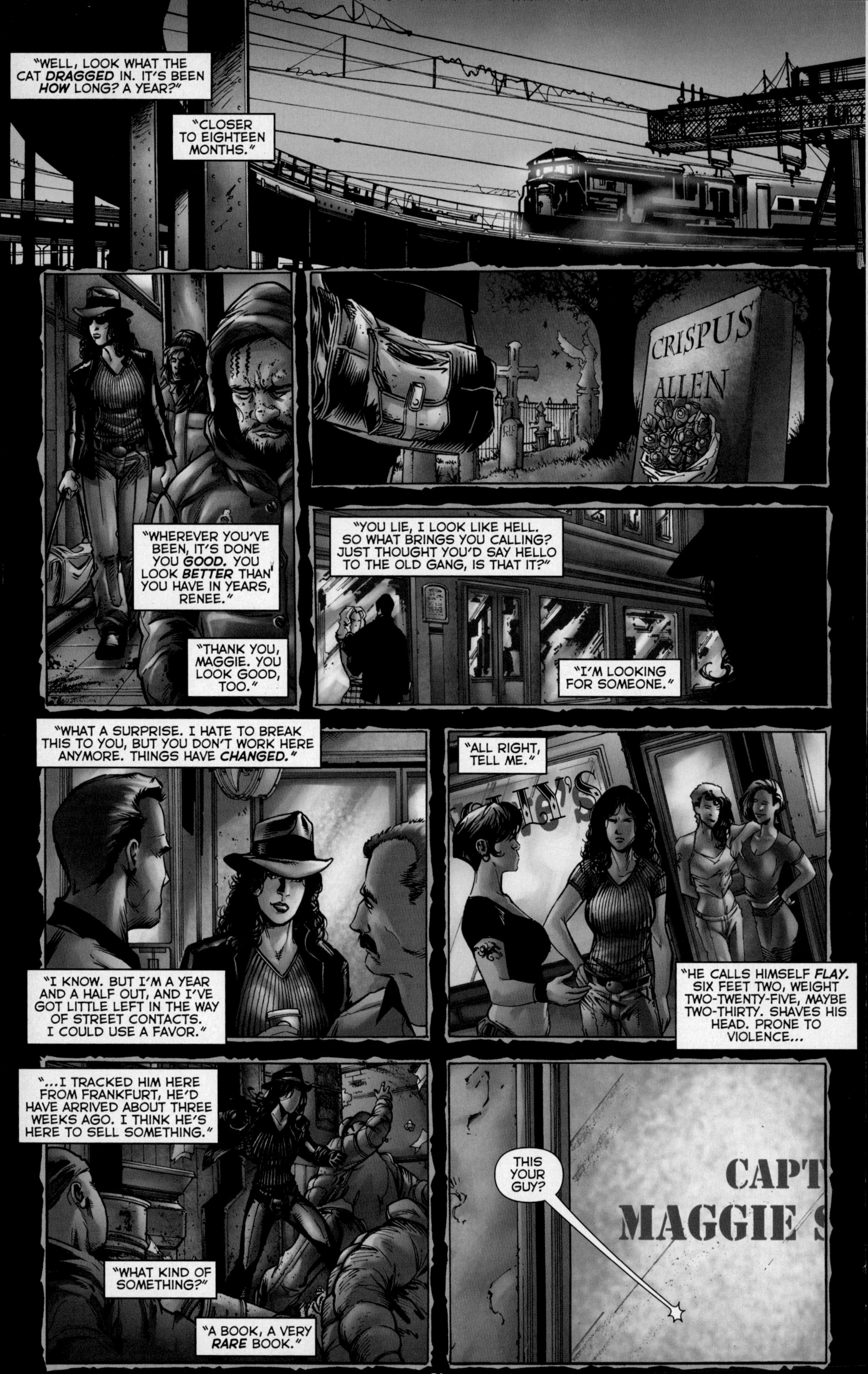
"WELL, LOOK WHAT THE CAT DRAGGED IN. IT'S BEEN HOW LONG? A YEAR?"
"CLOSER TO EIGHTEEN MONTHS."
CRISPUS ALLEN
"WHEREVER YOU'VE BEEN, IT'S DONE YOU GOOD. YOU LOOK BETTER THAN YOU HAVE IN YEARS, RENEE."
"THANK YOU, MAGGIE. YOU LOOK GOOD, TOO."
"YOU LIE, I LOOK LIKE HELL. SO WHAT BRINGS YOU CALLING? JUST THOUGHT YOU'D SAY HELLO TO THE OLD GANG, IS THAT IT?"
"I'M LOOKING FOR SOMEONE."
"WHAT A SURPRISE. I HATE TO BREAK THIS TO YOU, BUT YOU DON'T WORK HERE ANYMORE. THINGS HAVE CHANGED."
"I KNOW. BUT I'M A YEAR AND A HALF OUT, AND I'VE GOT LITTLE LEFT IN THE WAY OF STREET CONTACTS. I COULD USE A FAVOR."
"ALL RIGHT, TELL ME."
"HE CALLS HIMSELF FLAY. SIX FEET TWO, WEIGHT TWO-TWENTY-FIVE, MAYBE TWO-THIRTY. SHAVES HIS HEAD. PRONE TO VIOLENCE..."
"...I TRACKED HIM HERE FROM FRANKFURT, HE'D HAVE ARRIVED ABOUT THREE WEEKS AGO. I THINK HE'S HERE TO SELL SOMETHING."
"WHAT KIND OF SOMETHING?"
"A BOOK, A VERY RARE BOOK."
THIS YOUR GUY?
CAPT
MAGGIE

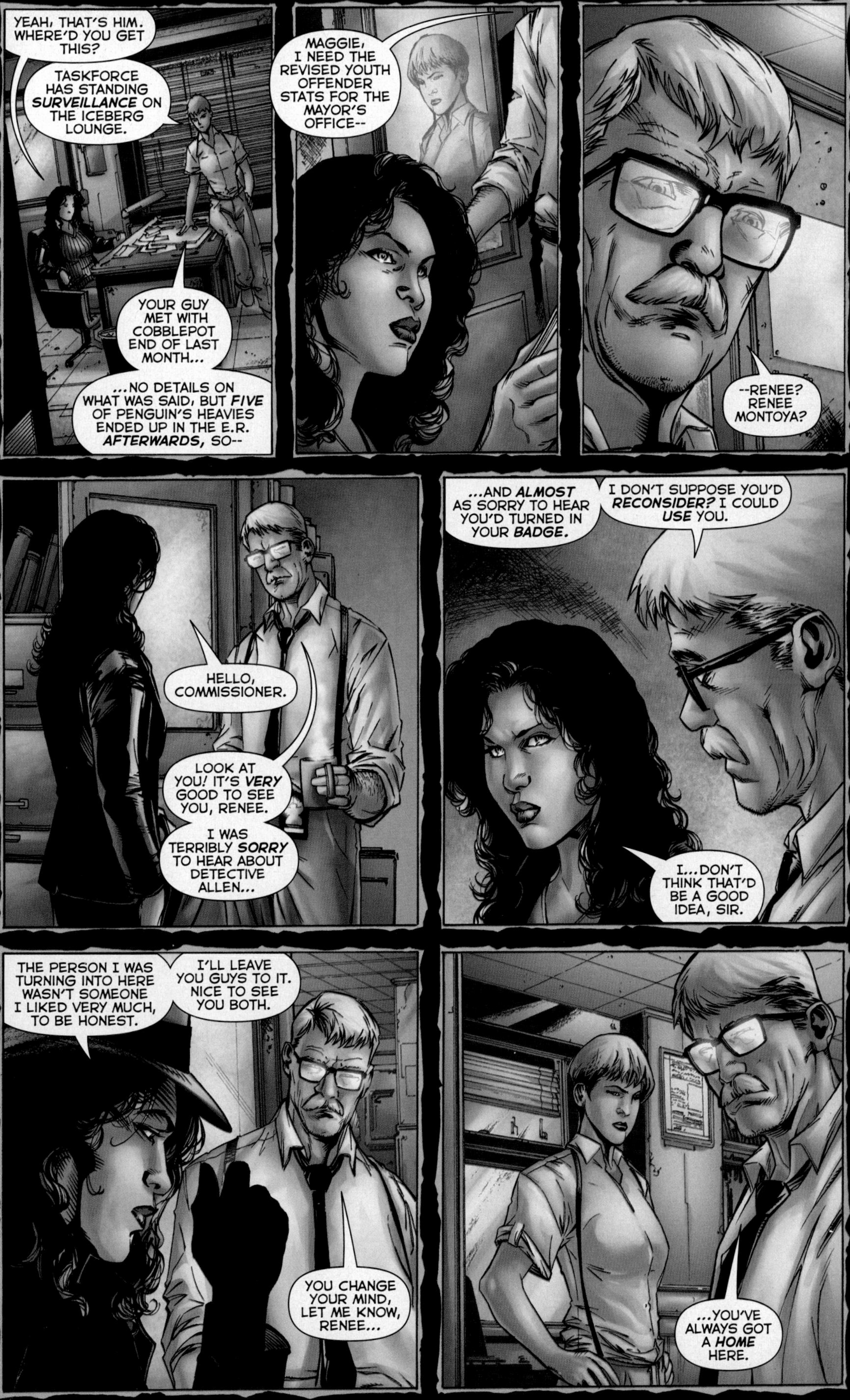
YEAH, THAT'S HIM. WHERE'D YOU GET THIS?
TASKFORCE HAS STANDING SURVEILLANCE ON THE ICEBERG LOUNGE.
YOUR GUY MET WITH COBBLEPOT END OF LAST MONTH...
...NO DETAILS ON WHAT WAS SAID, BUT FIVE OF PENGUIN'S HEAVIES ENDED UP IN THE E.R. AFTERWARDS, SO--
MAGGIE, I NEED THE REVISED YOUTH OFFENDER STATS FOR THE MAYOR'S OFFICE--
--RENEE? RENEE MONTOYA?
HELLO, COMMISSIONER.
LOOK AT YOU! IT'S VERY GOOD TO SEE YOU, RENEE.
I WAS TERRIBLY SORRY TO HEAR ABOUT DETECTIVE ALLEN...
...AND ALMOST AS SORRY TO HEAR YOU'D TURNED IN YOUR BADGE.
I DON'T SUPPOSE YOU'D RECONSIDER? I COULD USE YOU.
I...DON'T THINK THAT'D BE A GOOD IDEA, SIR.
THE PERSON I WAS TURNING INTO HERE WASN'T SOMEONE I LIKED VERY MUCH, TO BE HONEST.
I'LL LEAVE YOU GUYS TO IT. NICE TO SEE YOU BOTH.
YOU CHANGE YOUR MIND, LET ME KNOW, RENEE...
...YOU'VE ALWAYS GOT A HOME HERE.

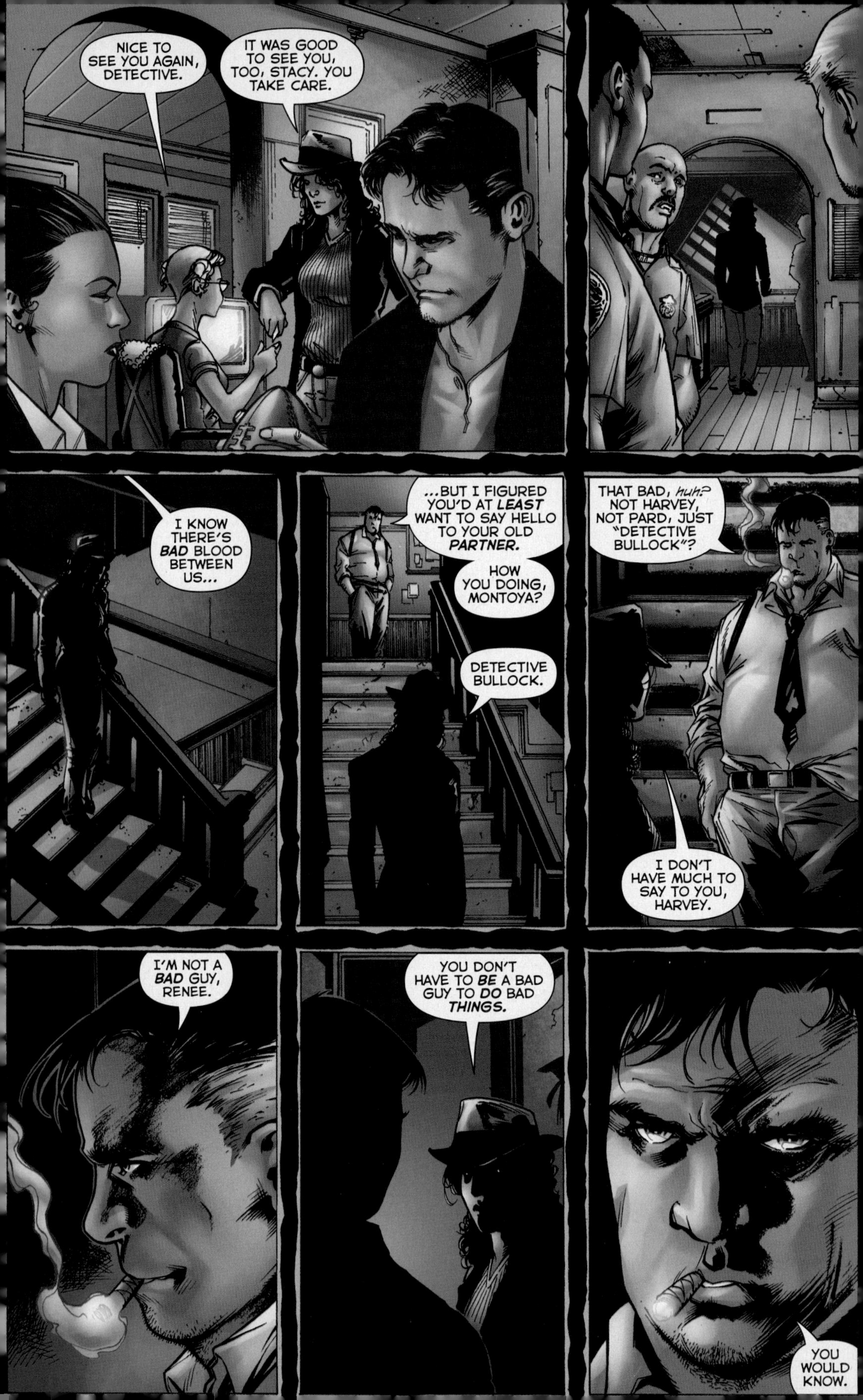
NICE TO SEE YOU AGAIN, DETECTIVE.
IT WAS GOOD TO SEE YOU, TOO, STACY. YOU TAKE CARE.
I KNOW THERE'S *BAD* BLOOD BETWEEN US...
...BUT I FIGURED YOU'D AT *LEAST* WANT TO SAY HELLO TO YOUR OLD *PARTNER.*
HOW YOU DOING, MONTOYA?
DETECTIVE BULLOCK.
THAT BAD, *huh?* NOT HARVEY, NOT PARD, JUST "DETECTIVE BULLOCK"?
I DON'T HAVE MUCH TO SAY TO YOU, HARVEY.
I'M NOT A *BAD* GUY, RENEE.
YOU DON'T HAVE TO *BE* A BAD GUY TO *DO* BAD *THINGS.*
YOU WOULD KNOW.

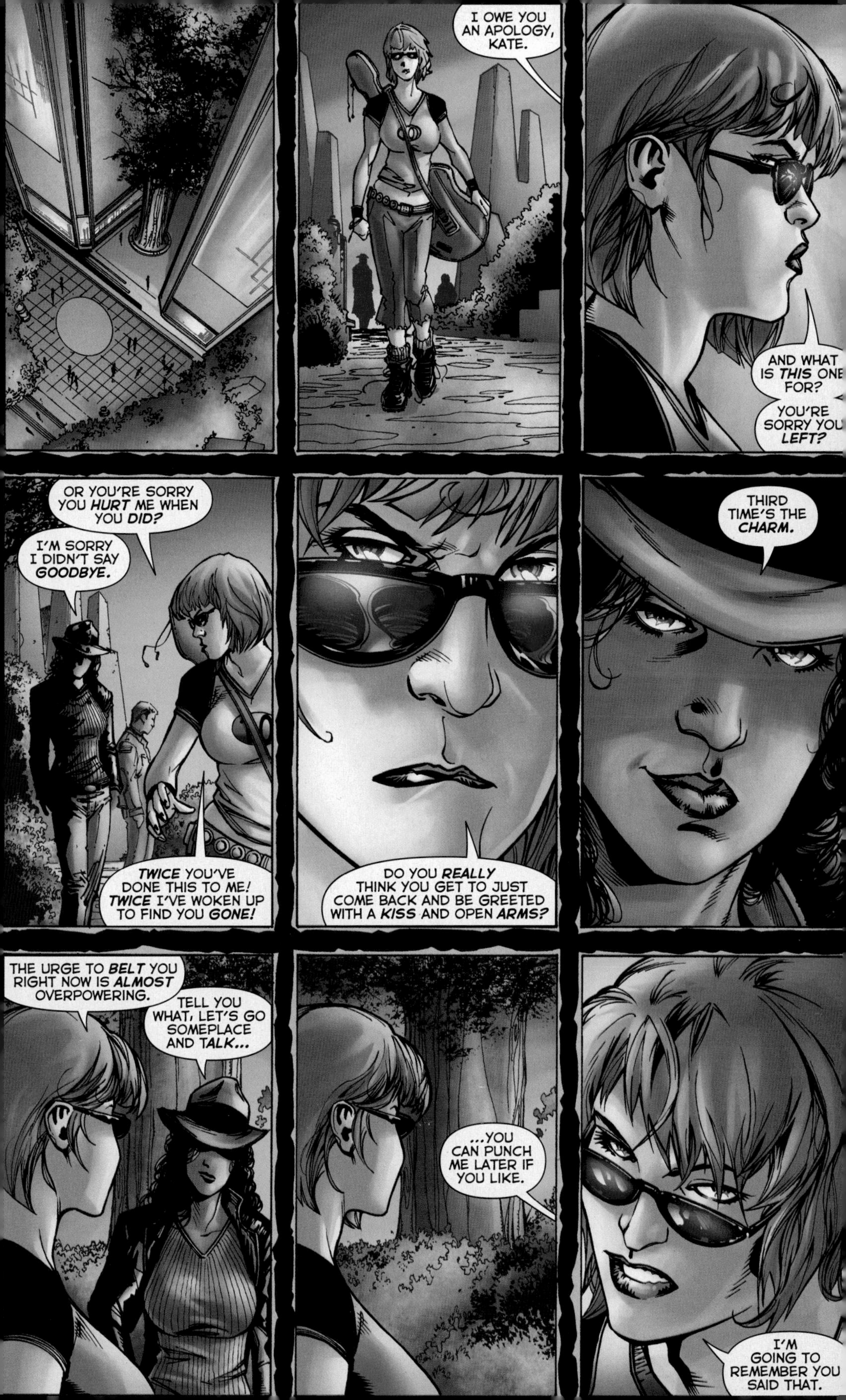

I OWE YOU AN APOLOGY, KATE.
AND WHAT IS *THIS* ONE FOR?
YOU'RE SORRY YOU *LEFT?*
OR YOU'RE SORRY YOU *HURT* ME WHEN YOU *DID?*
I'M SORRY I DIDN'T SAY *GOODBYE.*
TWICE YOU'VE DONE THIS TO ME! *TWICE* I'VE WOKEN UP TO FIND YOU *GONE!*
DO YOU *REALLY* THINK YOU GET TO JUST COME BACK AND BE GREETED WITH A *KISS* AND OPEN *ARMS?*
THIRD TIME'S THE *CHARM.*
THE URGE TO *BELT* YOU RIGHT NOW IS *ALMOST* OVERPOWERING.
TELL YOU WHAT, LET'S GO SOMEPLACE AND *TALK...*
...YOU CAN PUNCH ME LATER IF YOU LIKE.
I'M GOING TO REMEMBER YOU SAID THAT.

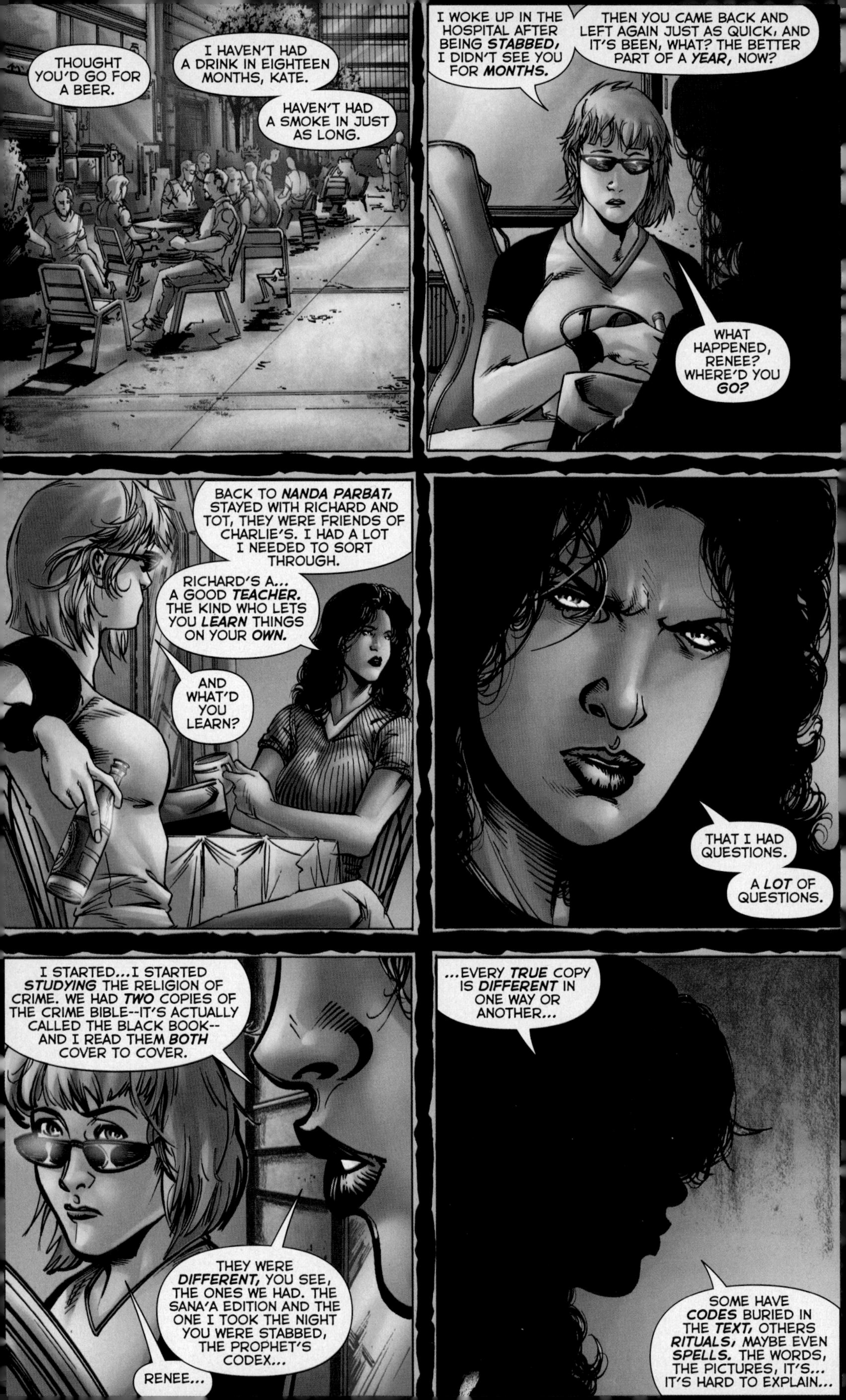
THOUGHT YOU'D GO FOR A BEER.
I HAVEN'T HAD A DRINK IN EIGHTEEN MONTHS, KATE.
HAVEN'T HAD A SMOKE IN JUST AS LONG.
I WOKE UP IN THE HOSPITAL AFTER BEING STABBED, I DIDN'T SEE YOU FOR MONTHS.
THEN YOU CAME BACK AND LEFT AGAIN JUST AS QUICK, AND IT'S BEEN, WHAT? THE BETTER PART OF A YEAR, NOW?
WHAT HAPPENED, RENEE? WHERE'D YOU GO?
BACK TO NANDA PARBAT, STAYED WITH RICHARD AND TOT, THEY WERE FRIENDS OF CHARLIE'S. I HAD A LOT I NEEDED TO SORT THROUGH.
RICHARD'S A... A GOOD TEACHER. THE KIND WHO LETS YOU LEARN THINGS ON YOUR OWN.
AND WHAT'D YOU LEARN?
THAT I HAD QUESTIONS.
A LOT OF QUESTIONS.
I STARTED...I STARTED STUDYING THE RELIGION OF CRIME. WE HAD TWO COPIES OF THE CRIME BIBLE--IT'S ACTUALLY CALLED THE BLACK BOOK--AND I READ THEM BOTH COVER TO COVER.
THEY WERE DIFFERENT, YOU SEE, THE ONES WE HAD. THE SANA'A EDITION AND THE ONE I TOOK THE NIGHT YOU WERE STABBED, THE PROPHET'S CODEX...
RENEE...
...EVERY TRUE COPY IS DIFFERENT IN ONE WAY OR ANOTHER...
SOME HAVE CODES BURIED IN THE TEXT, OTHERS RITUALS, MAYBE EVEN SPELLS. THE WORDS, THE PICTURES, IT'S... IT'S HARD TO EXPLAIN...

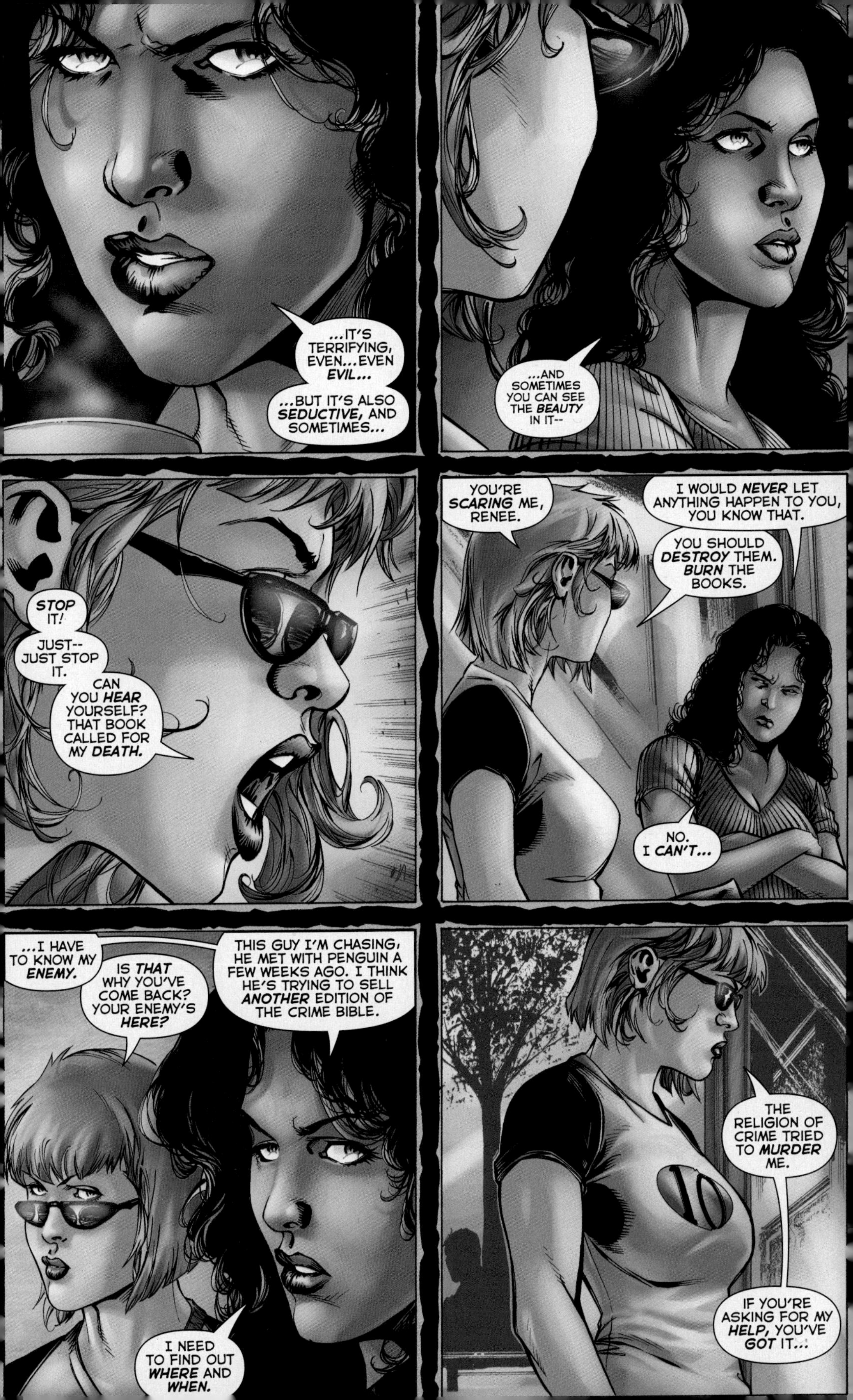
...IT'S TERRIFYING, EVEN...EVEN EVIL...
...BUT IT'S ALSO SEDUCTIVE, AND SOMETIMES...
...AND SOMETIMES YOU CAN SEE THE BEAUTY IN IT--
STOP IT!
JUST-- JUST STOP IT.
CAN YOU HEAR YOURSELF? THAT BOOK CALLED FOR MY DEATH.
YOU'RE SCARING ME, RENEE.
I WOULD NEVER LET ANYTHING HAPPEN TO YOU, YOU KNOW THAT.
YOU SHOULD DESTROY THEM. BURN THE BOOKS.
NO. I CAN'T...
...I HAVE TO KNOW MY ENEMY.
IS THAT WHY YOU'VE COME BACK? YOUR ENEMY'S HERE?
THIS GUY I'M CHASING, HE MET WITH PENGUIN A FEW WEEKS AGO. I THINK HE'S TRYING TO SELL ANOTHER EDITION OF THE CRIME BIBLE.
I NEED TO FIND OUT WHERE AND WHEN.
THE RELIGION OF CRIME TRIED TO MURDER ME.
IF YOU'RE ASKING FOR MY HELP, YOU'VE GOT IT...

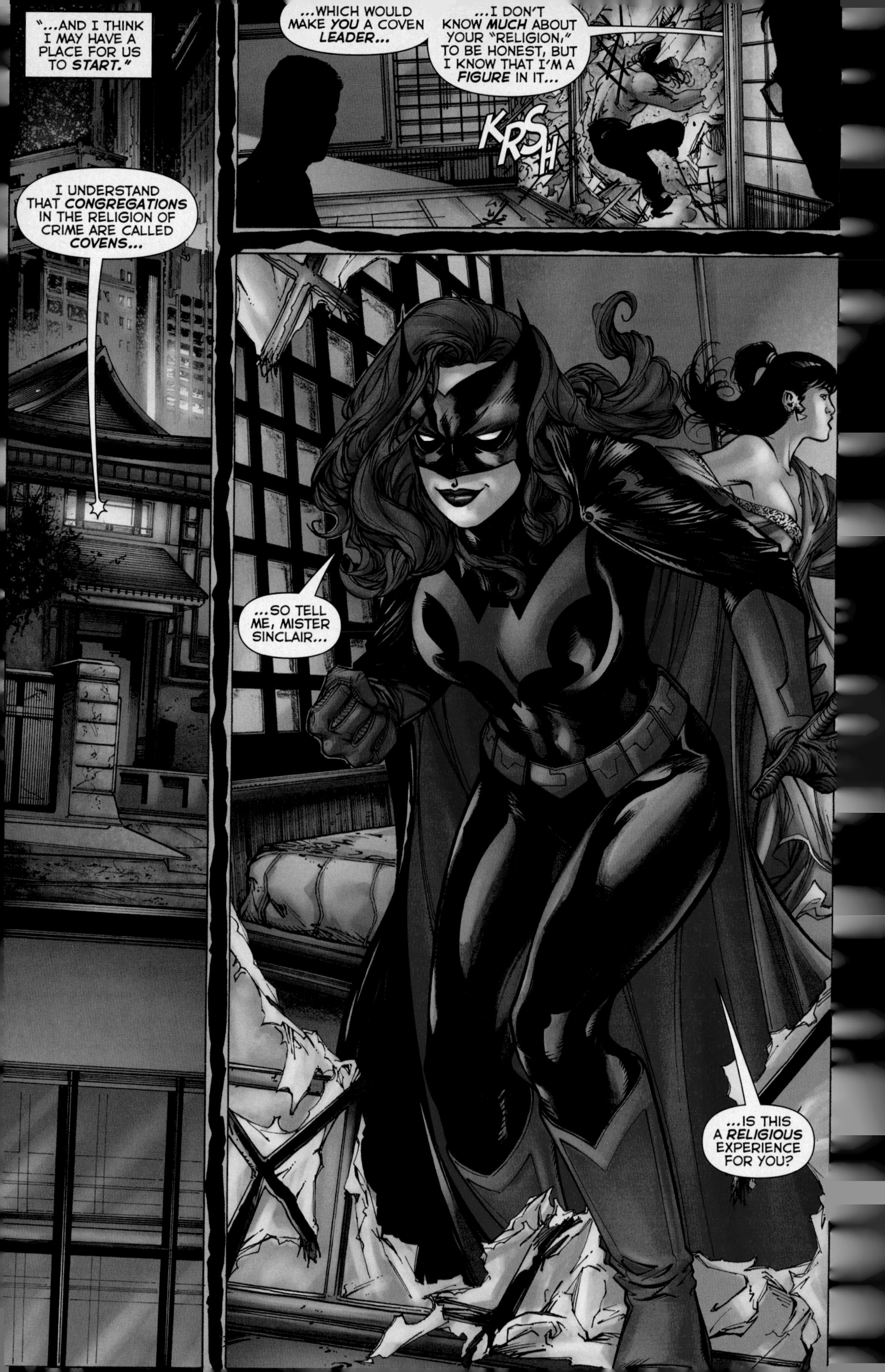
"...AND I THINK I MAY HAVE A PLACE FOR US TO START."
I UNDERSTAND THAT CONGREGATIONS IN THE RELIGION OF CRIME ARE CALLED COVENS...
...WHICH WOULD MAKE YOU A COVEN LEADER...
...I DON'T KNOW MUCH ABOUT YOUR "RELIGION," TO BE HONEST, BUT I KNOW THAT I'M A FIGURE IN IT...
KRSH
...SO TELL ME, MISTER SINCLAIR...
...IS THIS A RELIGIOUS EXPERIENCE FOR YOU?

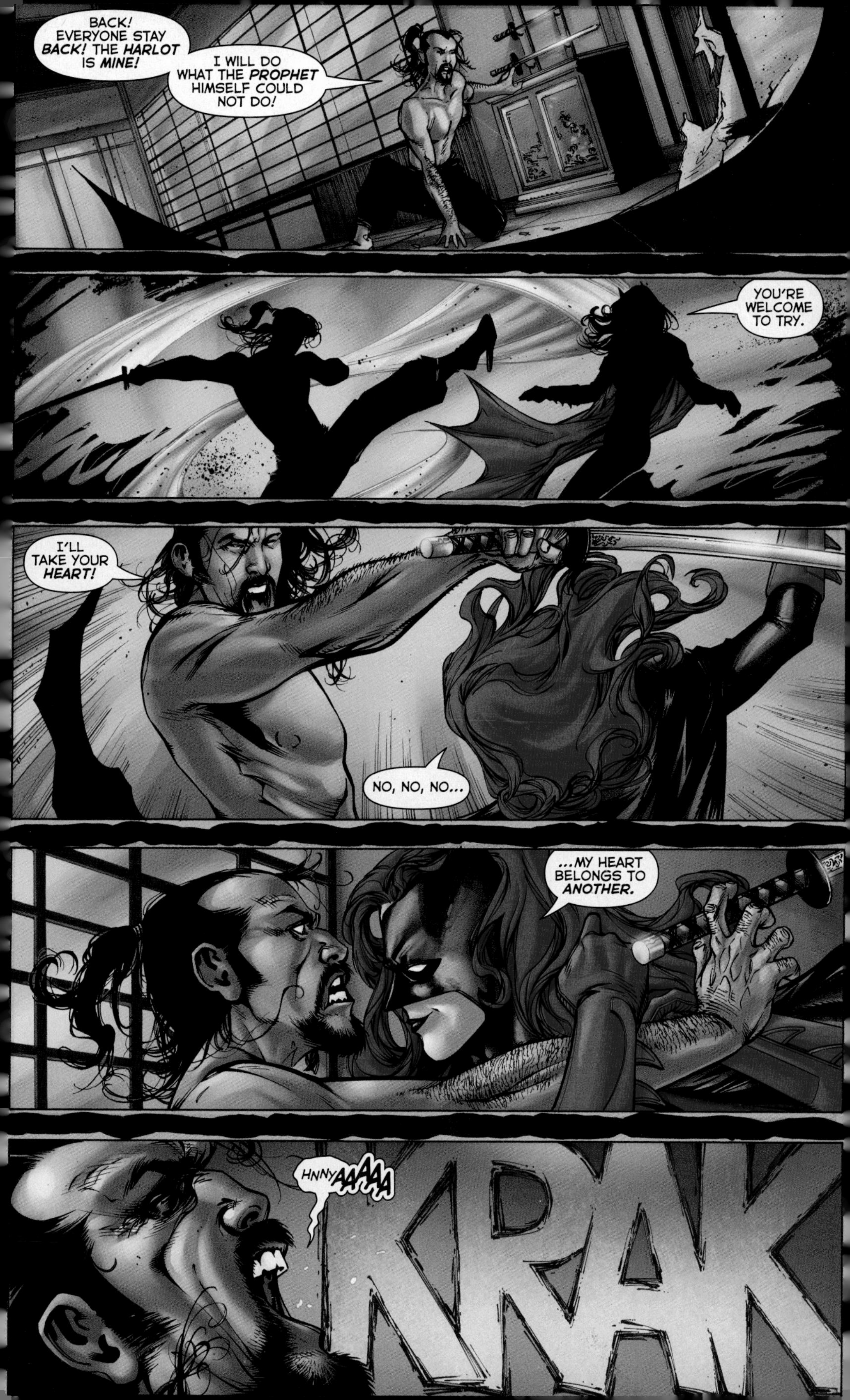
BACK! EVERYONE STAY BACK! THE HARLOT IS MINE!
I WILL DO WHAT THE PROPHET HIMSELF COULD NOT DO!
YOU'RE WELCOME TO TRY.
I'LL TAKE YOUR HEART!
NO, NO, NO...
...MY HEART BELONGS TO ANOTHER.
HNNYAAAAA
KRAK

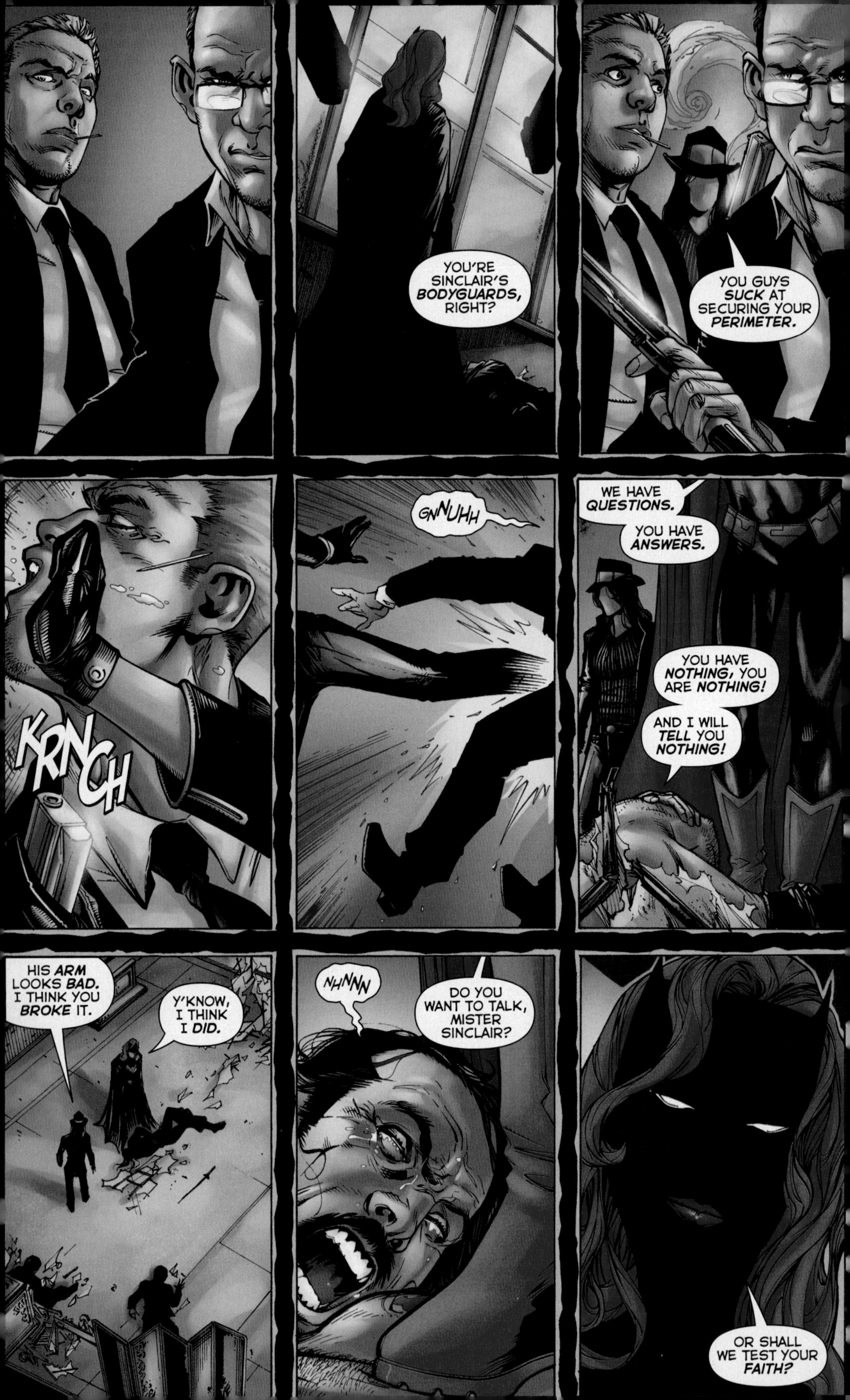
YOU'RE SINCLAIR'S BODYGUARDS, RIGHT?
YOU GUYS SUCK AT SECURING YOUR PERIMETER.
KRNCH
GNNUHH
WE HAVE QUESTIONS.
YOU HAVE ANSWERS.
YOU HAVE NOTHING, YOU ARE NOTHING!
AND I WILL TELL YOU NOTHING!
HIS ARM LOOKS BAD. I THINK YOU BROKE IT.
Y'KNOW, I THINK I DID.
NHNNN
DO YOU WANT TO TALK, MISTER SINCLAIR?
OR SHALL WE TEST YOUR FAITH?

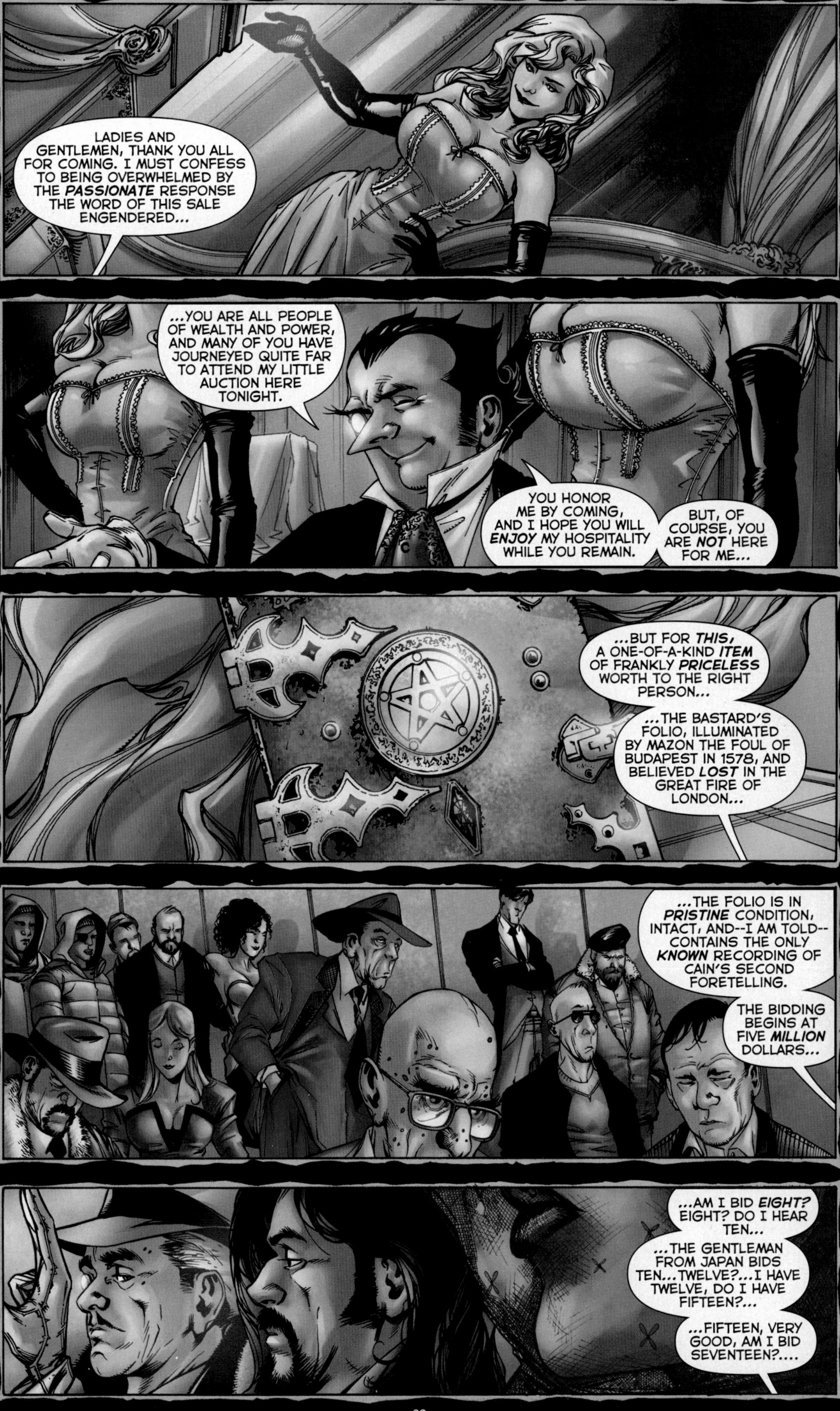

LADIES AND GENTLEMEN, THANK YOU ALL FOR COMING. I MUST CONFESS TO BEING OVERWHELMED BY THE *PASSIONATE* RESPONSE THE WORD OF THIS SALE ENGENDERED...
...YOU ARE ALL PEOPLE OF WEALTH AND POWER, AND MANY OF YOU HAVE JOURNEYED QUITE FAR TO ATTEND MY LITTLE AUCTION HERE TONIGHT.
YOU HONOR ME BY COMING, AND I HOPE YOU WILL *ENJOY* MY HOSPITALITY WHILE YOU REMAIN.
BUT, OF COURSE, YOU ARE *NOT* HERE FOR ME...
...BUT FOR *THIS,* A ONE-OF-A-KIND *ITEM* OF FRANKLY *PRICELESS* WORTH TO THE RIGHT PERSON...
...THE BASTARD'S FOLIO, ILLUMINATED BY MAZON THE FOUL OF BUDAPEST IN 1578, AND BELIEVED *LOST* IN THE GREAT FIRE OF LONDON...
...THE FOLIO IS IN *PRISTINE* CONDITION, INTACT, AND--I AM TOLD--CONTAINS THE ONLY *KNOWN* RECORDING OF CAIN'S SECOND FORETELLING.
THE BIDDING BEGINS AT FIVE *MILLION* DOLLARS...
...AM I BID *EIGHT?* EIGHT? DO I HEAR TEN...
...THE GENTLEMAN FROM JAPAN BIDS TEN...TWELVE?...I HAVE TWELVE, DO I HAVE FIFTEEN?...
...FIFTEEN, VERY GOOD, AM I BID SEVENTEEN?....

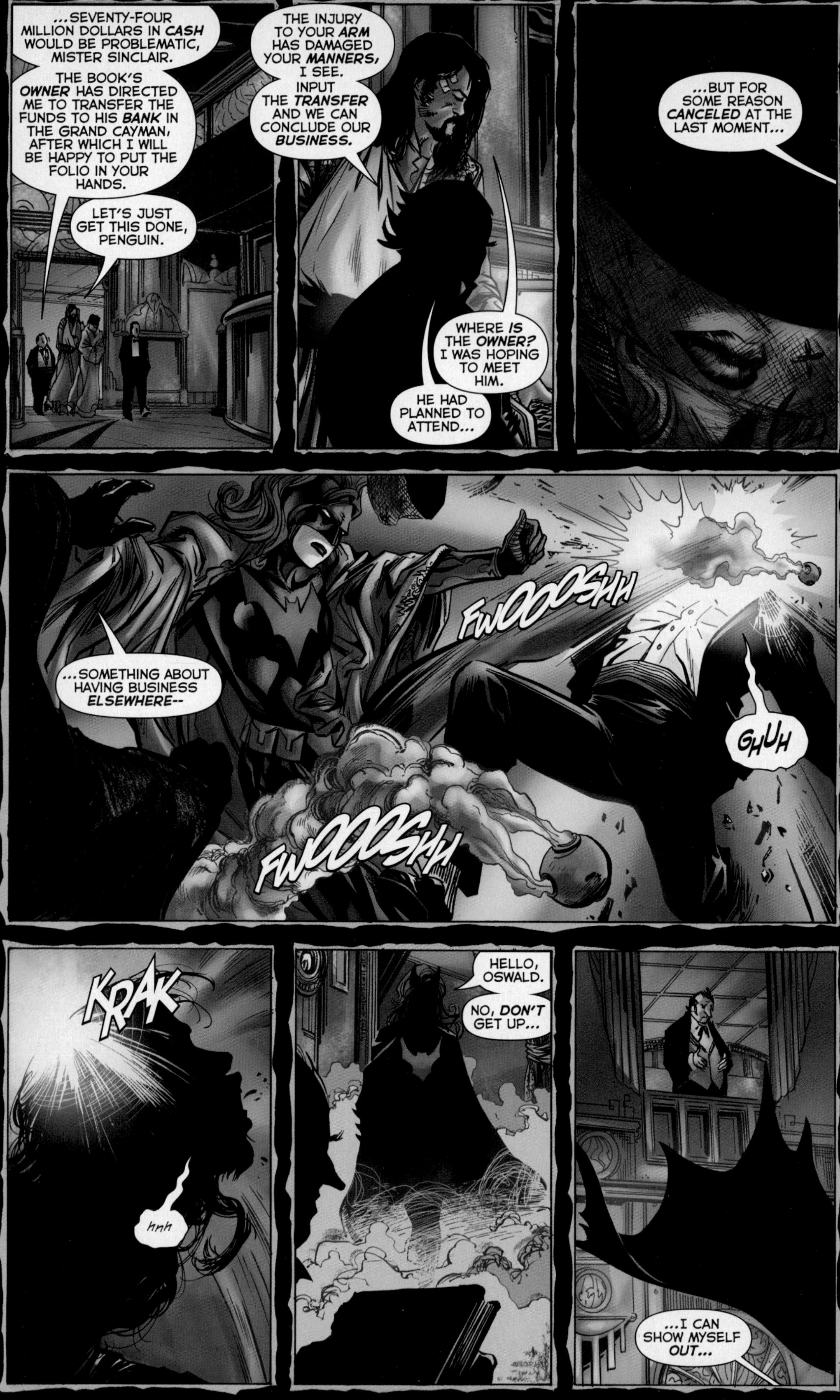

...SEVENTY-FOUR MILLION DOLLARS IN CASH WOULD BE PROBLEMATIC, MISTER SINCLAIR.
THE BOOK'S OWNER HAS DIRECTED ME TO TRANSFER THE FUNDS TO HIS BANK IN THE GRAND CAYMAN, AFTER WHICH I WILL BE HAPPY TO PUT THE FOLIO IN YOUR HANDS.
LET'S JUST GET THIS DONE, PENGUIN.
THE INJURY TO YOUR ARM HAS DAMAGED YOUR MANNERS, I SEE.
INPUT THE TRANSFER AND WE CAN CONCLUDE OUR BUSINESS.
WHERE IS THE OWNER? I WAS HOPING TO MEET HIM.
HE HAD PLANNED TO ATTEND...
...BUT FOR SOME REASON CANCELED AT THE LAST MOMENT...
...SOMETHING ABOUT HAVING BUSINESS ELSEWHERE--
FWOOOOSHH
GHUH
FWOOOOSHH
KRAK
hnh
HELLO, OSWALD.
NO, DON'T GET UP...
...I CAN SHOW MYSELF OUT...

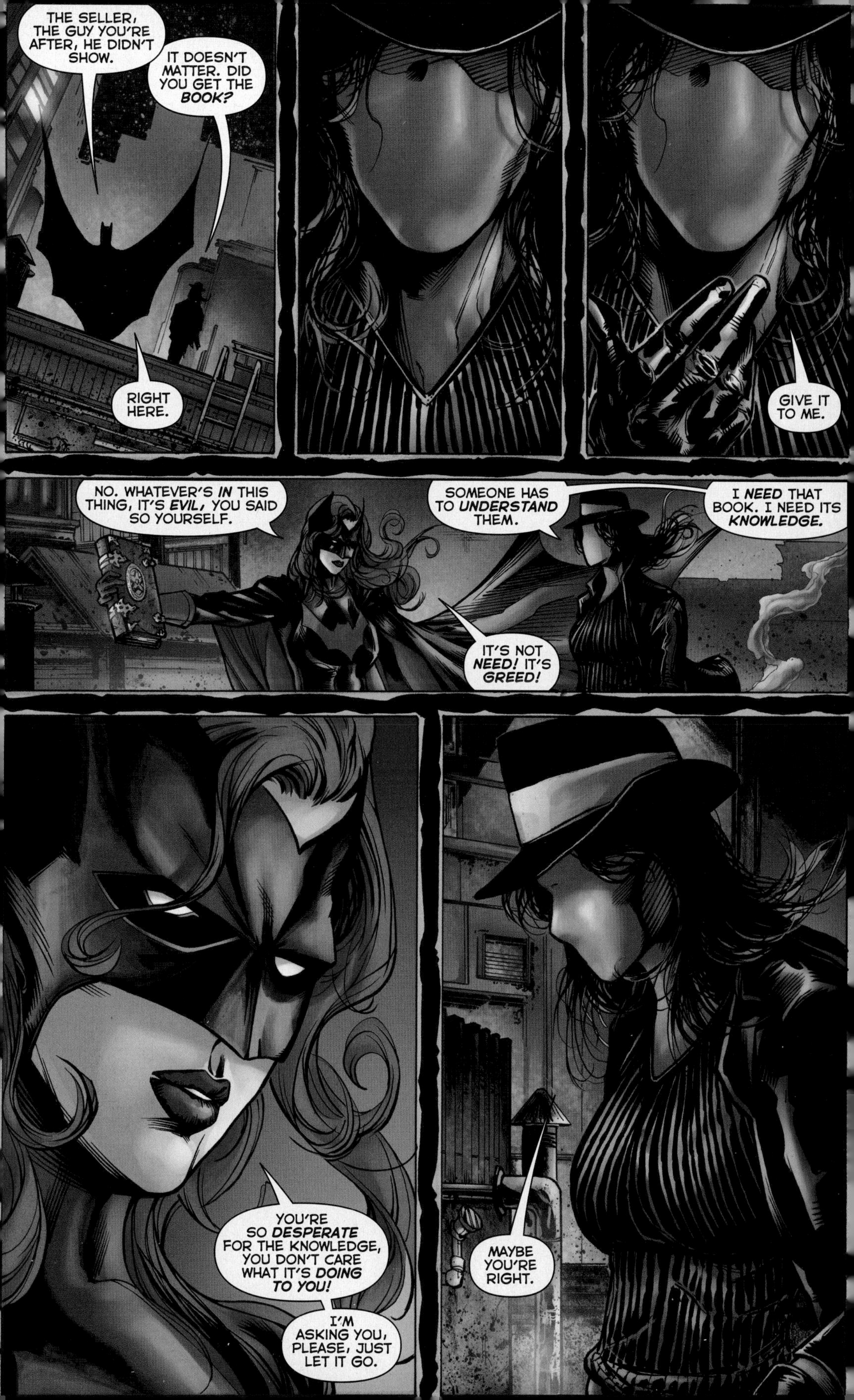
THE SELLER, THE GUY YOU'RE AFTER, HE DIDN'T SHOW.
IT DOESN'T MATTER. DID YOU GET THE *BOOK?*
RIGHT HERE.
GIVE IT TO ME.
NO. WHATEVER'S *IN* THIS THING, IT'S *EVIL,* YOU SAID SO YOURSELF.
SOMEONE HAS TO *UNDERSTAND* THEM.
I *NEED* THAT BOOK. I NEED ITS *KNOWLEDGE.*
IT'S NOT *NEED!* IT'S *GREED!*
YOU'RE SO *DESPERATE* FOR THE KNOWLEDGE, YOU DON'T CARE WHAT IT'S *DOING TO YOU!*
I'M ASKING YOU, PLEASE, JUST LET IT GO.
MAYBE YOU'RE RIGHT.

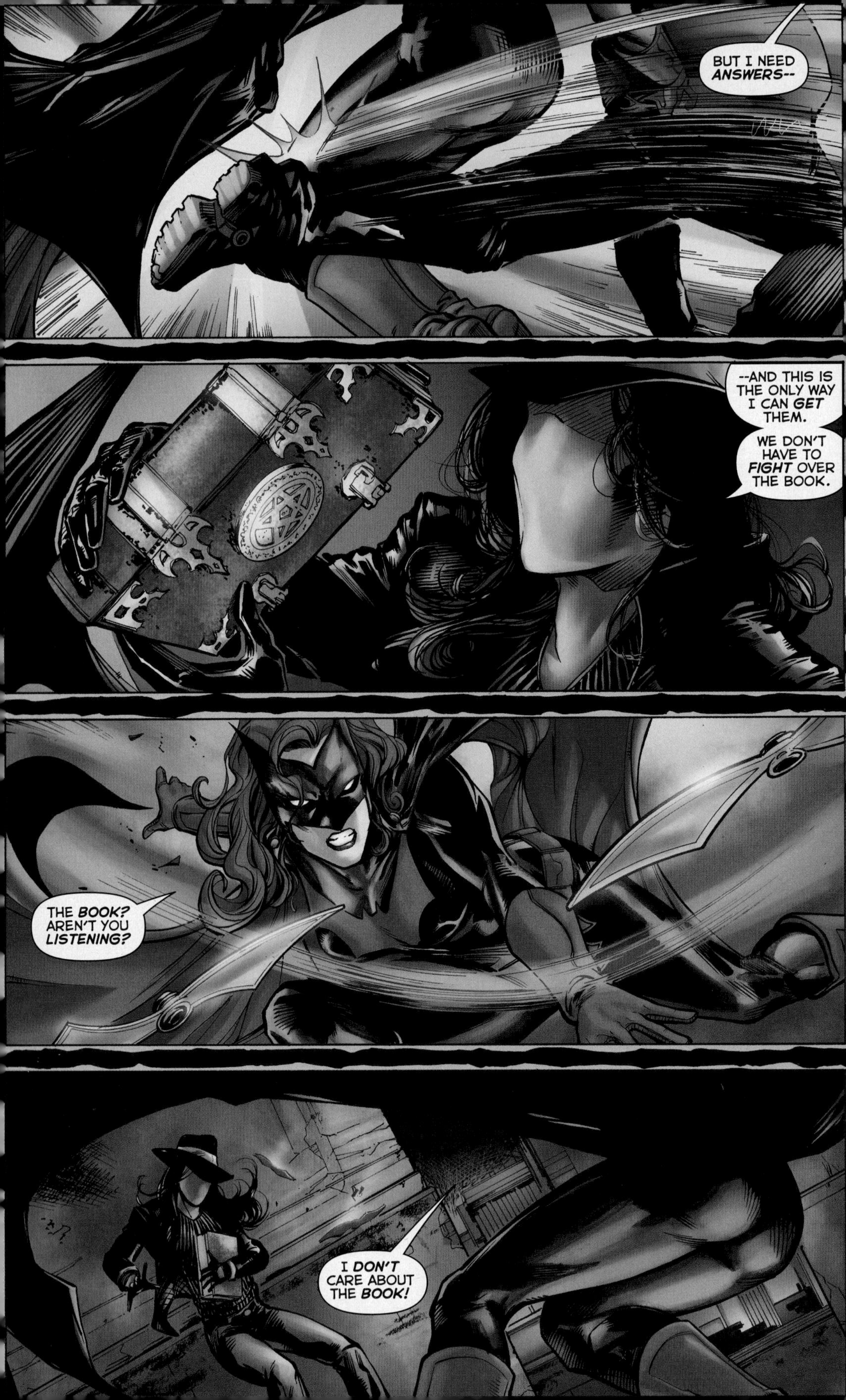

BUT I NEED ANSWERS--
--AND THIS IS THE ONLY WAY I CAN GET THEM.
WE DON'T HAVE TO FIGHT OVER THE BOOK.
THE BOOK? AREN'T YOU LISTENING?
I DON'T CARE ABOUT THE BOOK!

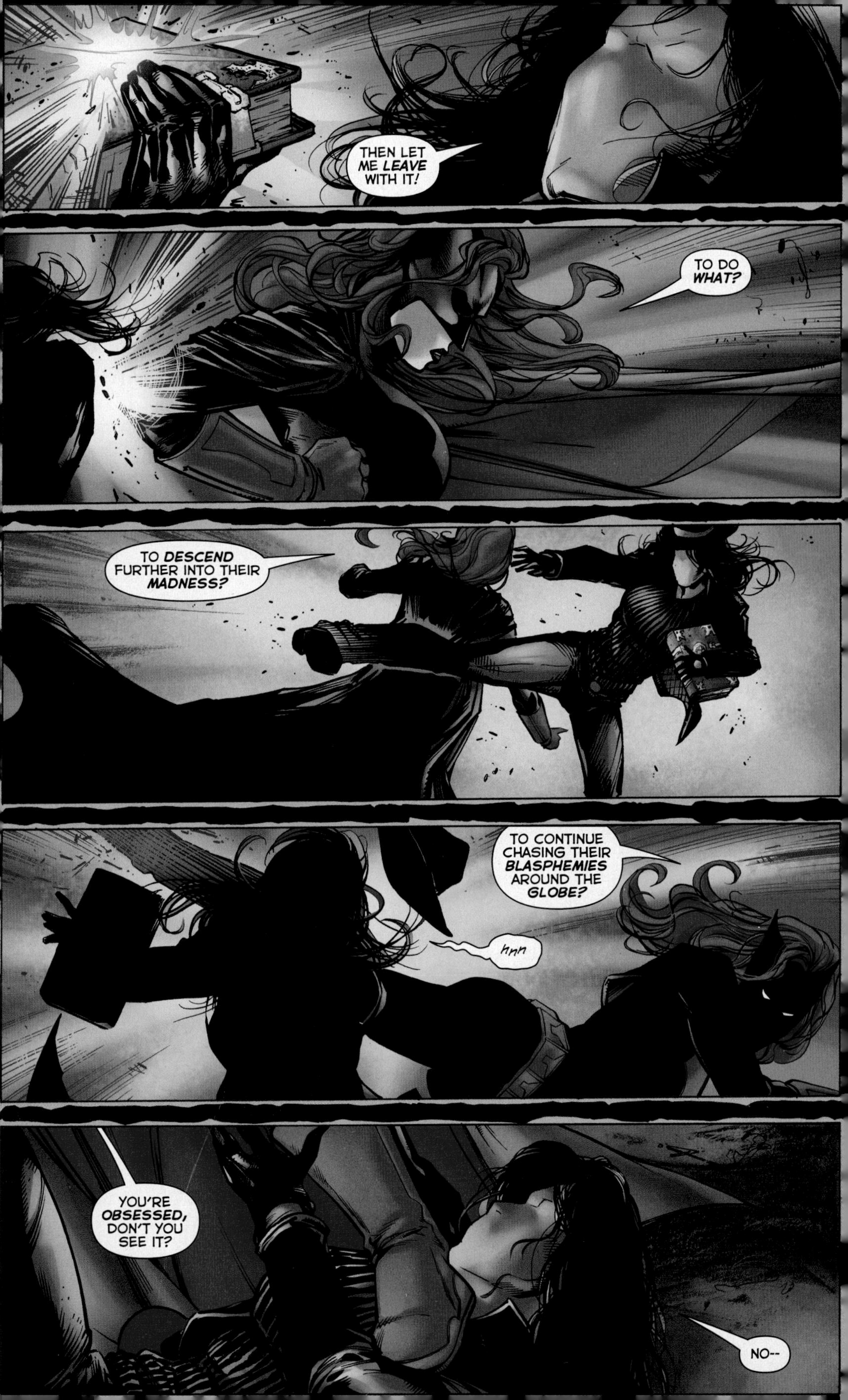
THEN LET ME LEAVE WITH IT!
TO DO WHAT?
TO DESCEND FURTHER INTO THEIR MADNESS?
TO CONTINUE CHASING THEIR BLASPHEMIES AROUND THE GLOBE?
hnn
YOU'RE OBSESSED, DON'T YOU SEE IT?
NO--

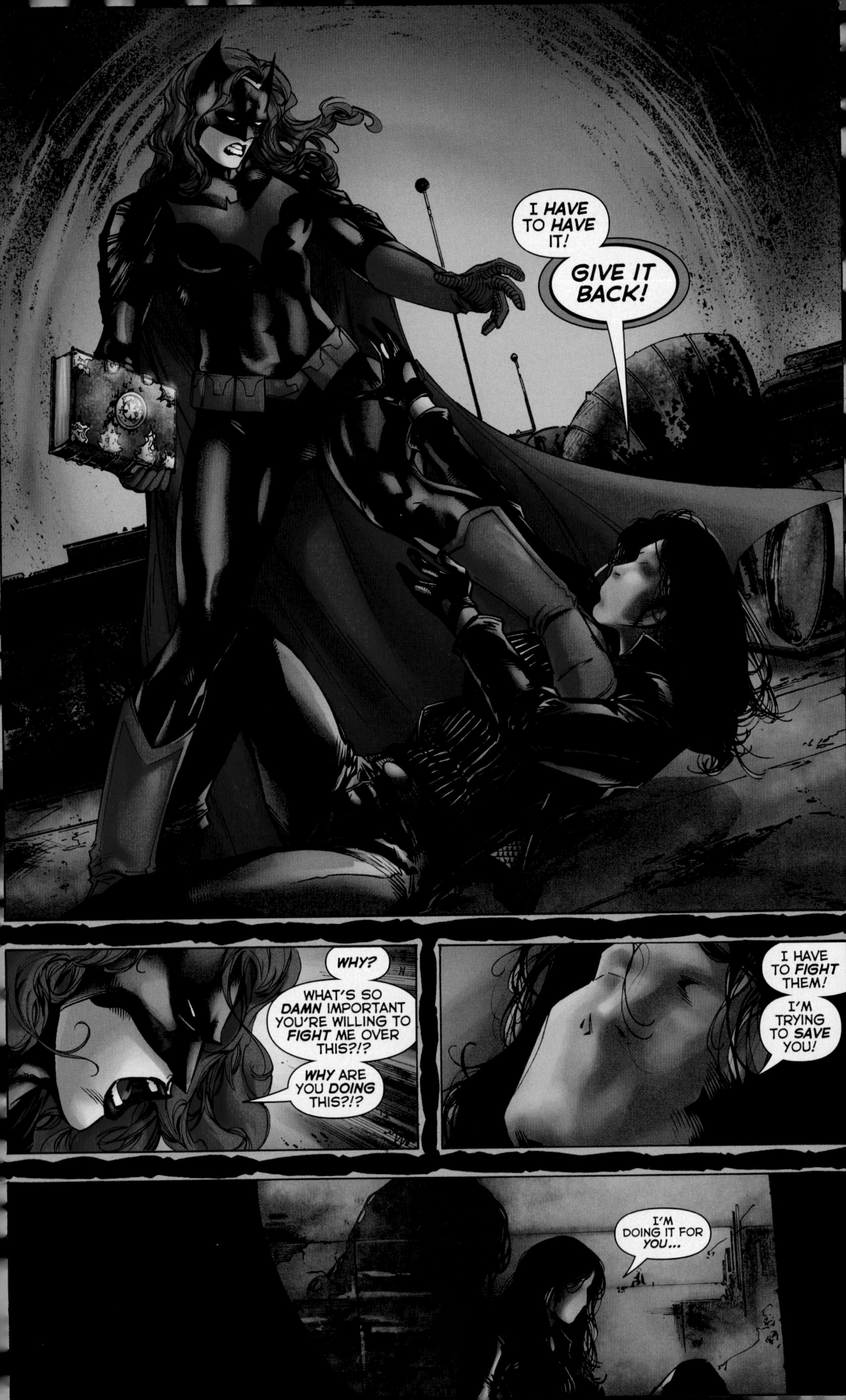
I HAVE TO HAVE IT!
GIVE IT BACK!
WHY?
WHAT'S SO DAMN IMPORTANT YOU'RE WILLING TO FIGHT ME OVER THIS?!?
WHY ARE YOU DOING THIS?!?
I HAVE TO FIGHT THEM!
I'M TRYING TO SAVE YOU!
I'M DOING IT FOR YOU...

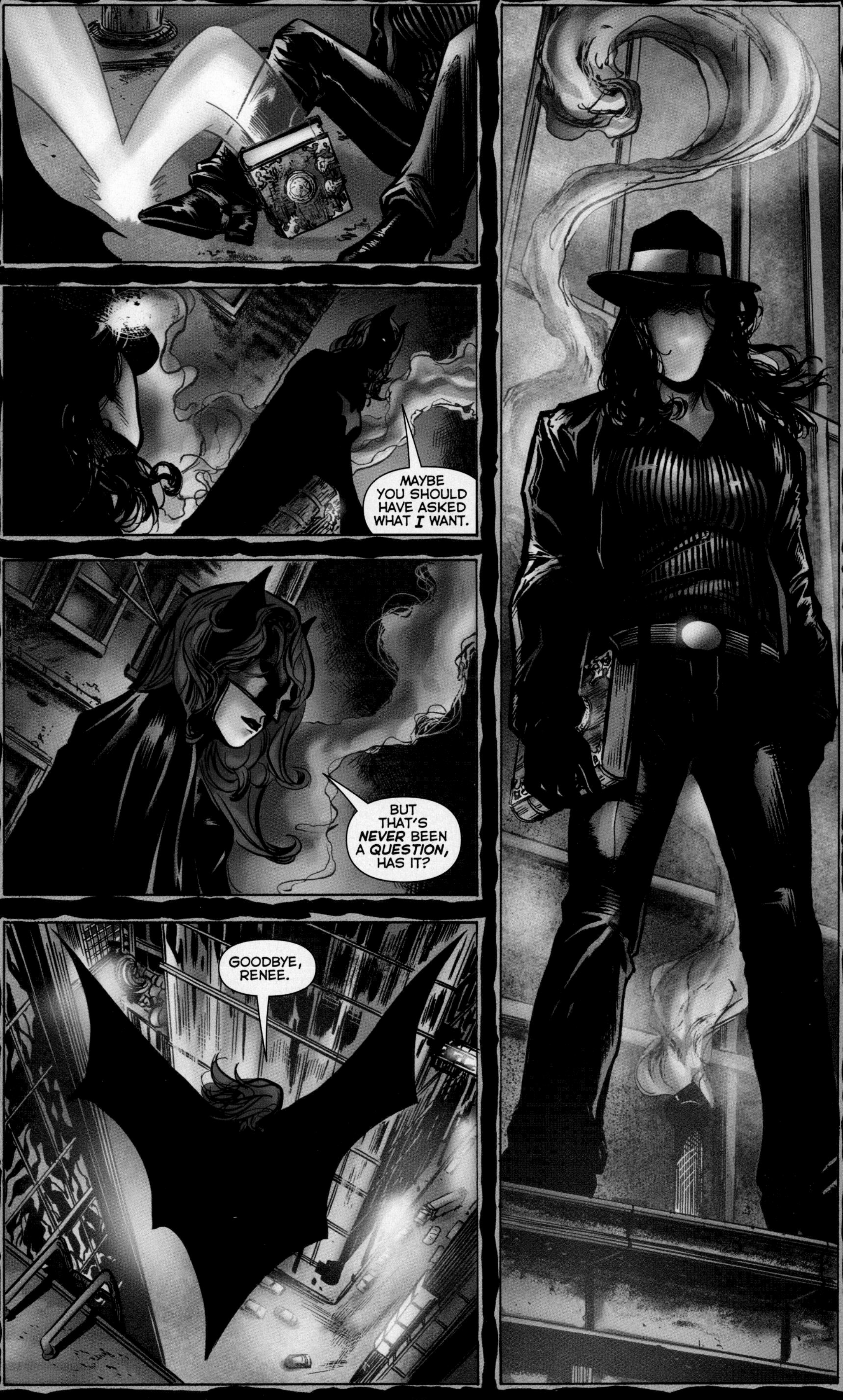
MAYBE YOU SHOULD HAVE ASKED WHAT I WANT.
BUT THAT'S NEVER BEEN A QUESTION, HAS IT?
GOODBYE, RENEE.

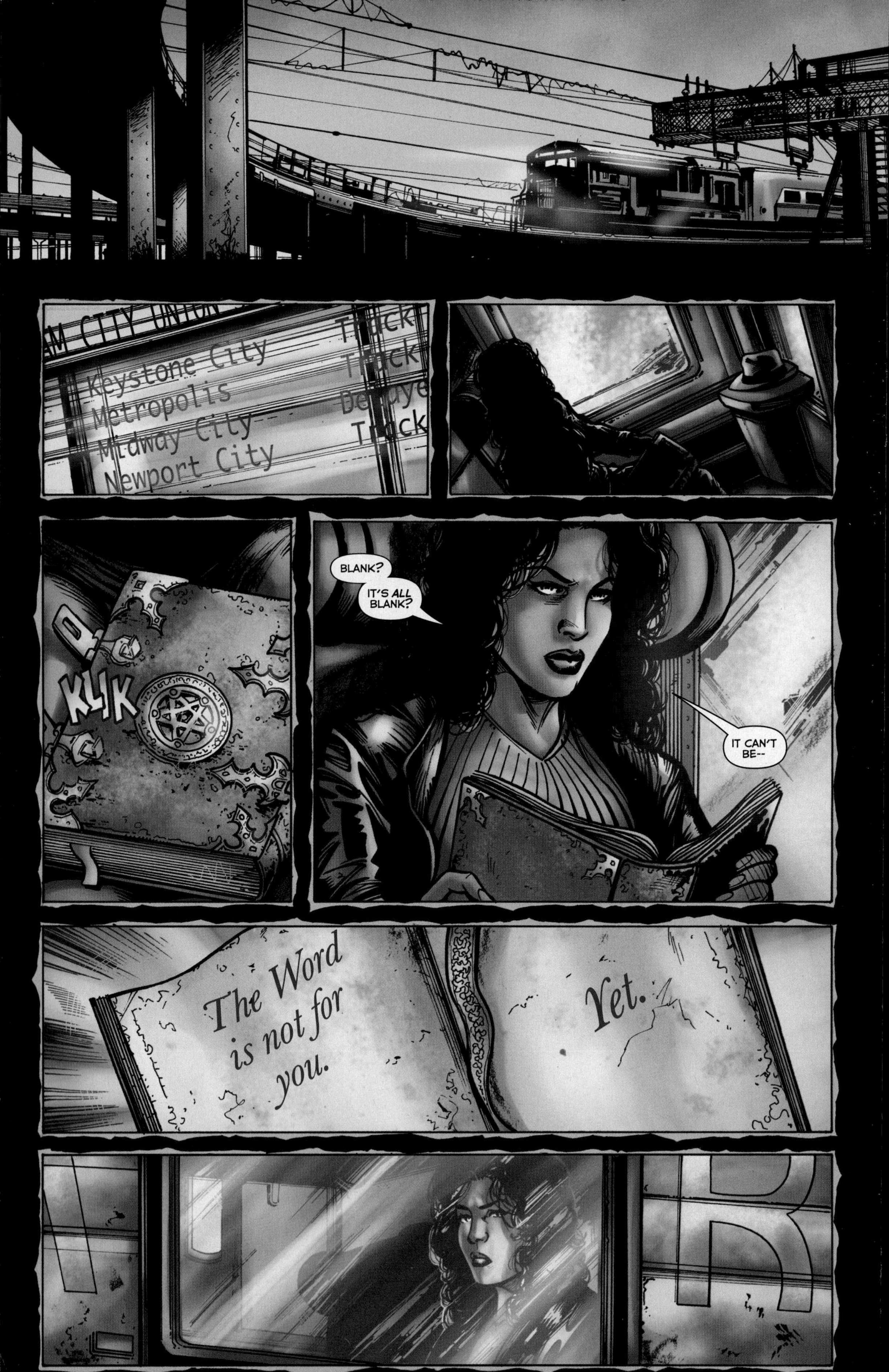

AM CITY UNION
Keystone City
Metropolis
Midway City
Newport City
KLIK
BLANK?
IT'S ALL BLANK?
IT CAN'T BE--
The Word is not for you.
Yet.

The Fourth Book of Blood

Chapter 3, Verses 1-12

¹ Now it was far beyond the lands of Lamech and outside their memory that the First wandered, for still He sought to complete Himself; for still was He a slave to the laws of the weak.

² And it came to pass that the First did leave the Waste and enter unto the House of the Pharisiacs, and there He saw those who took the name of Righteous and Good; and amongst them He didst spy the one-eyed Caitiff, besieged and much confused.

³ And the First said unto the Caitiff, Why doth thou dwell here amongst these who would practice Deceit upon thee, and deny us our worth?

⁴ And the House of Pharisiacs saw then who it was amongst them, and begged of Him to repent His devotion, and become as they.

⁵ And the First said, Nay, for my worth I do measure alone, above all gods, and none else who takes it shall have matter to me.

⁶ And still didst they entreat of Him, and so did fail, and thus turned to pleas, and begged Him to serve as they.

⁷ And their mewling words did so offend Him that His vision did once more fill with blood, and the First knew the Red Rage again, and knowing, did give Himself to it all complete and without regret; with blade, fist, and shard did He give Himself to it, and so scoured them of that which they were too weak to hold.

⁸ And this the First did until the one-eyed Caitiff alone remained to draw breath.

⁹ And the First gazed upon what He had wrought, and knew it as the Fourth Lesson of Blood; and He did weep with joy at His freedom now completed.

¹⁰ And the First didst turn to the Caitiff, and did anoint him with the blood that lay there, saying, This, then, is the Fourth of the Four, the last of all Lessons; for if ye cannot take life, ye lack all claim to keep of it, nor master over it.

¹¹ Thus do I mark thee, that ye might practice Murder and take that of which the weak have no need, and so earn thy right to live.

¹² And in this way was the one-eyed Caitiff sent forth, to teach the Fourth Lesson to the world.

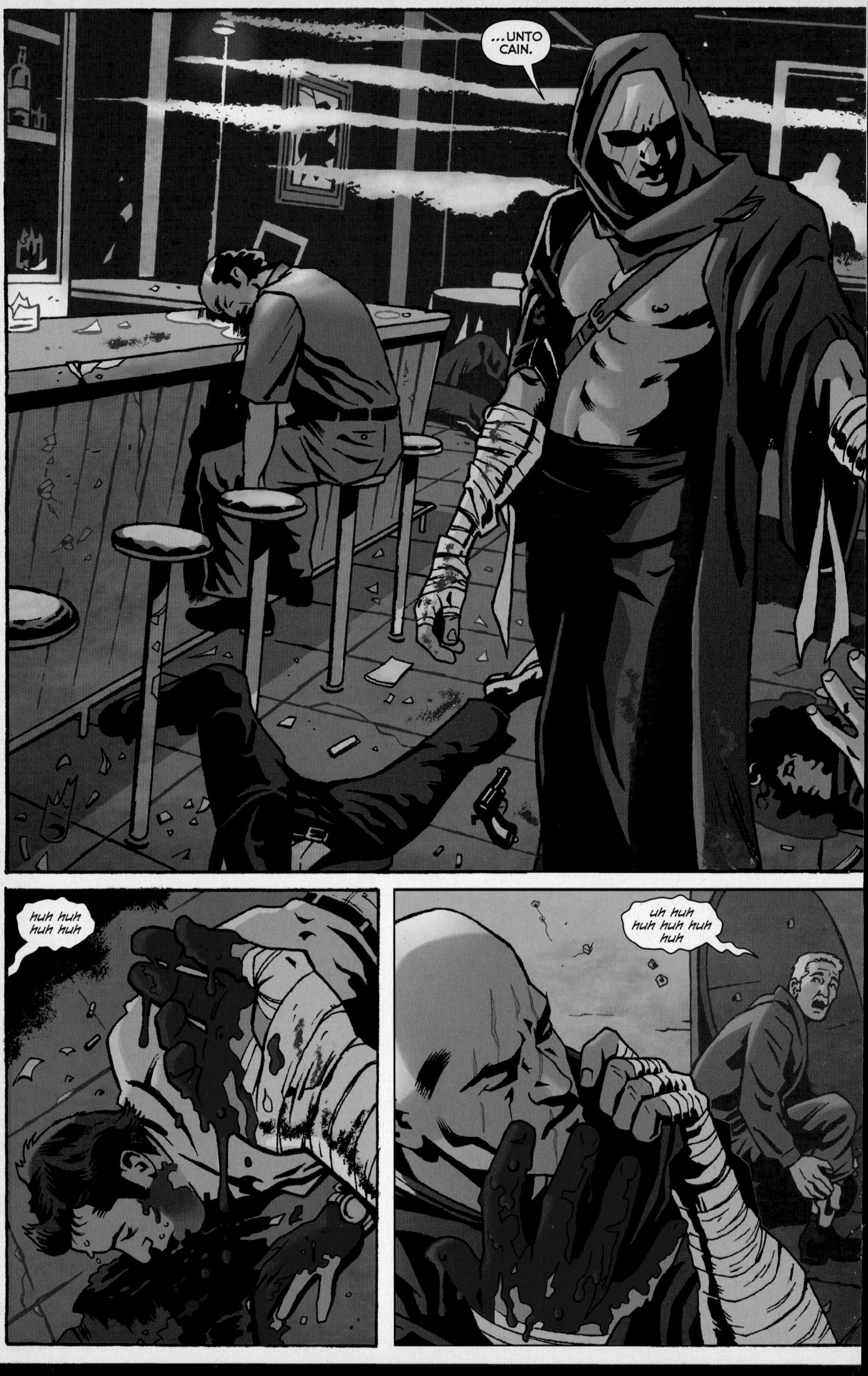
...UNTO CAIN.
huh huh huh huh
uh huh huh huh huh huh

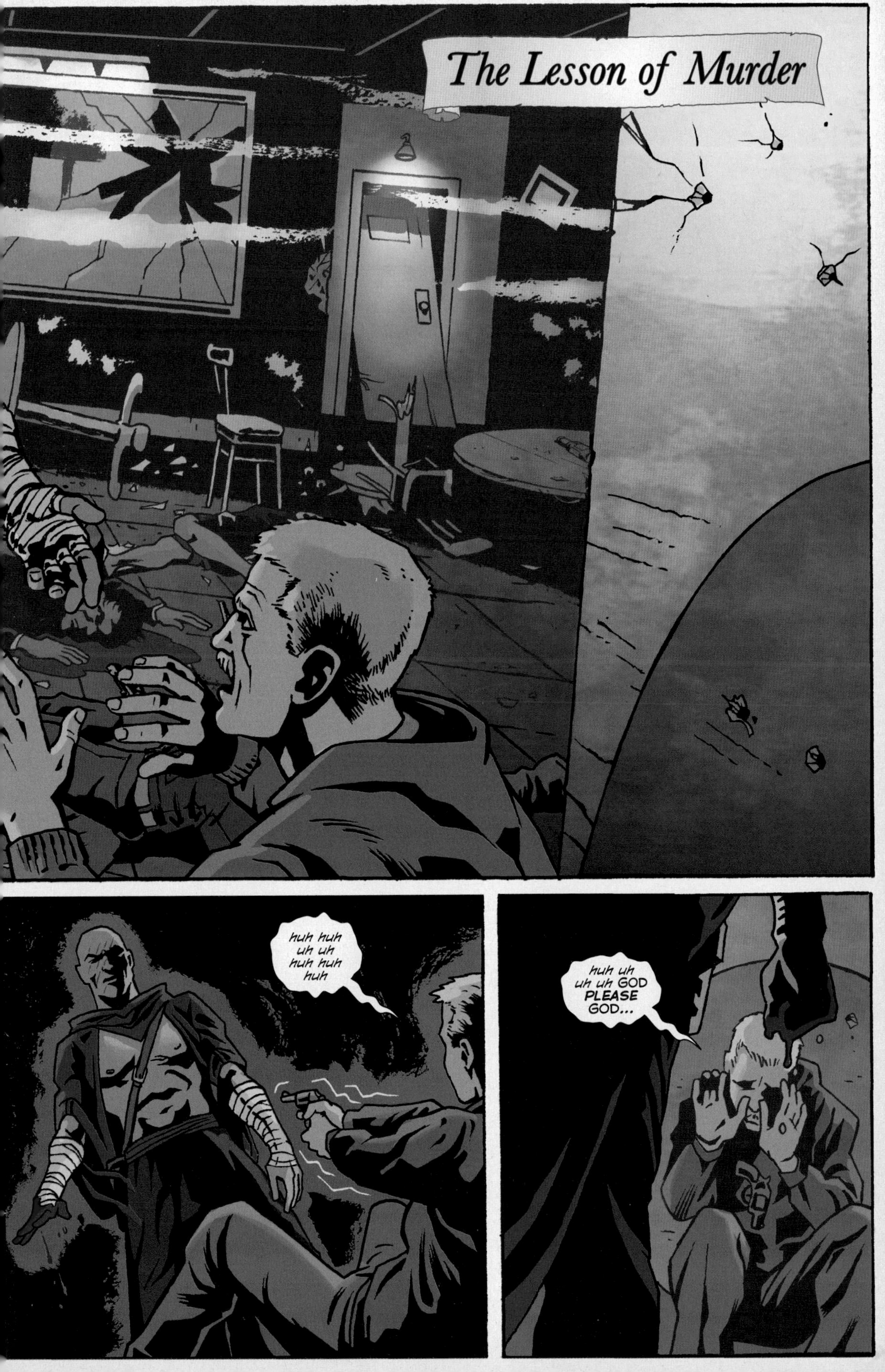
The Lesson of Murder
huh huh uh uh huh huh huh
huh uh uh uh GOD PLEASE GOD...

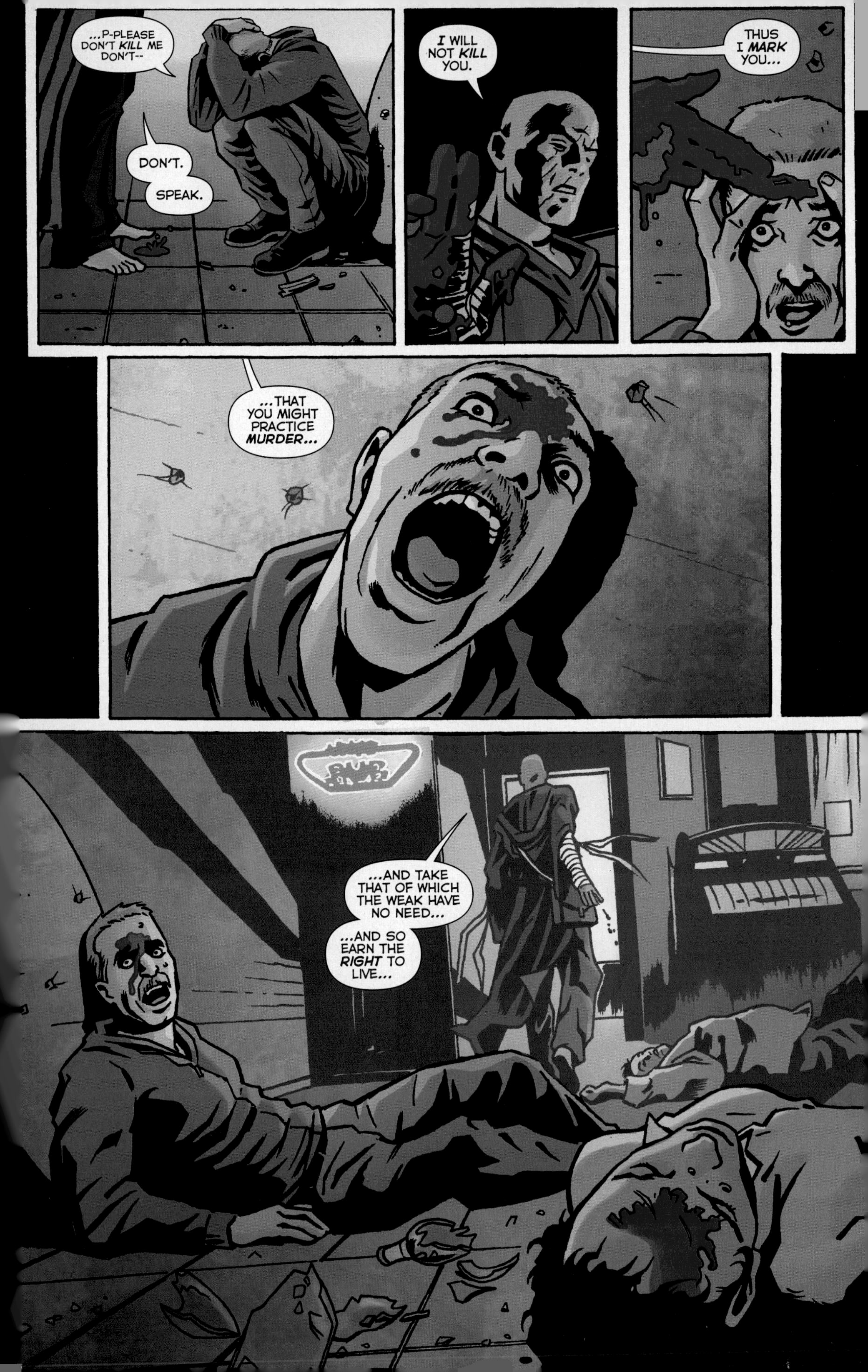
...P-PLEASE DON'T KILL ME DON'T--
DON'T.
SPEAK.
I WILL NOT KILL YOU.
THUS I MARK YOU...
...THAT YOU MIGHT PRACTICE MURDER...
...AND TAKE THAT OF WHICH THE WEAK HAVE NO NEED...
...AND SO EARN THE RIGHT TO LIVE...

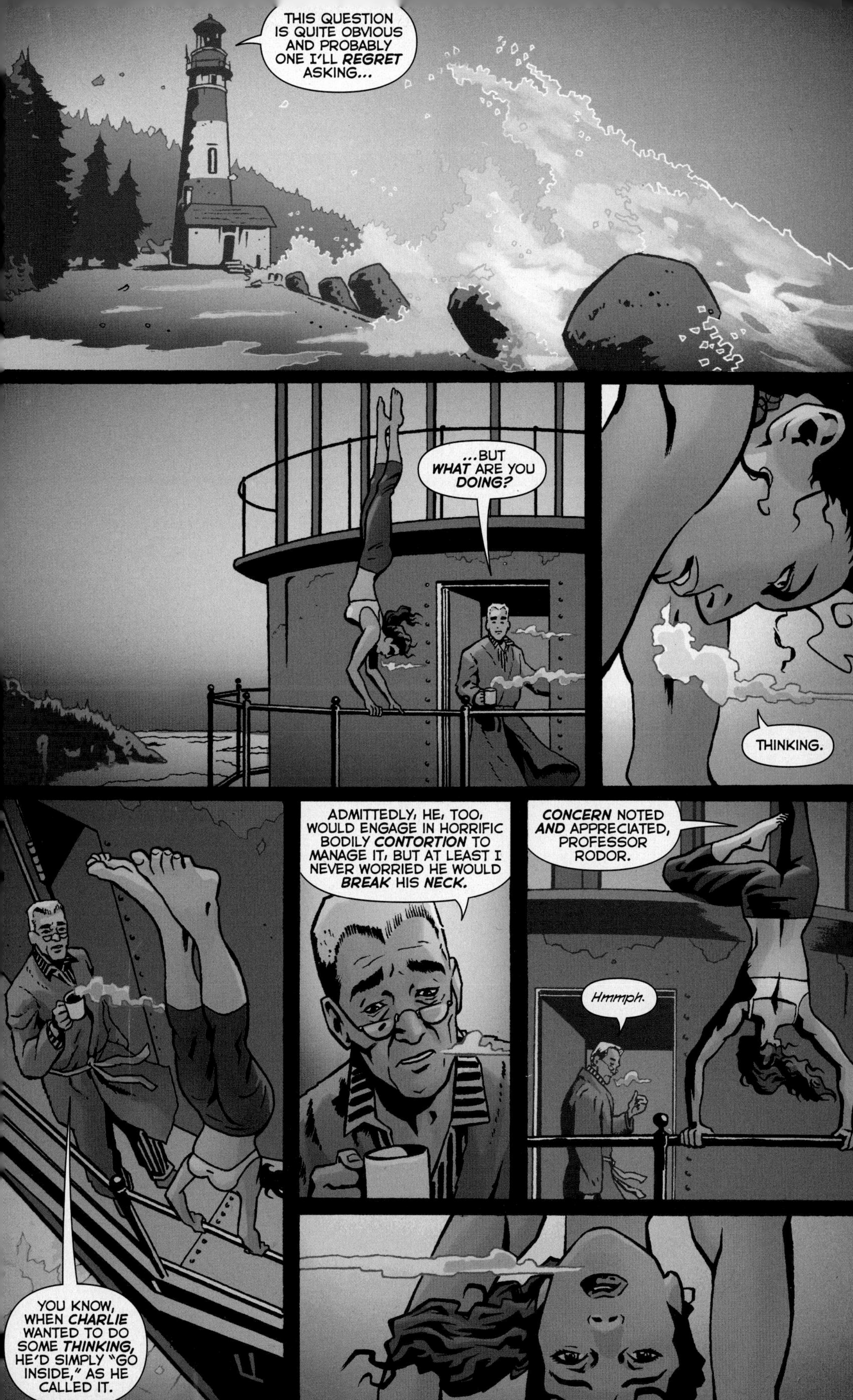
THIS QUESTION IS QUITE OBVIOUS AND PROBABLY ONE I'LL REGRET ASKING...
...BUT WHAT ARE YOU DOING?
THINKING.
YOU KNOW, WHEN CHARLIE WANTED TO DO SOME THINKING, HE'D SIMPLY "GO INSIDE," AS HE CALLED IT.
ADMITTEDLY, HE, TOO, WOULD ENGAGE IN HORRIFIC BODILY CONTORTION TO MANAGE IT, BUT AT LEAST I NEVER WORRIED HE WOULD BREAK HIS NECK.
CONCERN NOTED AND APPRECIATED, PROFESSOR RODOR.
Hmmph.

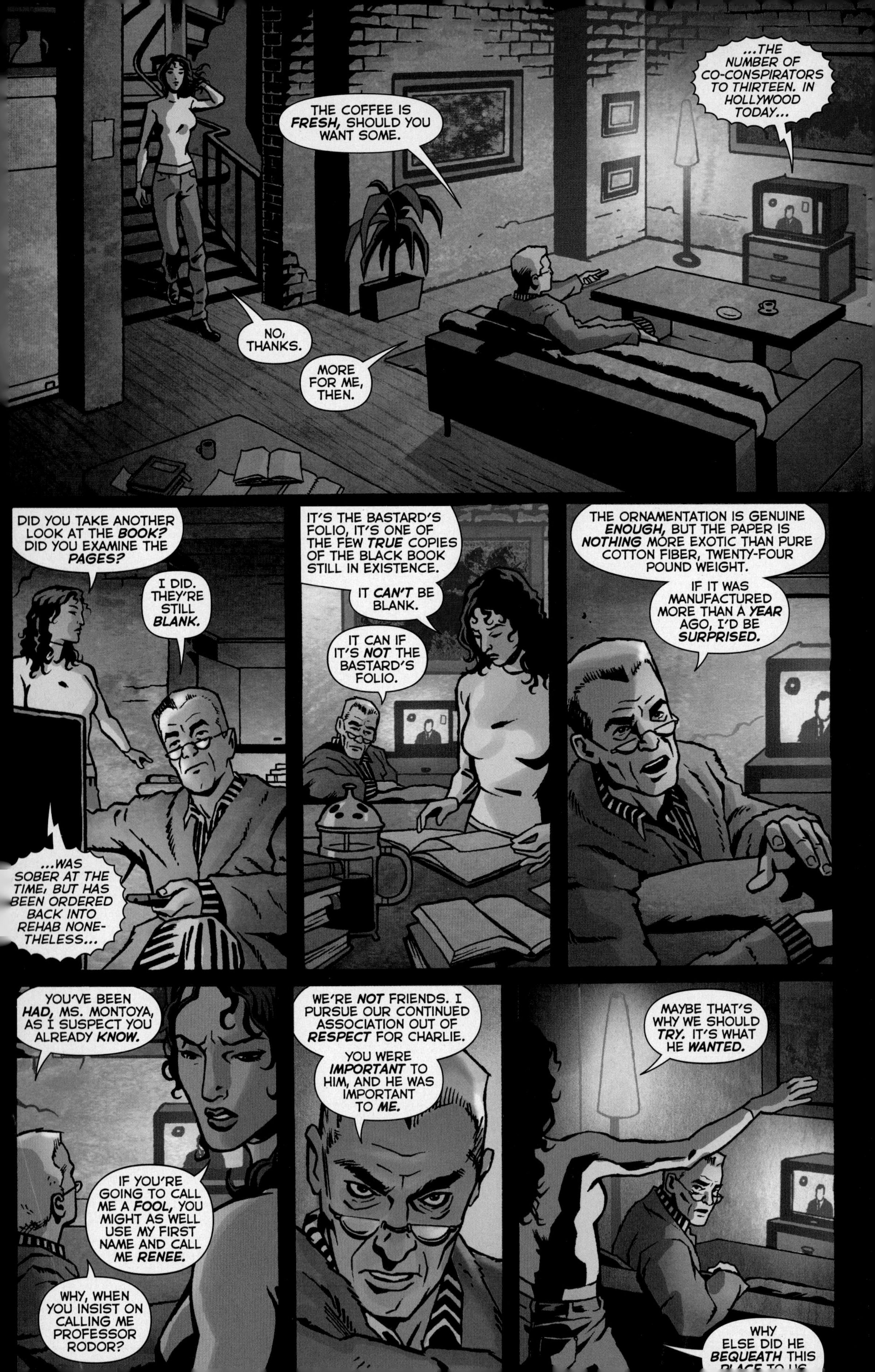

THE COFFEE IS FRESH, SHOULD YOU WANT SOME.
...THE NUMBER OF CO-CONSPIRATORS TO THIRTEEN. IN HOLLYWOOD TODAY...
NO, THANKS.
MORE FOR ME, THEN.
DID YOU TAKE ANOTHER LOOK AT THE BOOK? DID YOU EXAMINE THE PAGES?
I DID. THEY'RE STILL BLANK.
...WAS SOBER AT THE TIME, BUT HAS BEEN ORDERED BACK INTO REHAB NONE-THELESS...
IT'S THE BASTARD'S FOLIO, IT'S ONE OF THE FEW TRUE COPIES OF THE BLACK BOOK STILL IN EXISTENCE.
IT CAN'T BE BLANK.
IT CAN IF IT'S NOT THE BASTARD'S FOLIO.
THE ORNAMENTATION IS GENUINE ENOUGH, BUT THE PAPER IS NOTHING MORE EXOTIC THAN PURE COTTON FIBER, TWENTY-FOUR POUND WEIGHT.
IF IT WAS MANUFACTURED MORE THAN A YEAR AGO, I'D BE SURPRISED.
YOU'VE BEEN HAD, MS. MONTOYA, AS I SUSPECT YOU ALREADY KNOW.
IF YOU'RE GOING TO CALL ME A FOOL, YOU MIGHT AS WELL USE MY FIRST NAME AND CALL ME RENEE.
WHY, WHEN YOU INSIST ON CALLING ME PROFESSOR RODOR?
WE'RE NOT FRIENDS. I PURSUE OUR CONTINUED ASSOCIATION OUT OF RESPECT FOR CHARLIE.
YOU WERE IMPORTANT TO HIM, AND HE WAS IMPORTANT TO ME.
MAYBE THAT'S WHY WE SHOULD TRY. IT'S WHAT HE WANTED.
WHY ELSE DID HE BEQUEATH THIS

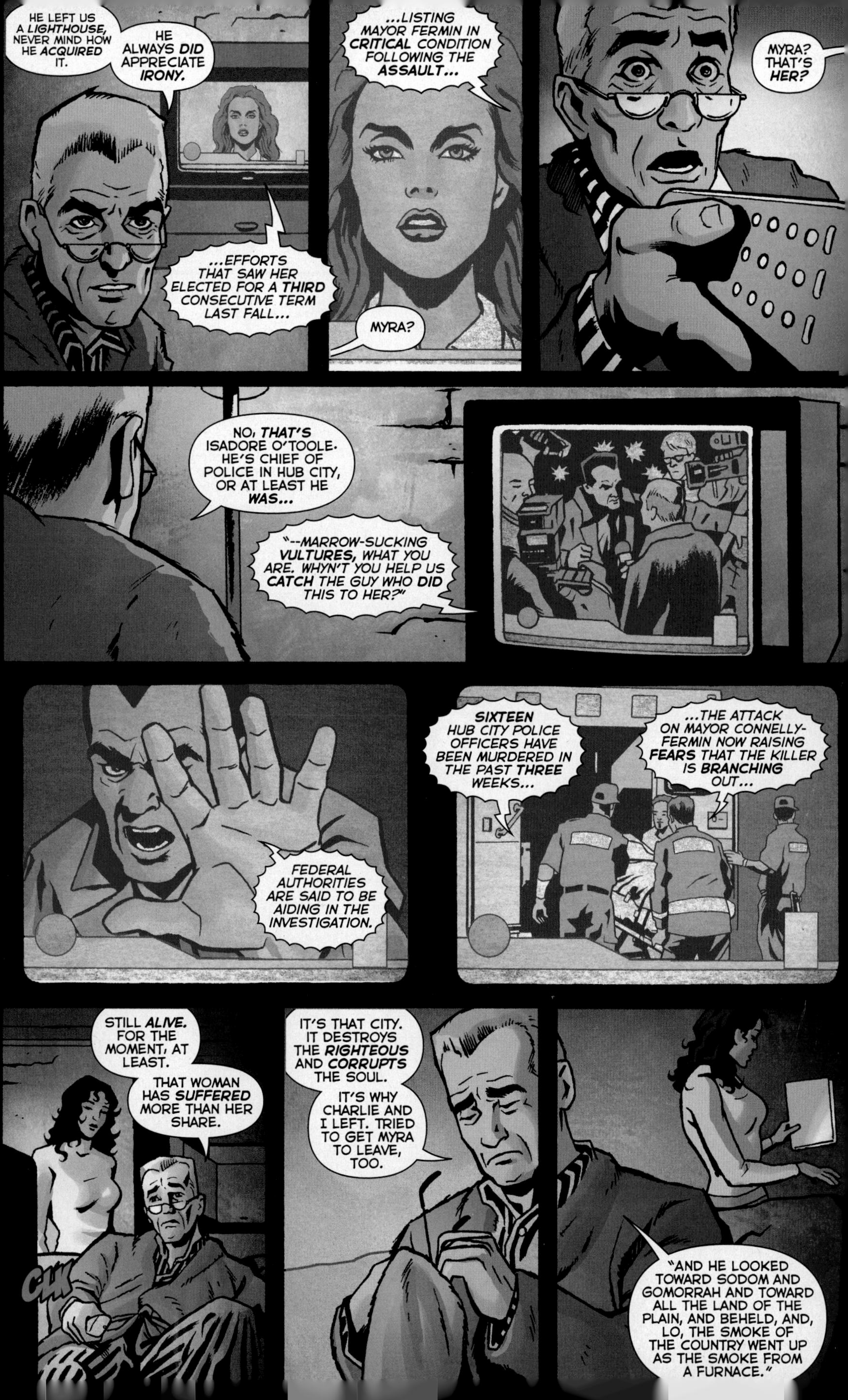
HE LEFT US A LIGHTHOUSE, NEVER MIND HOW HE ACQUIRED IT.
HE ALWAYS DID APPRECIATE IRONY.
...EFFORTS THAT SAW HER ELECTED FOR A THIRD CONSECUTIVE TERM LAST FALL...
...LISTING MAYOR FERMIN IN CRITICAL CONDITION FOLLOWING THE ASSAULT...
MYRA?
MYRA? THAT'S HER?
NO, THAT'S ISADORE O'TOOLE. HE'S CHIEF OF POLICE IN HUB CITY, OR AT LEAST HE WAS...
"--MARROW-SUCKING VULTURES, WHAT YOU ARE. WHYN'T YOU HELP US CATCH THE GUY WHO DID THIS TO HER?"
FEDERAL AUTHORITIES ARE SAID TO BE AIDING IN THE INVESTIGATION.
SIXTEEN HUB CITY POLICE OFFICERS HAVE BEEN MURDERED IN THE PAST THREE WEEKS...
...THE ATTACK ON MAYOR CONNELLY-FERMIN NOW RAISING FEARS THAT THE KILLER IS BRANCHING OUT...
STILL ALIVE. FOR THE MOMENT, AT LEAST.
THAT WOMAN HAS SUFFERED MORE THAN HER SHARE.
IT'S THAT CITY. IT DESTROYS THE RIGHTEOUS AND CORRUPTS THE SOUL.
IT'S WHY CHARLIE AND I LEFT. TRIED TO GET MYRA TO LEAVE, TOO.
"AND HE LOOKED TOWARD SODOM AND GOMORRAH AND TOWARD ALL THE LAND OF THE PLAIN, AND BEHELD, AND, LO, THE SMOKE OF THE COUNTRY WENT UP AS THE SMOKE FROM A FURNACE."

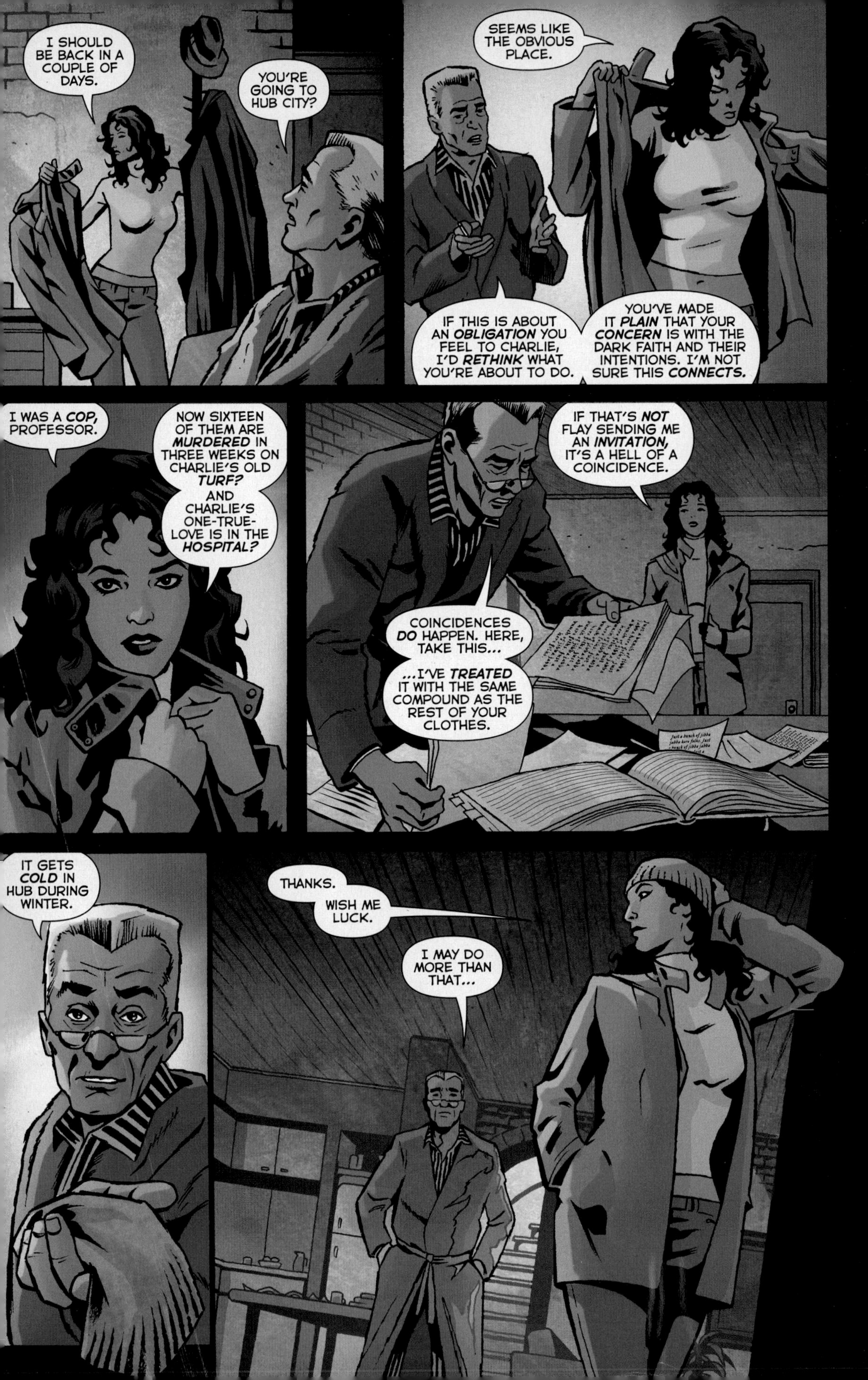
I SHOULD BE BACK IN A COUPLE OF DAYS.
YOU'RE GOING TO HUB CITY?
SEEMS LIKE THE OBVIOUS PLACE.
IF THIS IS ABOUT AN OBLIGATION YOU FEEL TO CHARLIE, I'D RETHINK WHAT YOU'RE ABOUT TO DO.
YOU'VE MADE IT PLAIN THAT YOUR CONCERN IS WITH THE DARK FAITH AND THEIR INTENTIONS. I'M NOT SURE THIS CONNECTS.
I WAS A COP, PROFESSOR.
NOW SIXTEEN OF THEM ARE MURDERED IN THREE WEEKS ON CHARLIE'S OLD TURF? AND CHARLIE'S ONE-TRUE-LOVE IS IN THE HOSPITAL?
IF THAT'S NOT FLAY SENDING ME AN INVITATION, IT'S A HELL OF A COINCIDENCE.
COINCIDENCES DO HAPPEN. HERE, TAKE THIS...
...I'VE TREATED IT WITH THE SAME COMPOUND AS THE REST OF YOUR CLOTHES.
IT GETS COLD IN HUB DURING WINTER.
THANKS.
WISH ME LUCK.
I MAY DO MORE THAN THAT...

"...I MAY ACTUALLY *PRAY*."

HAIL MARY, FULL OF GRACE...

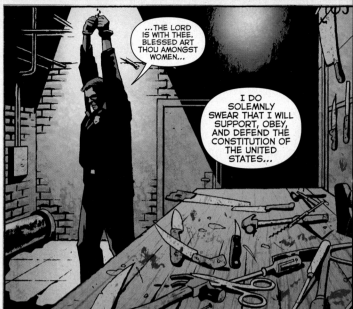

...THE LORD IS WITH THEE. BLESSED ART THOU AMONGST WOMEN...

I DO SOLEMNLY SWEAR THAT I WILL SUPPORT, OBEY, AND DEFEND THE CONSTITUTION OF THE UNITED STATES...

...AND BLESSED IS THE FRUIT OF THY...THY WOMB...

...AND WILL WITH DILIGENCE DISCHARGE THE DUTIES ENTRUSTED TO ME TO *UPHOLD* THE LAWS, *PROTECT* THE CITIZENRY, AND *SERVE* THE COMMUNITY...

...OF HUB CITY WITH *HONESTY* AND *FAITH* BEFITTING MY AUTHORITY AS A POLICE OFFICER.

...PLEASE...

BUT *YOU CAN'T* PROTECT THEM. YOU'RE *WEAK*...

hnNn

...THE *BADGE* MAKES YOU *WEAK*...

--Nhapl-- PLEASE NHAAA AAHHhhhk kkhkk

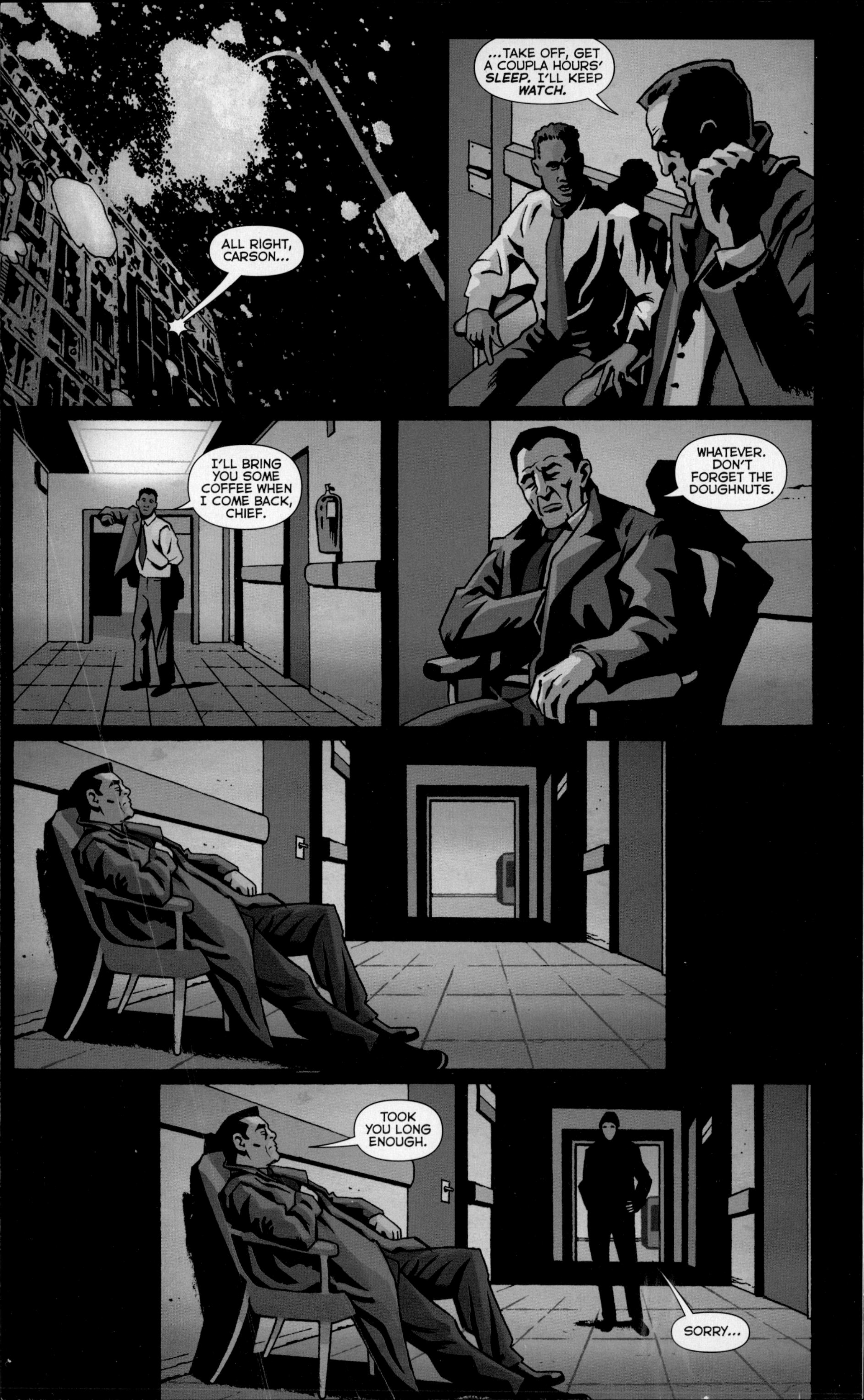
ALL RIGHT, CARSON...
...TAKE OFF, GET A COUPLA HOURS' SLEEP. I'LL KEEP WATCH.
I'LL BRING YOU SOME COFFEE WHEN I COME BACK, CHIEF.
WHATEVER. DON'T FORGET THE DOUGHNUTS.
TOOK YOU LONG ENOUGH.
SORRY...

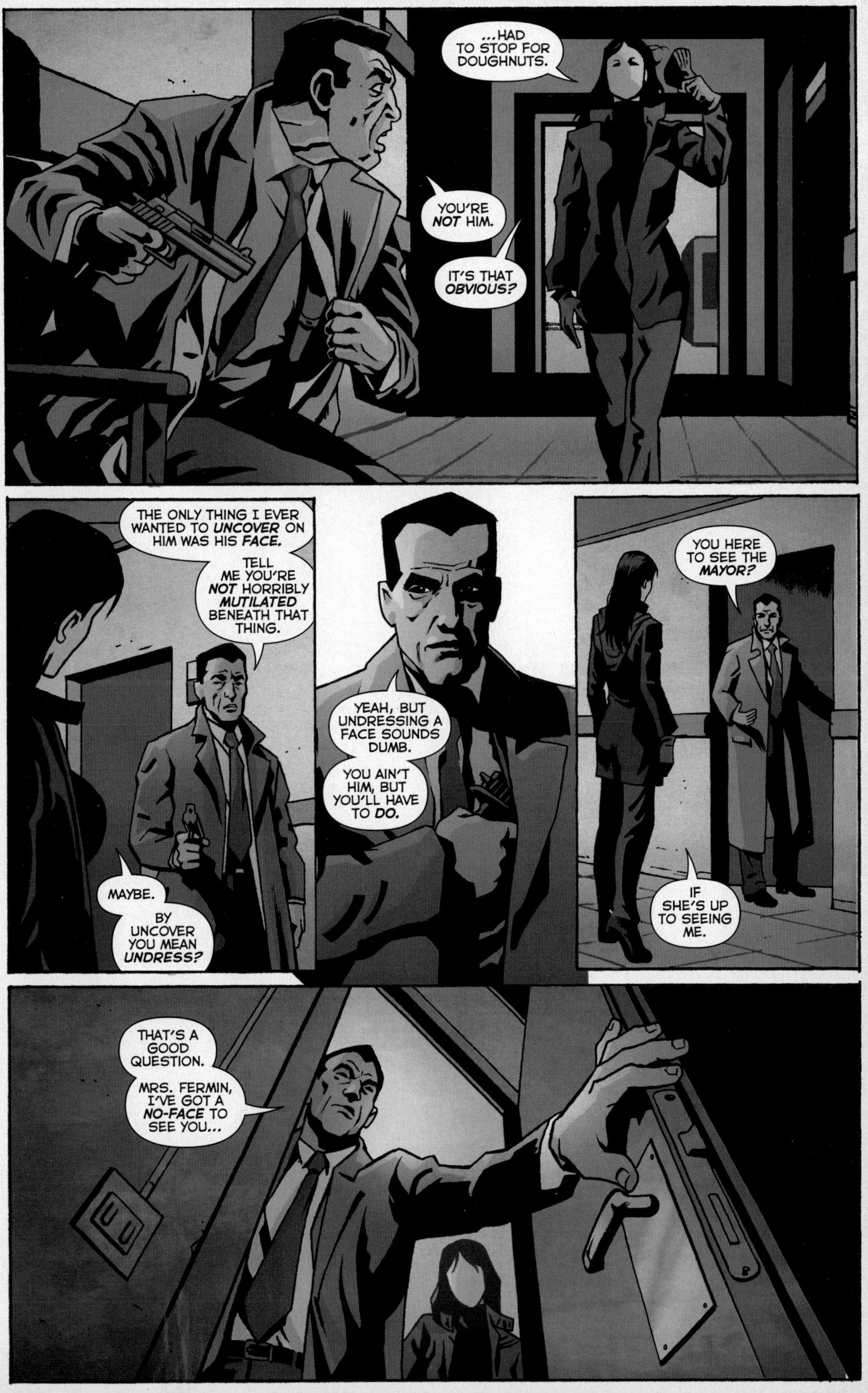
...HAD TO STOP FOR DOUGHNUTS.
YOU'RE NOT HIM.
IT'S THAT OBVIOUS?
THE ONLY THING I EVER WANTED TO UNCOVER ON HIM WAS HIS FACE.
TELL ME YOU'RE NOT HORRIBLY MUTILATED BENEATH THAT THING.
MAYBE.
BY UNCOVER YOU MEAN UNDRESS?
YEAH, BUT UNDRESSING A FACE SOUNDS DUMB.
YOU AIN'T HIM, BUT YOU'LL HAVE TO DO.
YOU HERE TO SEE THE MAYOR?
IF SHE'S UP TO SEEING ME.
THAT'S A GOOD QUESTION.
MRS. FERMIN, I'VE GOT A NO-FACE TO SEE YOU...

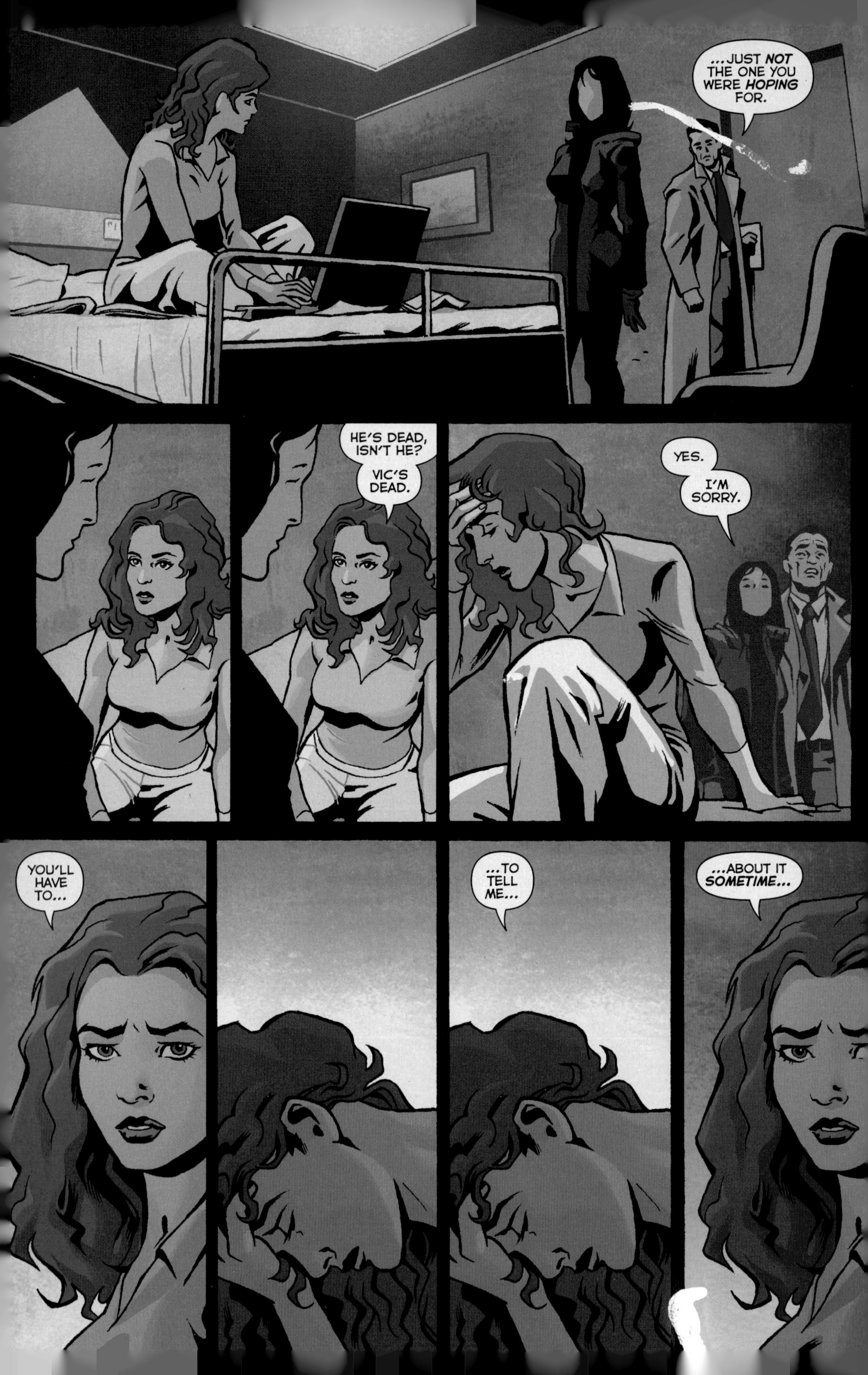
...JUST NOT THE ONE YOU WERE HOPING FOR.
HE'S DEAD, ISN'T HE?
VIC'S DEAD.
YES.
I'M SORRY.
YOU'LL HAVE TO...
...TO TELL ME...
...ABOUT IT SOMETIME...

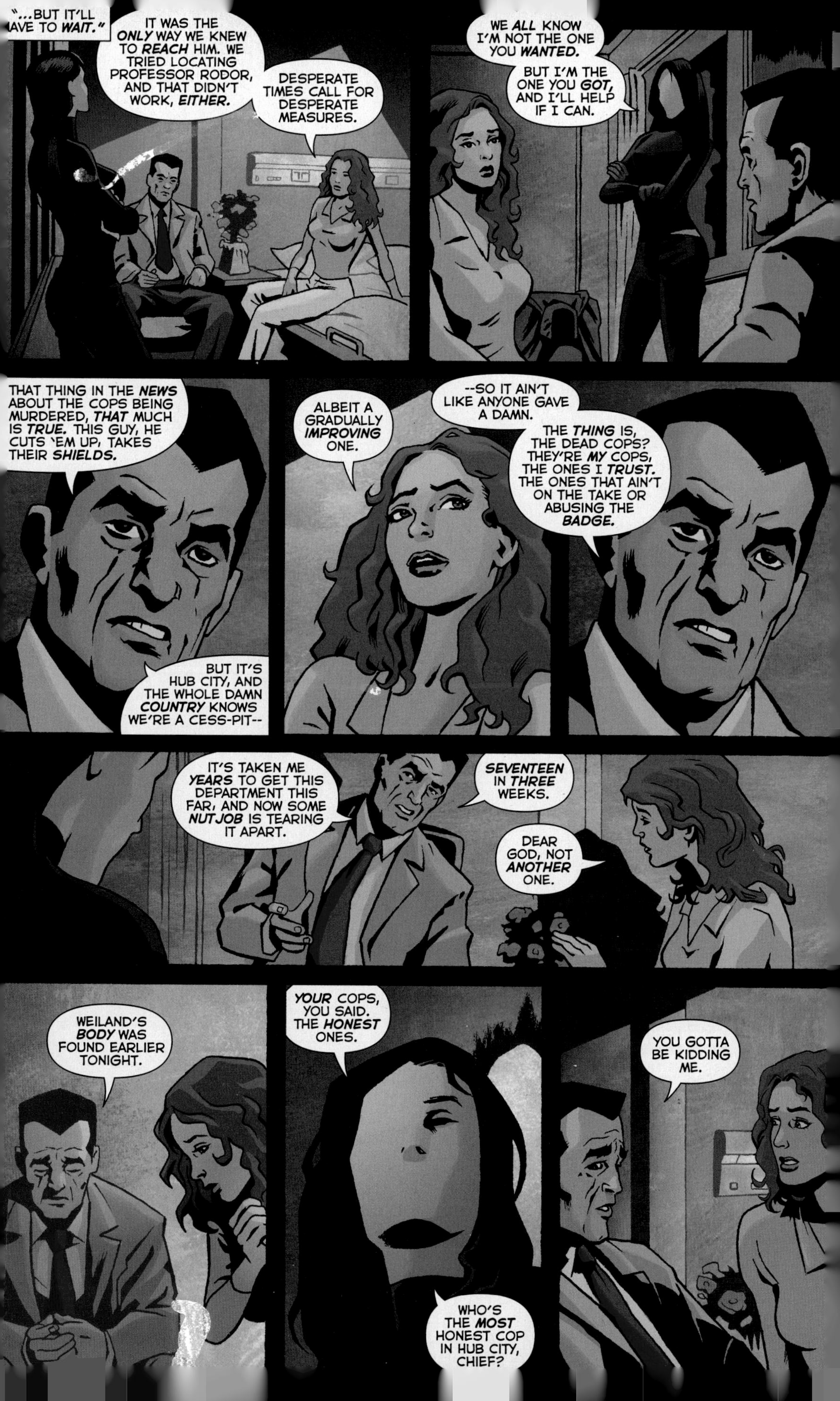
"...BUT IT'LL HAVE TO WAIT."
IT WAS THE ONLY WAY WE KNEW TO REACH HIM. WE TRIED LOCATING PROFESSOR RODOR, AND THAT DIDN'T WORK, EITHER.
DESPERATE TIMES CALL FOR DESPERATE MEASURES.
WE ALL KNOW I'M NOT THE ONE YOU WANTED.
BUT I'M THE ONE YOU GOT, AND I'LL HELP IF I CAN.
THAT THING IN THE NEWS ABOUT THE COPS BEING MURDERED, THAT MUCH IS TRUE. THIS GUY, HE CUTS 'EM UP, TAKES THEIR SHIELDS.
BUT IT'S HUB CITY, AND THE WHOLE DAMN COUNTRY KNOWS WE'RE A CESS-PIT--
ALBEIT A GRADUALLY IMPROVING ONE.
--SO IT AIN'T LIKE ANYONE GAVE A DAMN.
THE THING IS, THE DEAD COPS? THEY'RE MY COPS, THE ONES I TRUST. THE ONES THAT AIN'T ON THE TAKE OR ABUSING THE BADGE.
IT'S TAKEN ME YEARS TO GET THIS DEPARTMENT THIS FAR, AND NOW SOME NUTJOB IS TEARING IT APART.
SEVENTEEN IN THREE WEEKS.
DEAR GOD, NOT ANOTHER ONE.
WEILAND'S BODY WAS FOUND EARLIER TONIGHT.
YOUR COPS, YOU SAID. THE HONEST ONES.
WHO'S THE MOST HONEST COP IN HUB CITY, CHIEF?
YOU GOTTA BE KIDDING ME.

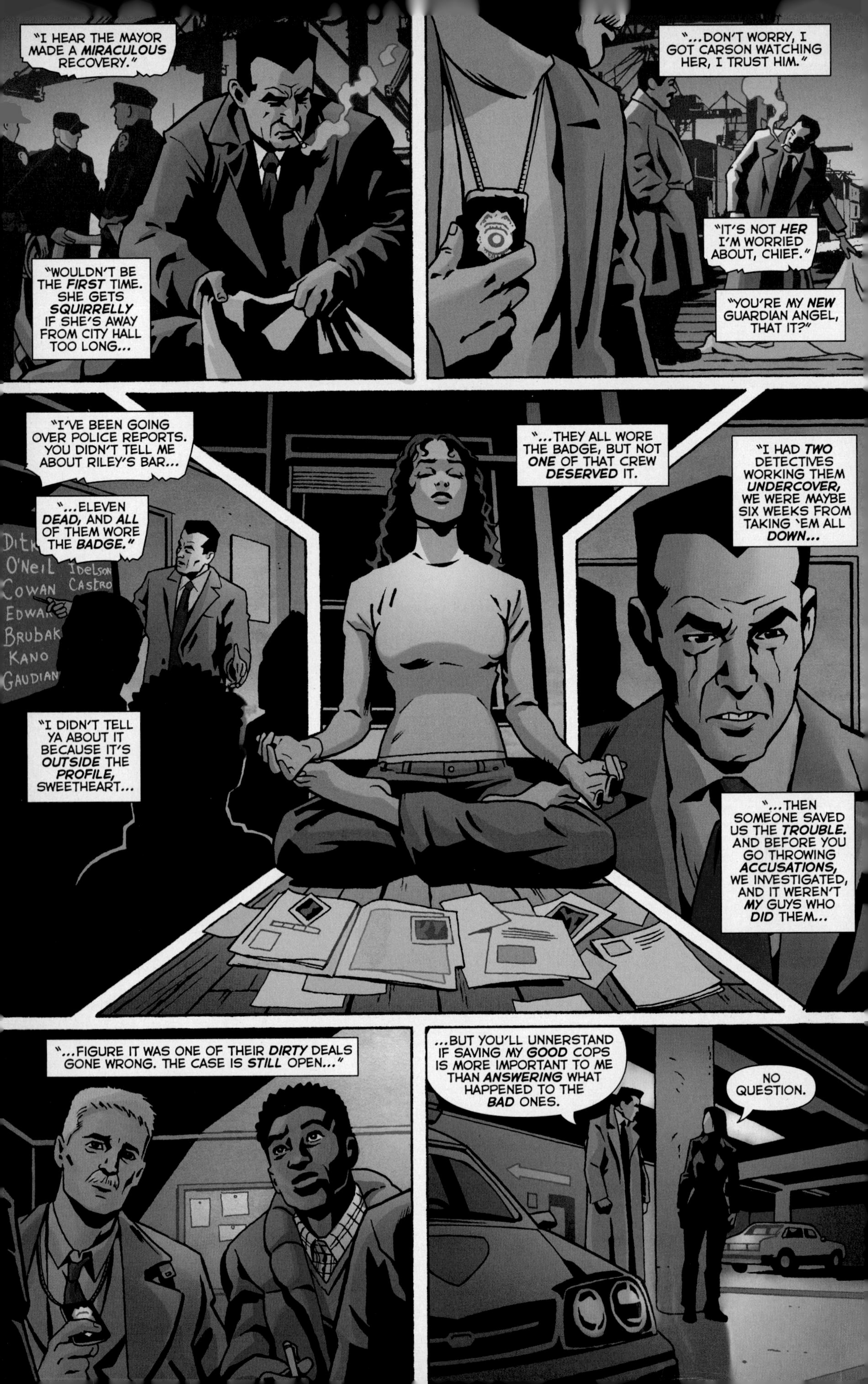
"I HEAR THE MAYOR MADE A MIRACULOUS RECOVERY."
"WOULDN'T BE THE FIRST TIME. SHE GETS SQUIRRELLY IF SHE'S AWAY FROM CITY HALL TOO LONG...
"...DON'T WORRY, I GOT CARSON WATCHING HER, I TRUST HIM."
"IT'S NOT HER I'M WORRIED ABOUT, CHIEF."
"YOU'RE MY NEW GUARDIAN ANGEL, THAT IT?"
"I'VE BEEN GOING OVER POLICE REPORTS. YOU DIDN'T TELL ME ABOUT RILEY'S BAR...
"...ELEVEN DEAD, AND ALL OF THEM WORE THE BADGE."
O'NEIL IDELSON
COWAN CASTRO
EDWA
BRUBAK
KANO
GAUDIAN
"I DIDN'T TELL YA ABOUT IT BECAUSE IT'S OUTSIDE THE PROFILE, SWEETHEART...
"...THEY ALL WORE THE BADGE, BUT NOT ONE OF THAT CREW DESERVED IT.
"I HAD TWO DETECTIVES WORKING THEM UNDERCOVER, WE WERE MAYBE SIX WEEKS FROM TAKING 'EM ALL DOWN...
"...THEN SOMEONE SAVED US THE TROUBLE. AND BEFORE YOU GO THROWING ACCUSATIONS, WE INVESTIGATED, AND IT WEREN'T MY GUYS WHO DID THEM...
"...FIGURE IT WAS ONE OF THEIR DIRTY DEALS GONE WRONG. THE CASE IS STILL OPEN..."
...BUT YOU'LL UNNERSTAND IF SAVING MY GOOD COPS IS MORE IMPORTANT TO ME THAN ANSWERING WHAT HAPPENED TO THE BAD ONES.
NO QUESTION.

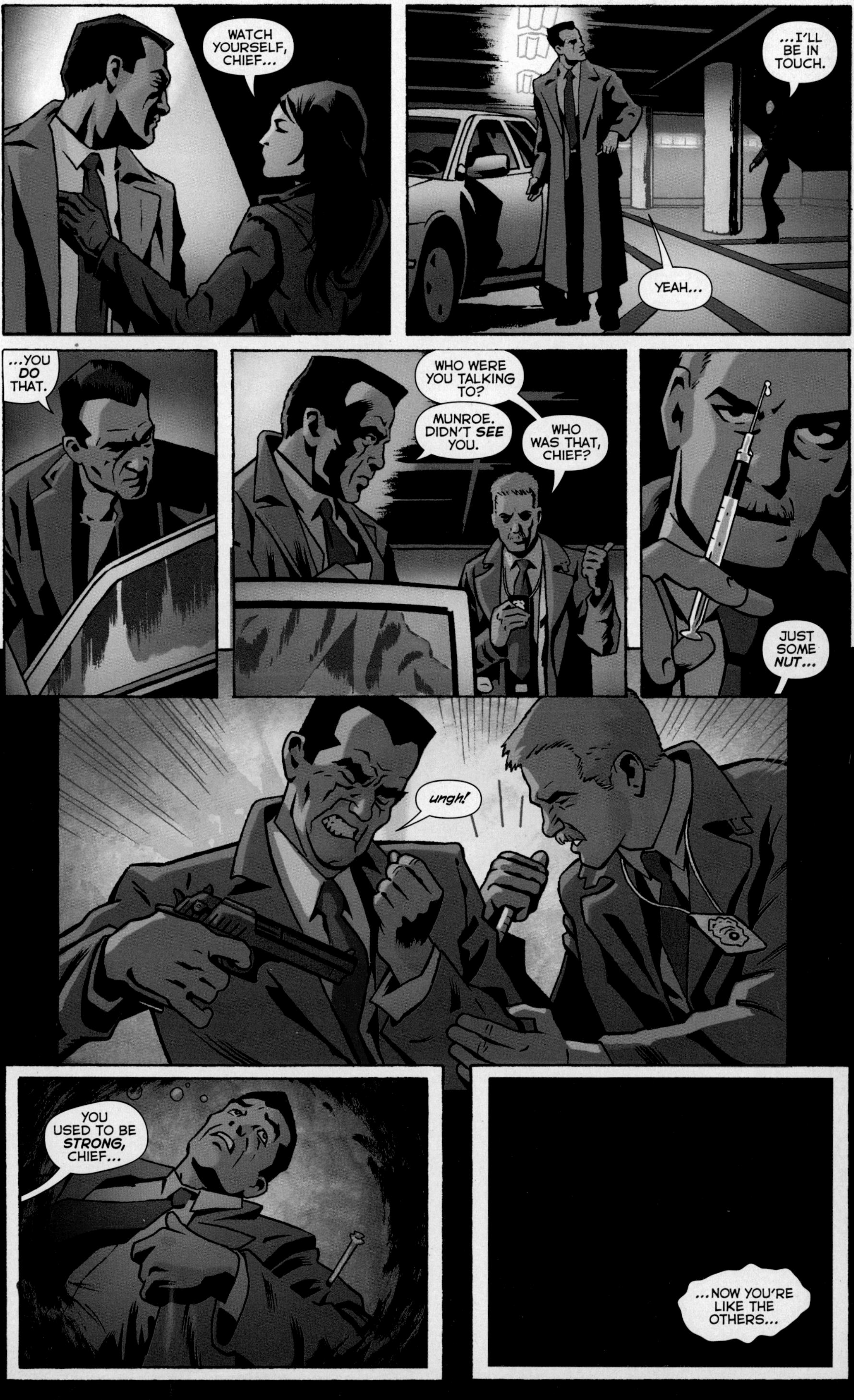
WATCH YOURSELF, CHIEF...
...I'LL BE IN TOUCH.
YEAH...
...YOU *DO* THAT.
WHO WERE YOU TALKING TO?
MUNROE. DIDN'T *SEE* YOU.
WHO WAS THAT, CHIEF?
JUST SOME *NUT*...
ungh!
YOU USED TO BE *STRONG*, CHIEF...
...NOW YOU'RE LIKE THE OTHERS...

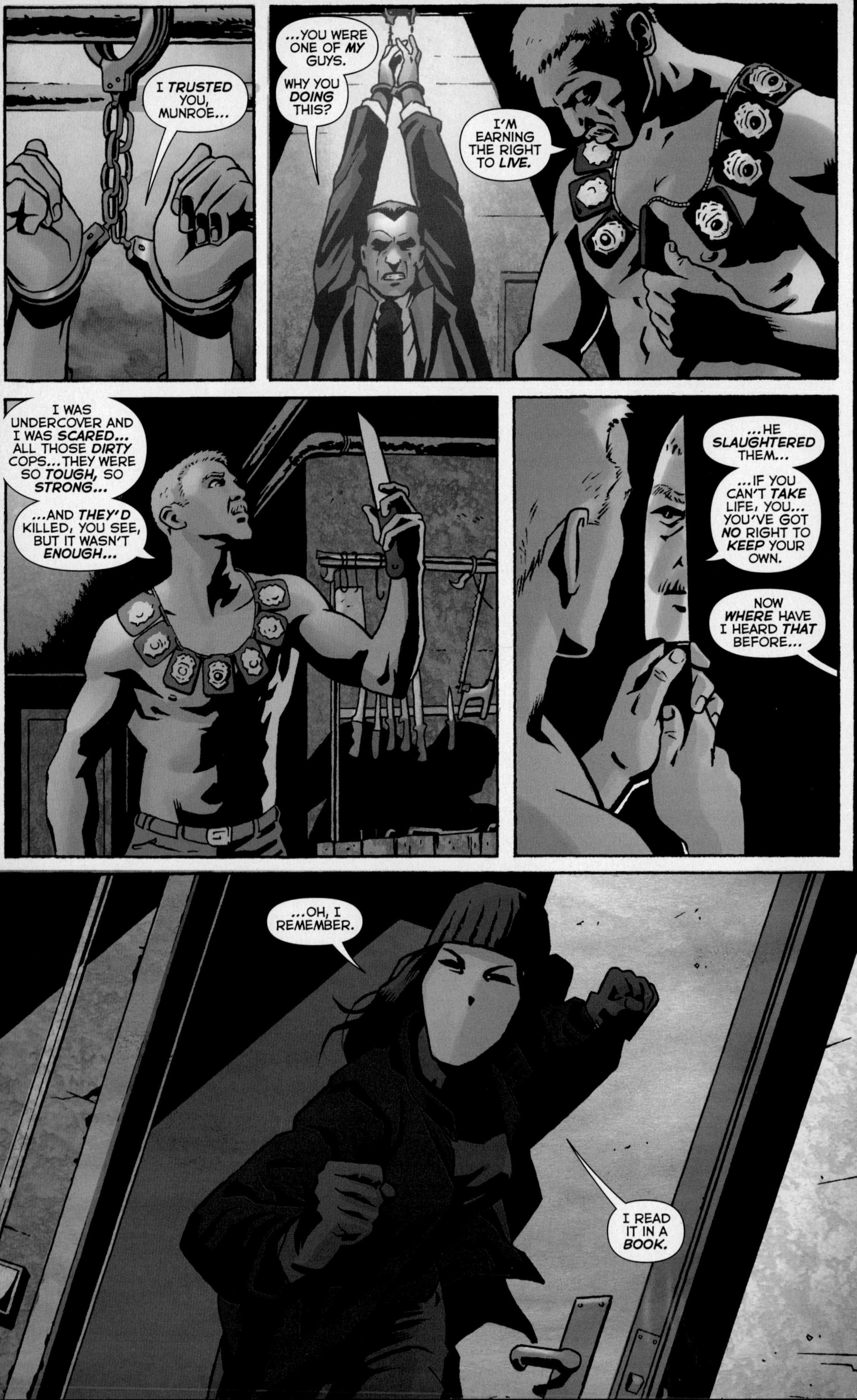
I TRUSTED YOU, MUNROE...
...YOU WERE ONE OF MY GUYS.
WHY YOU DOING THIS?
I'M EARNING THE RIGHT TO LIVE.
I WAS UNDERCOVER AND I WAS SCARED... ALL THOSE DIRTY COPS...THEY WERE SO TOUGH, SO STRONG...
...AND THEY'D KILLED, YOU SEE, BUT IT WASN'T ENOUGH...
...HE SLAUGHTERED THEM...
...IF YOU CAN'T TAKE LIFE, YOU... YOU'VE GOT NO RIGHT TO KEEP YOUR OWN.
NOW WHERE HAVE I HEARD THAT BEFORE...
...OH, I REMEMBER.
I READ IT IN A BOOK.

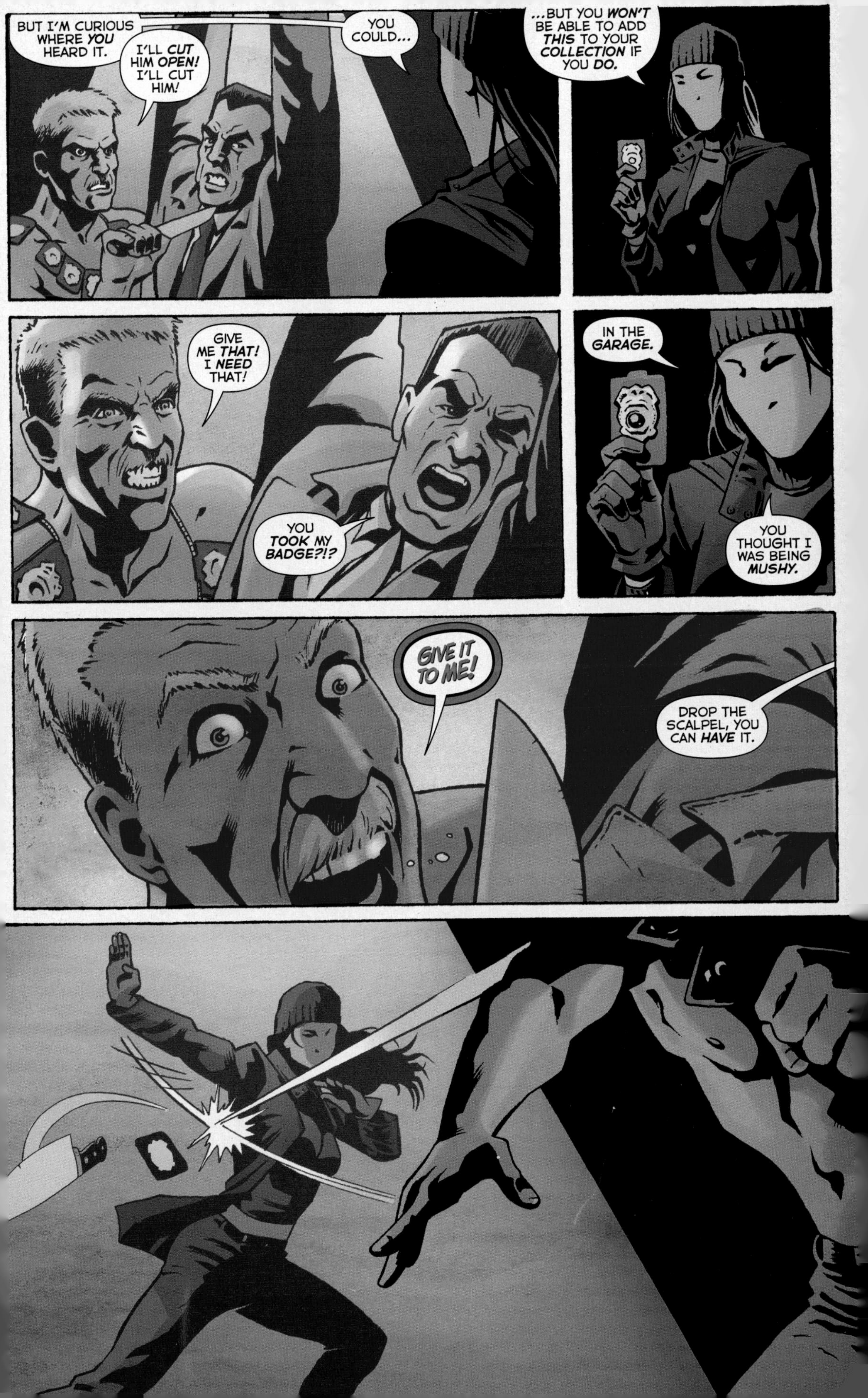
BUT I'M CURIOUS WHERE YOU HEARD IT.
I'LL CUT HIM OPEN! I'LL CUT HIM!
YOU COULD...
...BUT YOU WON'T BE ABLE TO ADD THIS TO YOUR COLLECTION IF YOU DO.
GIVE ME THAT! I NEED THAT!
YOU TOOK MY BADGE?!?
IN THE GARAGE.
YOU THOUGHT I WAS BEING MUSHY.
GIVE IT TO ME!
DROP THE SCALPEL, YOU CAN HAVE IT.

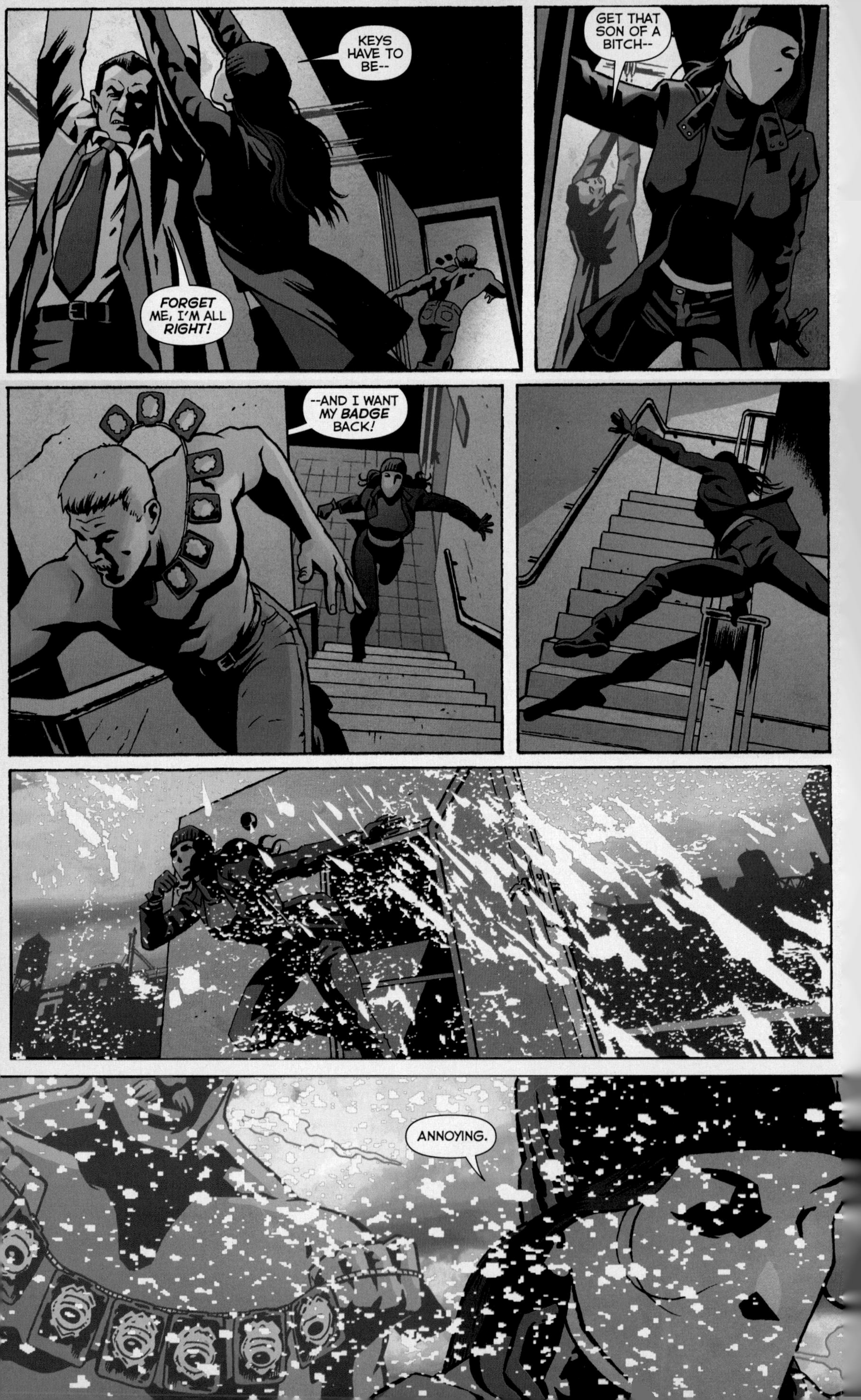

KEYS HAVE TO BE--
FORGET ME, I'M ALL RIGHT!
GET THAT SON OF A BITCH--
--AND I WANT MY BADGE BACK!
ANNOYING.

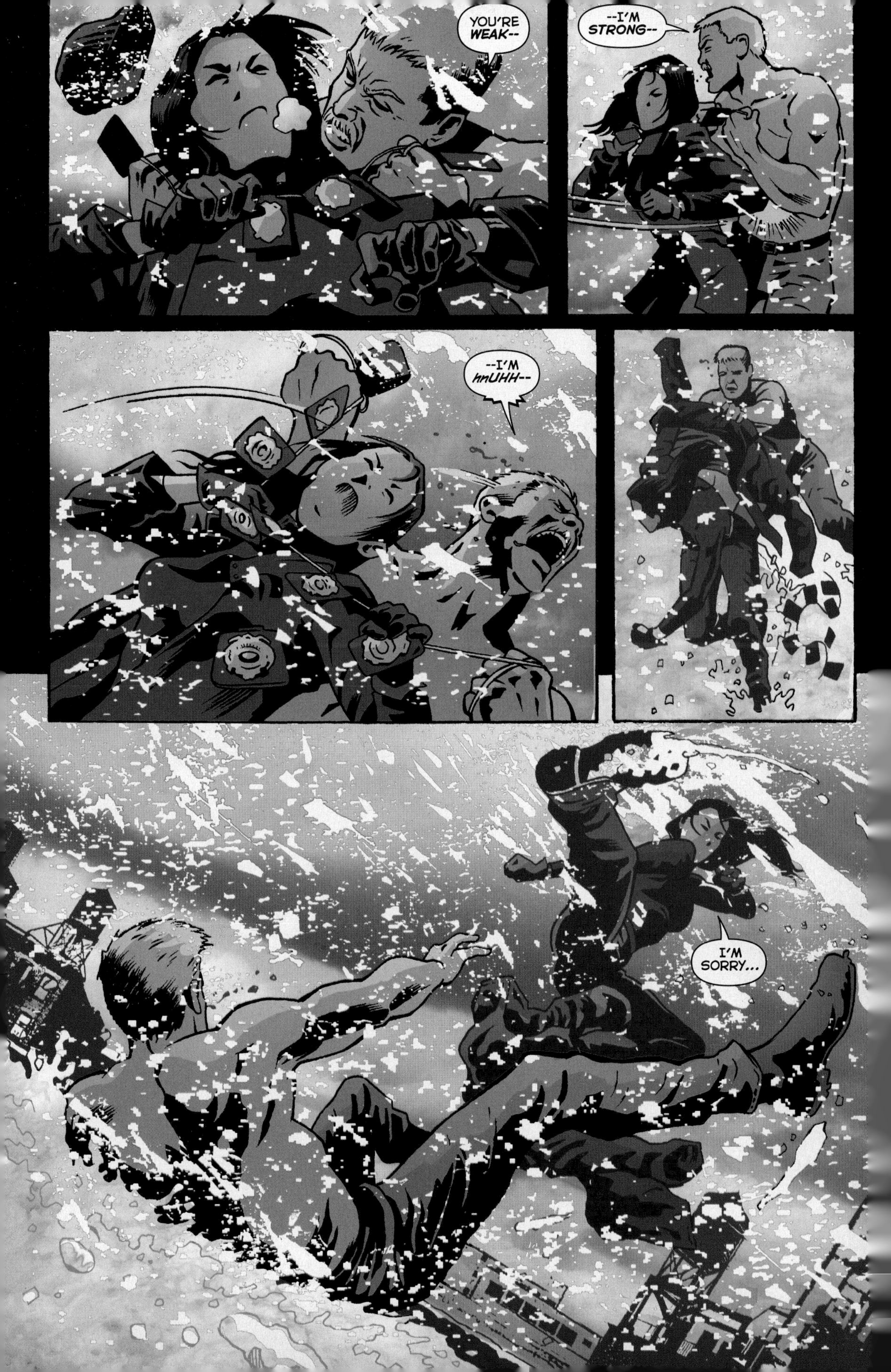
YOU'RE WEAK--
--I'M STRONG--
--I'M hnUHH--
I'M SORRY...

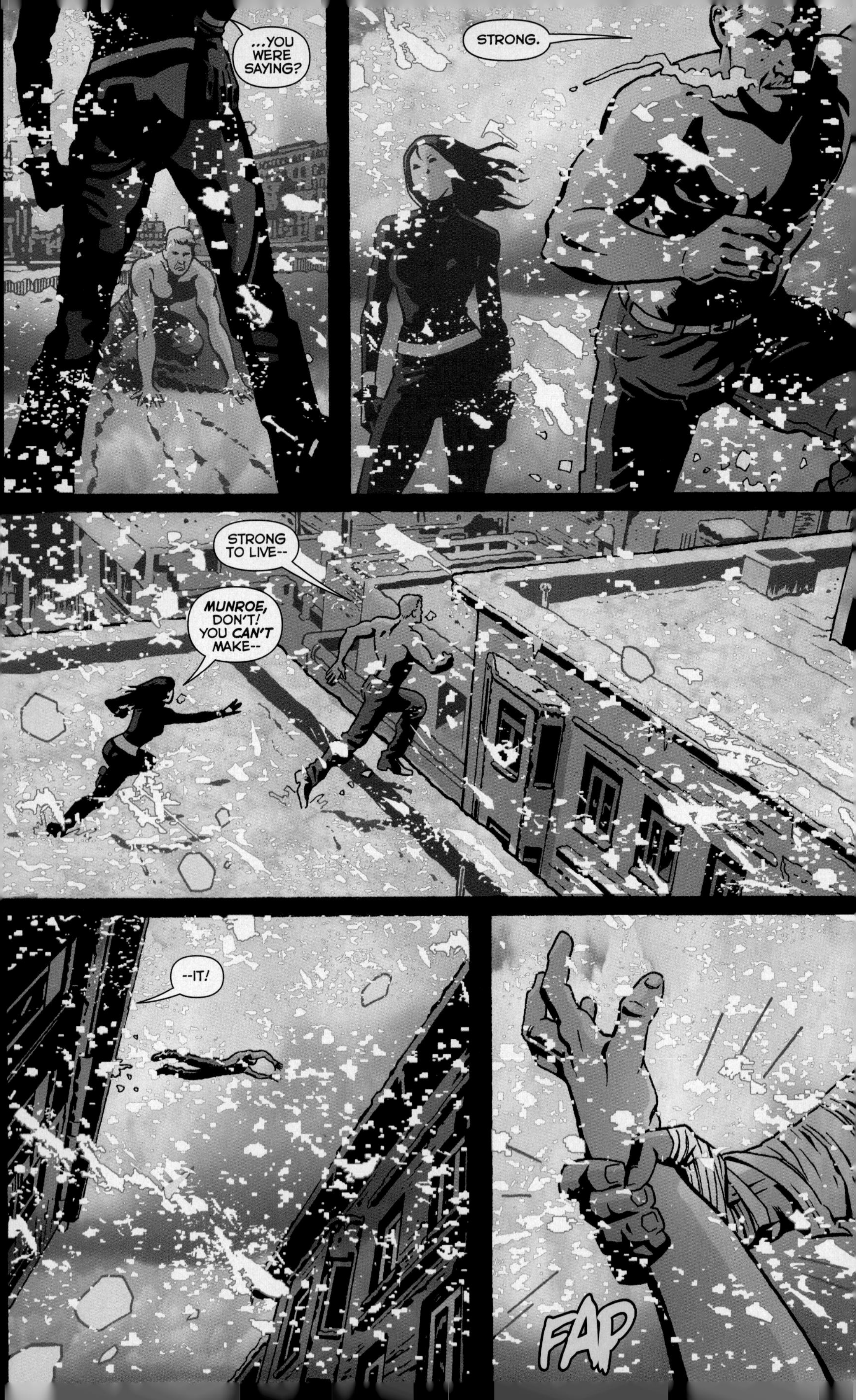
...YOU WERE SAYING?
STRONG.
STRONG TO LIVE--
MUNROE, DON'T! YOU *CAN'T* MAKE--
--IT!
FAP

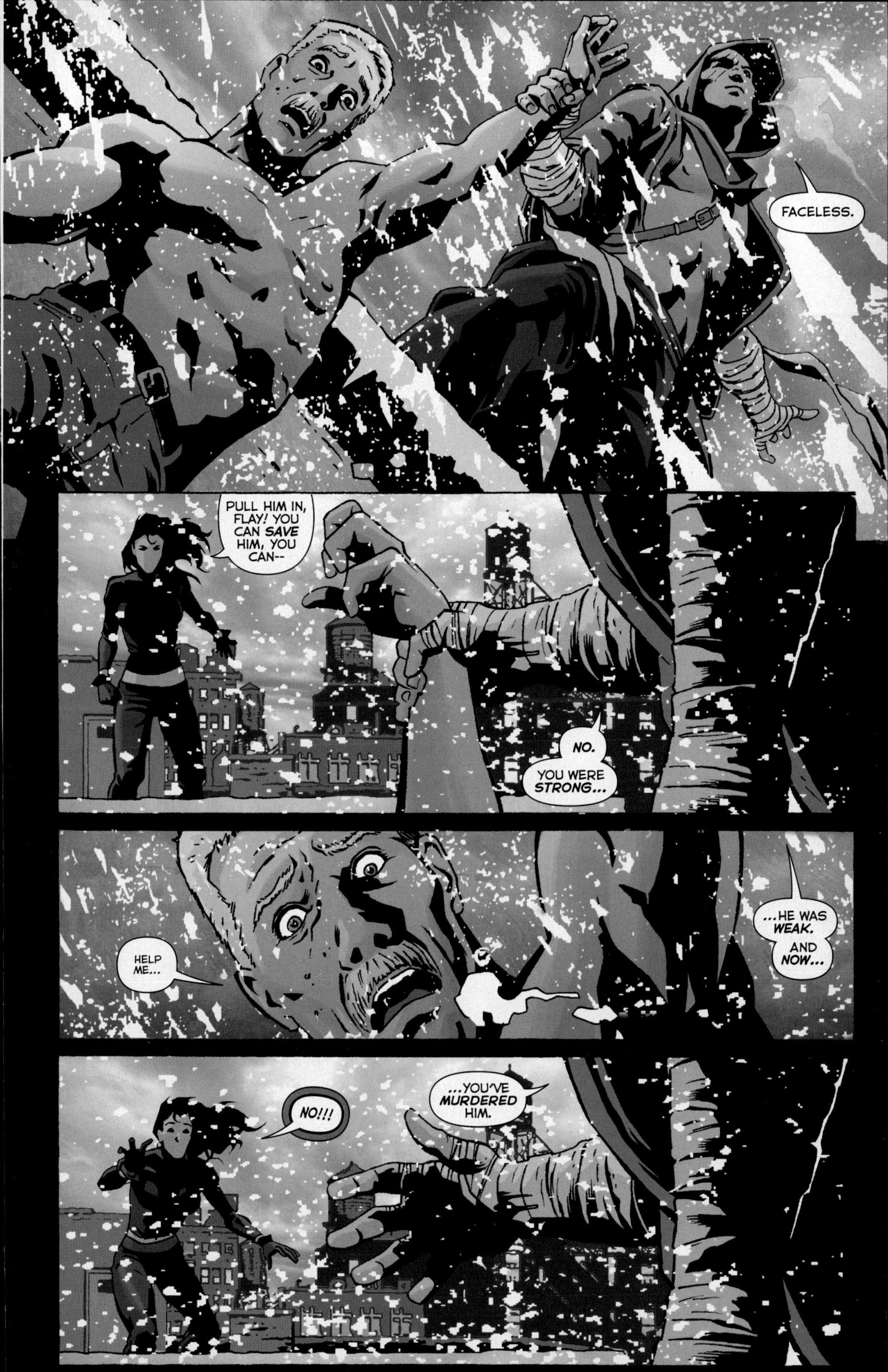
FACELESS.
PULL HIM IN, FLAY! YOU CAN SAVE HIM, YOU CAN--
NO.
YOU WERE STRONG...
HELP ME...
...HE WAS WEAK.
AND NOW...
NO!!!
...YOU'VE MURDERED HIM.

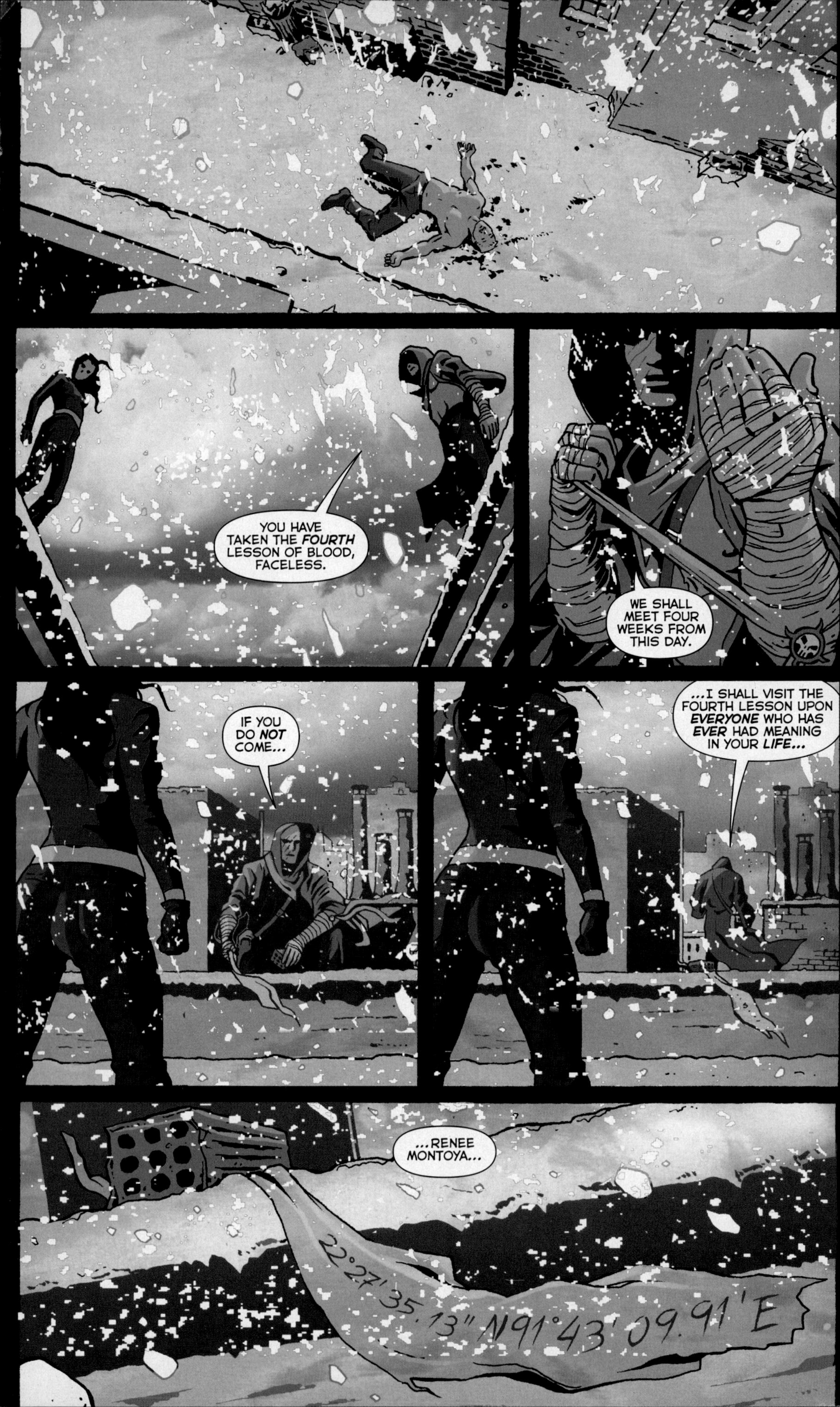

YOU HAVE TAKEN THE FOURTH LESSON OF BLOOD, FACELESS.
WE SHALL MEET FOUR WEEKS FROM THIS DAY.
IF YOU DO NOT COME...
...I SHALL VISIT THE FOURTH LESSON UPON EVERYONE WHO HAS EVER HAD MEANING IN YOUR LIFE...
...RENEE MONTOYA...
22°27'35.13"N91°43'09.91'E

The Fifth Book of Blood

Chapter 27, Verses 17-34

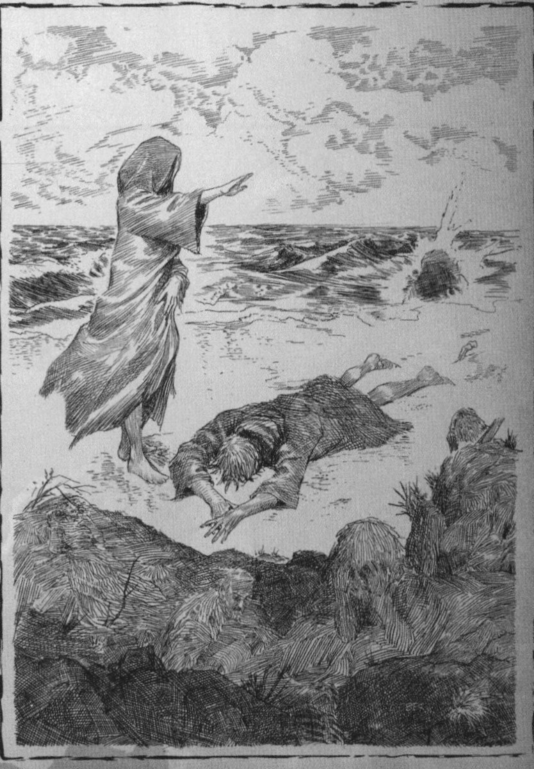

17 *Then returned to Har-Mammon the one-eyed*
Caitiff, and entered he the City of Night, the skies full
of smoke and the flames that joined heavens to Hell.
18 *And there the Caitiff found the face-less and*
wise alike, their celebration and joy greater even
than that of the Cities Made Salt; and being
marked by the First, he was brought before Lilith,
who did leadeth there.
19 *And Lilith did gaze upon the Caitiff, and with*
vision saw upon him the sojourn he had made, and
the sojourns yet to be made; and Lilith did grace the
Caitiff a kiss upon his lost eye, and blessed him a
portion of her guidance, that he might go forth and
follow in the steps of the First, and spread His word
with most-praise and new vision.
20 *So it was that the Caitiff did receive the blessing*
of Lilith, and thus sojourned forth from great
Har-Mammon and into the desert; and amongst
all the peoples he didst teach the Lessons, and
prepare them, and those he left with breath within
them were made stronger for his passing.
21 *And it came to pass that, on the shores of the abandoned, the Caitiff didst spy a woman alone, and with blessed*
eye, took her for a wanderer such as he; and finding her comely, and heeding his lessons, he called out to her.
22 *Sister, do you wander as I, and seek to master the lessons of our teacher? For I see in you one like*
myself, with hardened fist and step certain, unyielding in your search; Come and tarry with me, that we
might learn of each other, and share much.
23 *And she said unto the Caitiff, I have wandered far in search of knowledge, but know not of your*
teacher or his lessons, for mine are the lessons of another; Pray speak of them, and I shall listen.
24 *And thus the Caitiff told her all of Cain, called the First, and of His Lessons; and the Caitiff spake*
of the First Lesson, and taught her of Deceit.
25 *And she asked unto the Caitiff, I know this lesson, but what is the Truth in it?*
26 *And thus the Caitiff spake of the Second Lesson, and taught her of Lust.*
27 *And she asked unto the Caitiff, I know this lesson, but what of Regret?*
28 *And thus it was the Caitiff spake of the Third Lesson, and taught her of Greed.*
29 *And she asked unto the Caitiff, I know this lesson, but is there no Charity?*
30 *And thus the Caitiff spake of the Fourth lesson, and taught her of Murder.*
31 *And she asked unto the Caitiff, I know this lesson, but where is Mercy?*
32 *And the Caitiff gazed upon her, and saw then that she was without faith, and empty; and too, he*
saw his reflection upon her face.
33 *And the Caitiff said unto her, Faithless I name thee, as once was I; come, sister, and sojourn with*
me, that I may teach you the ways of my master, and so answer your questions all.
34 *And in this way did the Faithless come to journey beside him.*

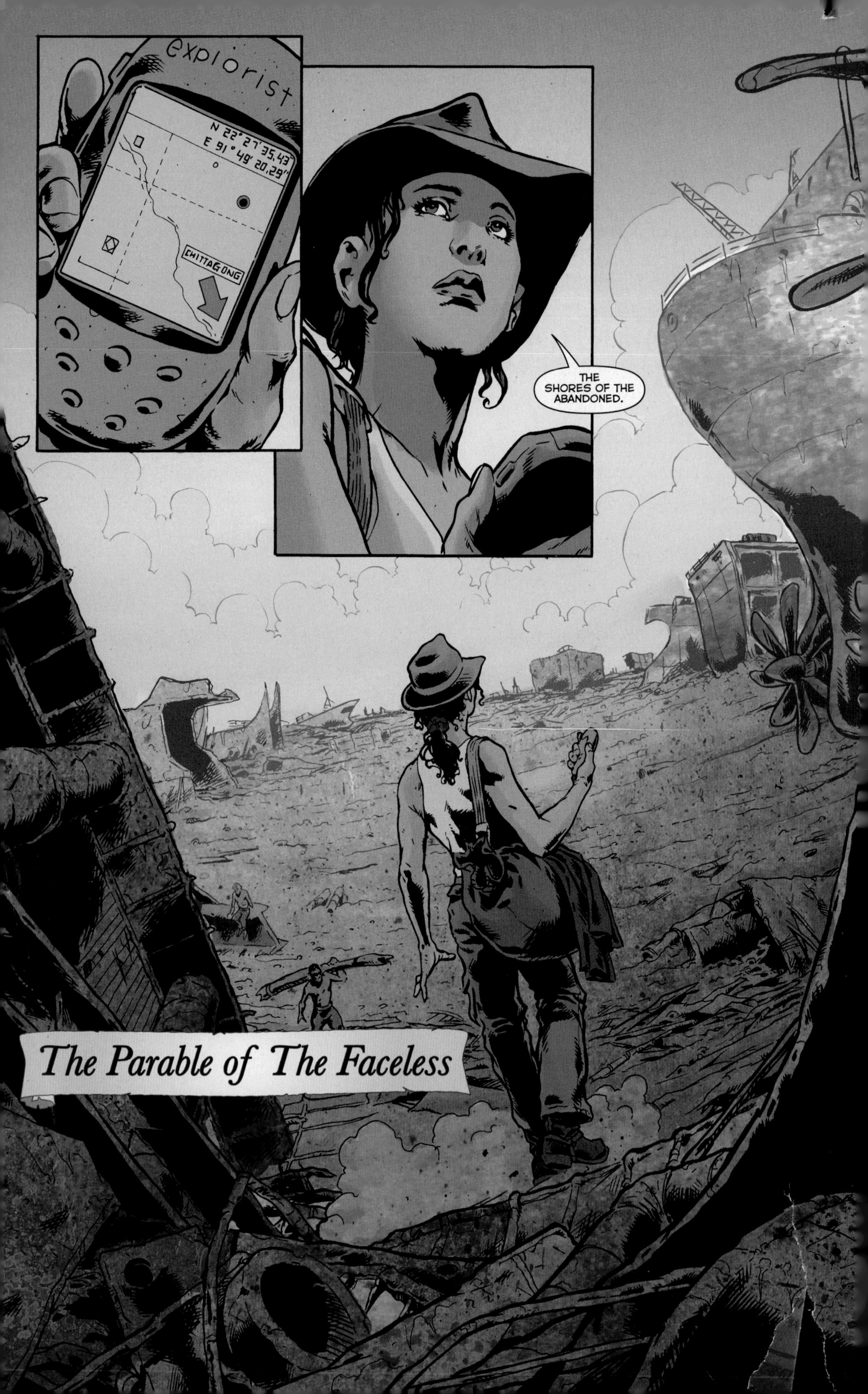
explorist
N 22° 27' 35.43"
E 91° 49' 20.29"
CHITTAGONG
THE SHORES OF THE ABANDONED.
The Parable of The Faceless

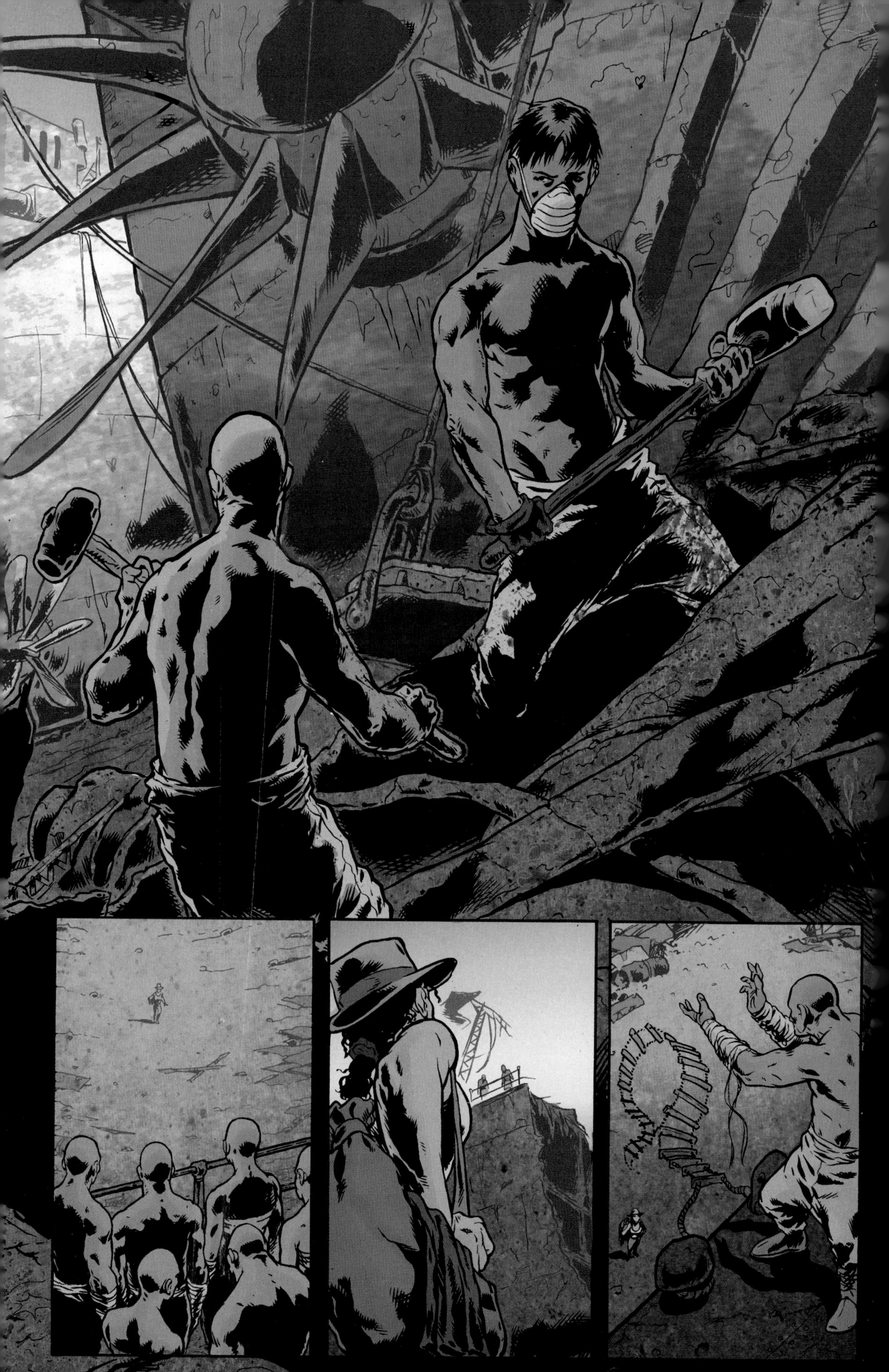

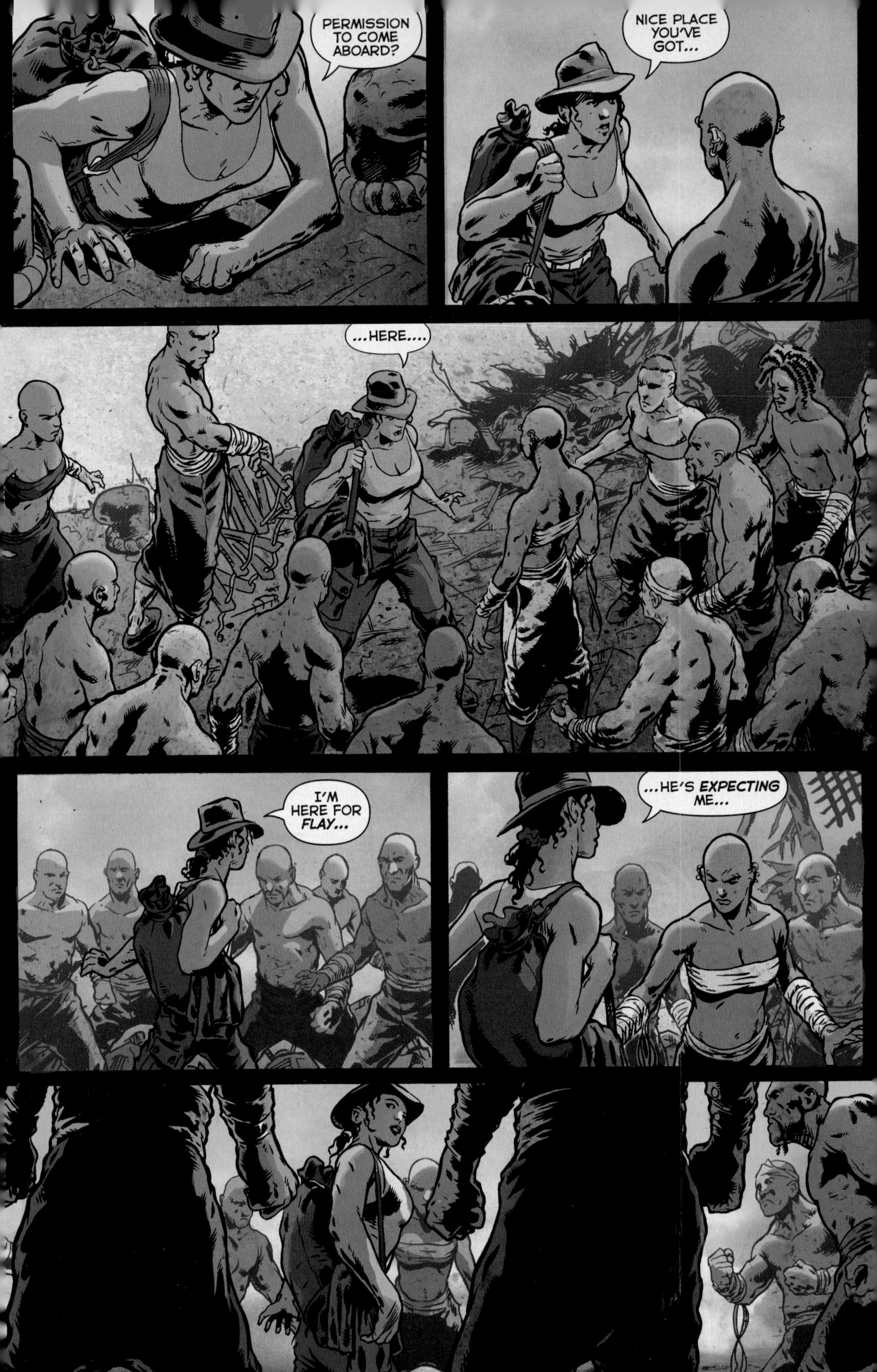
PERMISSION TO COME ABOARD?
NICE PLACE YOU'VE GOT...
...HERE....
I'M HERE FOR *FLAY*...
...HE'S *EXPECTING* ME...

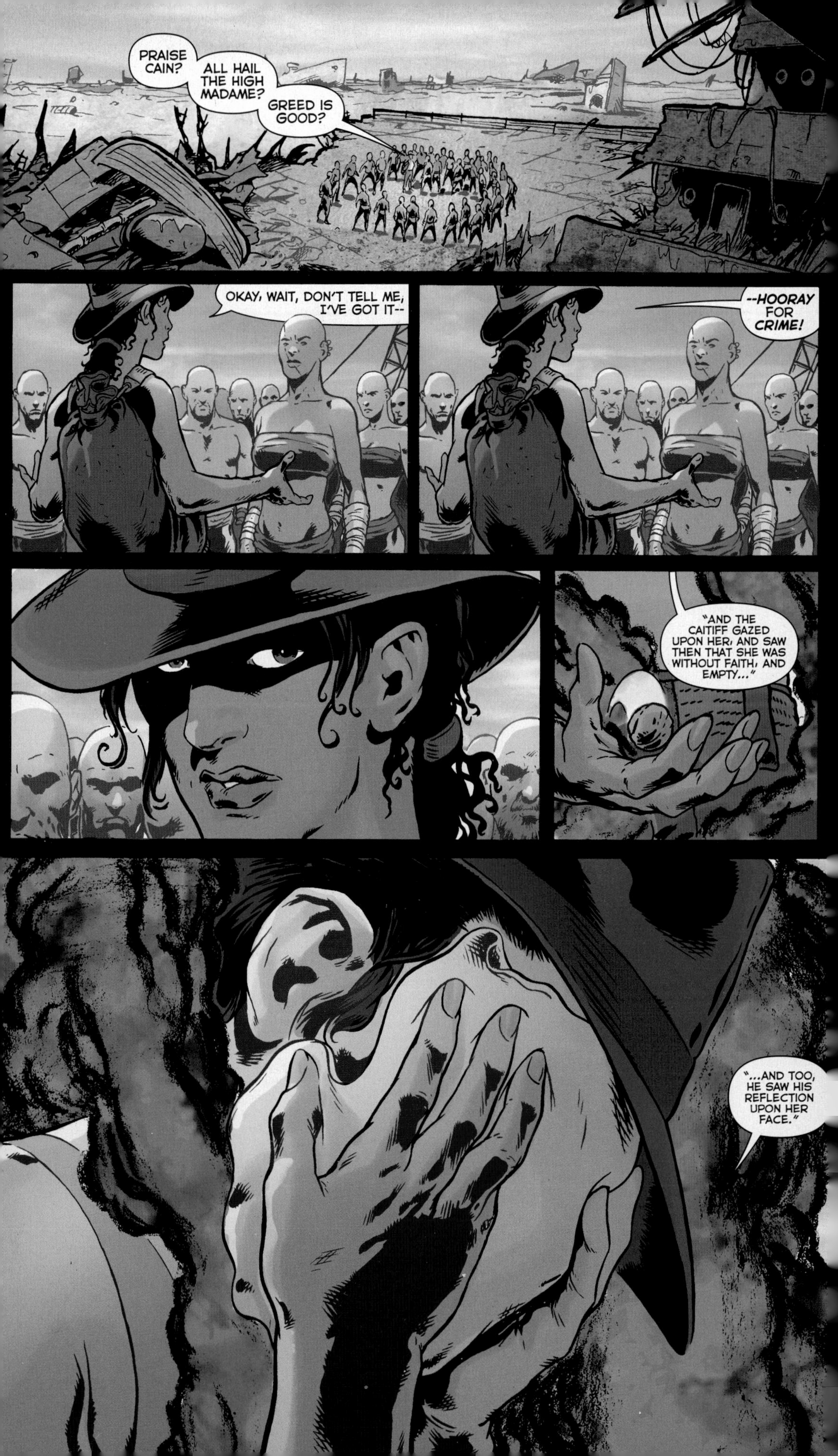
PRAISE CAIN?
ALL HAIL THE HIGH MADAME?
GREED IS GOOD?
OKAY, WAIT, DON'T TELL ME, I'VE GOT IT--
--HOORAY FOR CRIME!
"AND THE CAITIFF GAZED UPON HER, AND SAW THEN THAT SHE WAS WITHOUT FAITH, AND EMPTY..."
"...AND TOO, HE SAW HIS REFLECTION UPON HER FACE."

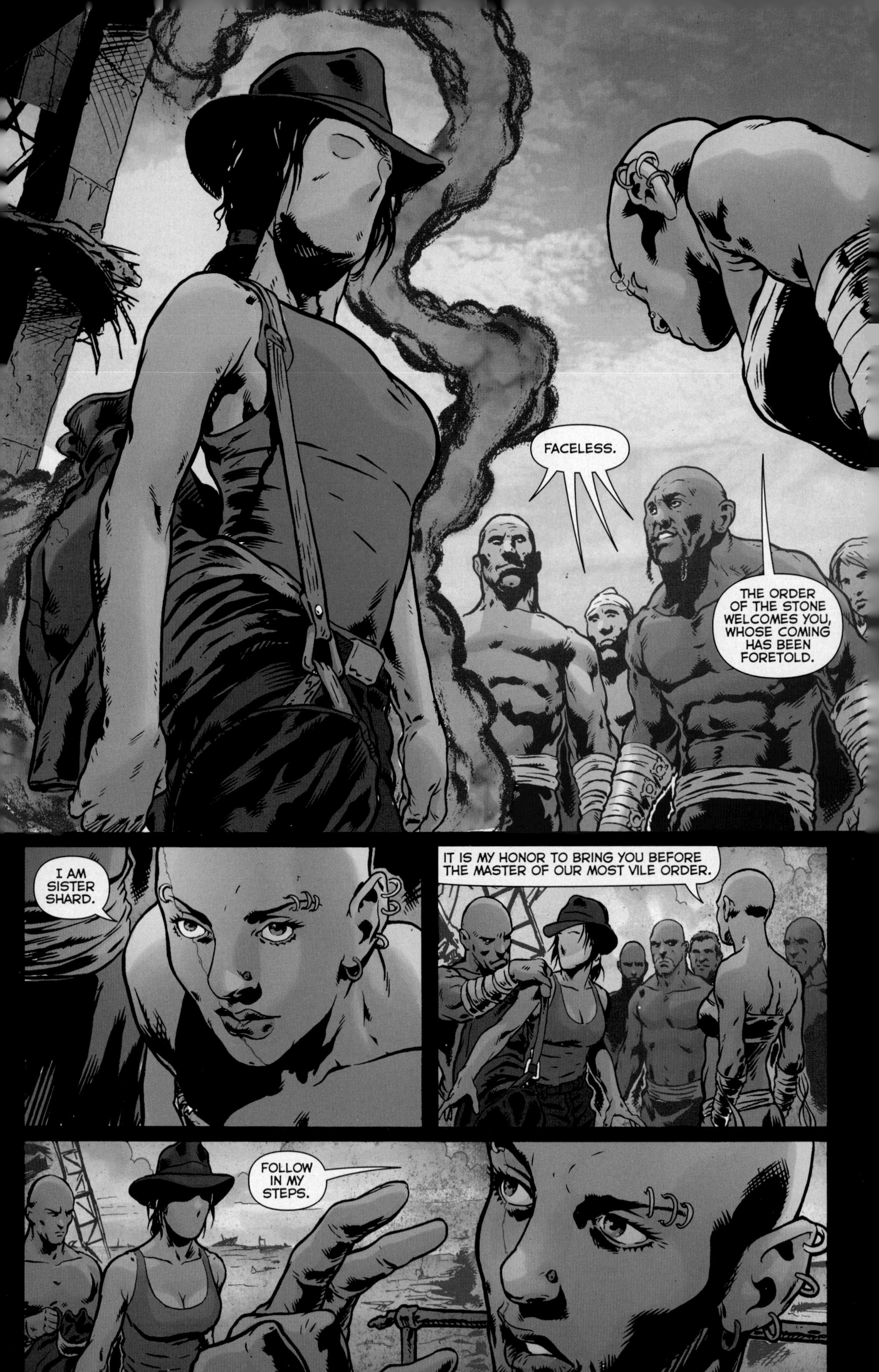
FACELESS.
THE ORDER OF THE STONE WELCOMES YOU, WHOSE COMING HAS BEEN FORETOLD.
I AM SISTER SHARD.
IT IS MY HONOR TO BRING YOU BEFORE THE MASTER OF OUR MOST VILE ORDER.
FOLLOW IN MY STEPS.

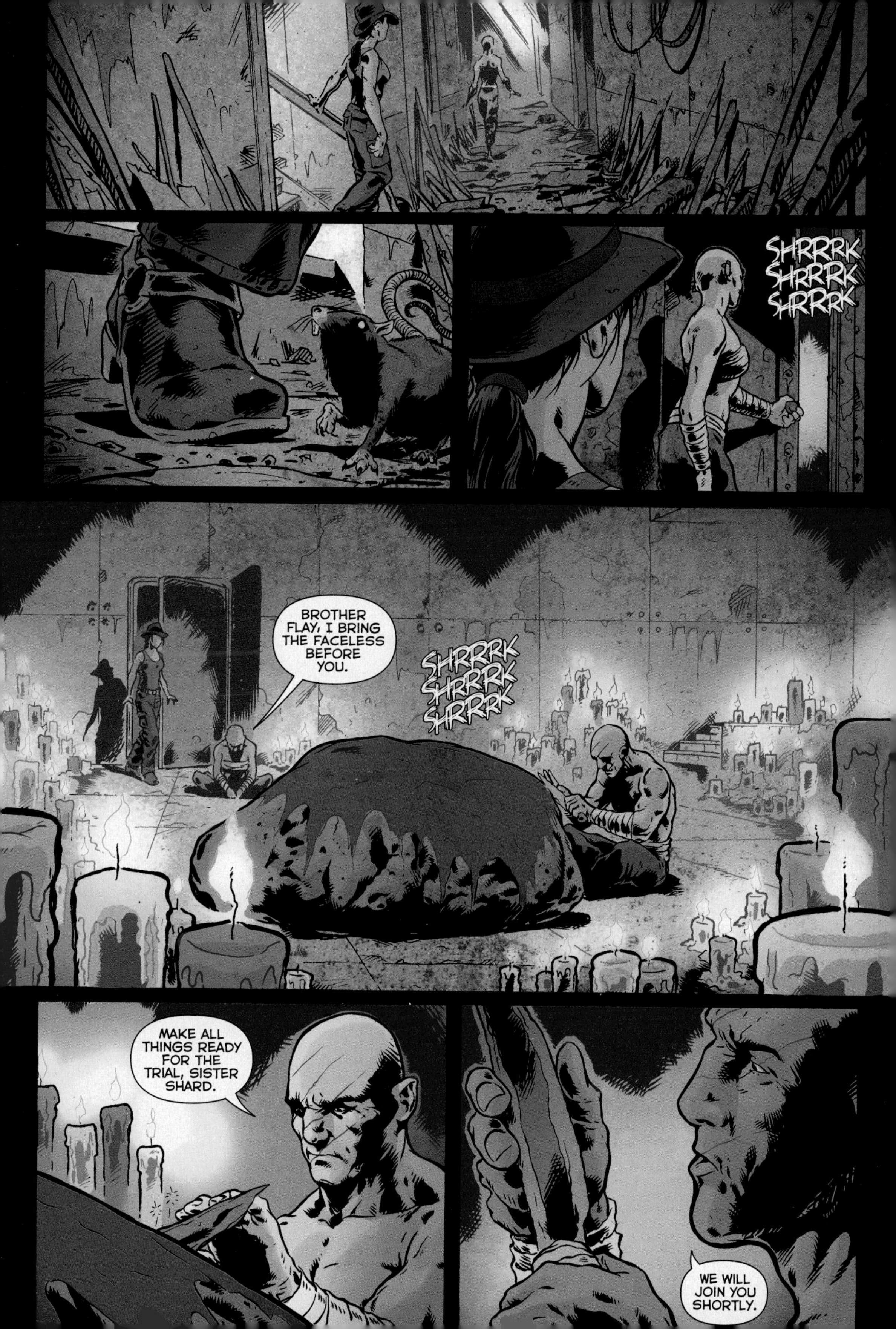
SHRRRK
SHRRRK
SHRRRK
BROTHER FLAY, I BRING THE FACELESS BEFORE YOU.
SHRRRK
SHRRRK
SHRRRK
MAKE ALL THINGS READY FOR THE TRIAL, SISTER SHARD.
WE WILL JOIN YOU SHORTLY.

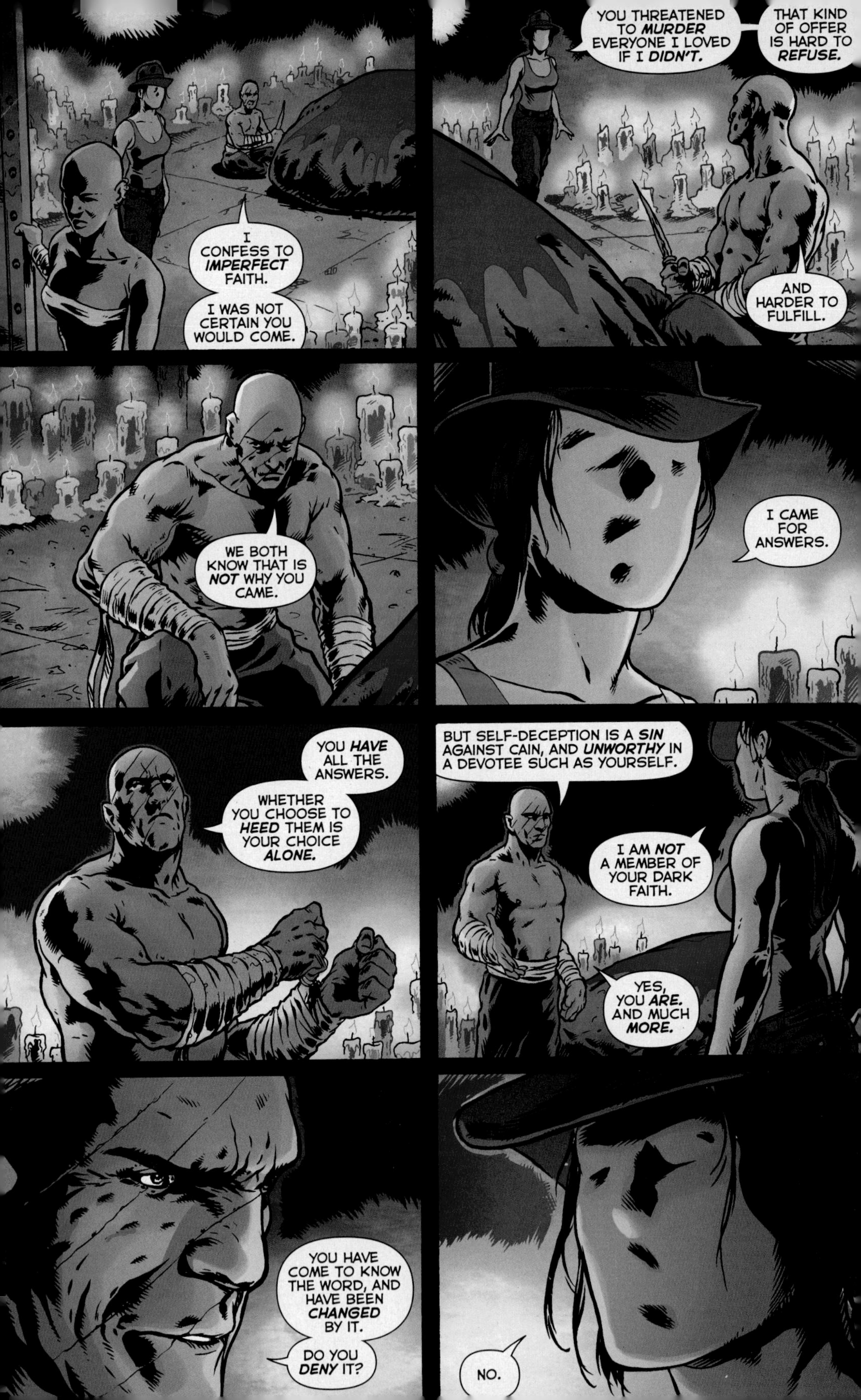

I CONFESS TO IMPERFECT FAITH.
I WAS NOT CERTAIN YOU WOULD COME.
YOU THREATENED TO MURDER EVERYONE I LOVED IF I DIDN'T.
THAT KIND OF OFFER IS HARD TO REFUSE.
AND HARDER TO FULFILL.
WE BOTH KNOW THAT IS NOT WHY YOU CAME.
I CAME FOR ANSWERS.
YOU HAVE ALL THE ANSWERS.
WHETHER YOU CHOOSE TO HEED THEM IS YOUR CHOICE ALONE.
BUT SELF-DECEPTION IS A SIN AGAINST CAIN, AND UNWORTHY IN A DEVOTEE SUCH AS YOURSELF.
I AM NOT A MEMBER OF YOUR DARK FAITH.
YES, YOU ARE. AND MUCH MORE.
YOU HAVE COME TO KNOW THE WORD, AND HAVE BEEN CHANGED BY IT.
DO YOU DENY IT?
NO.

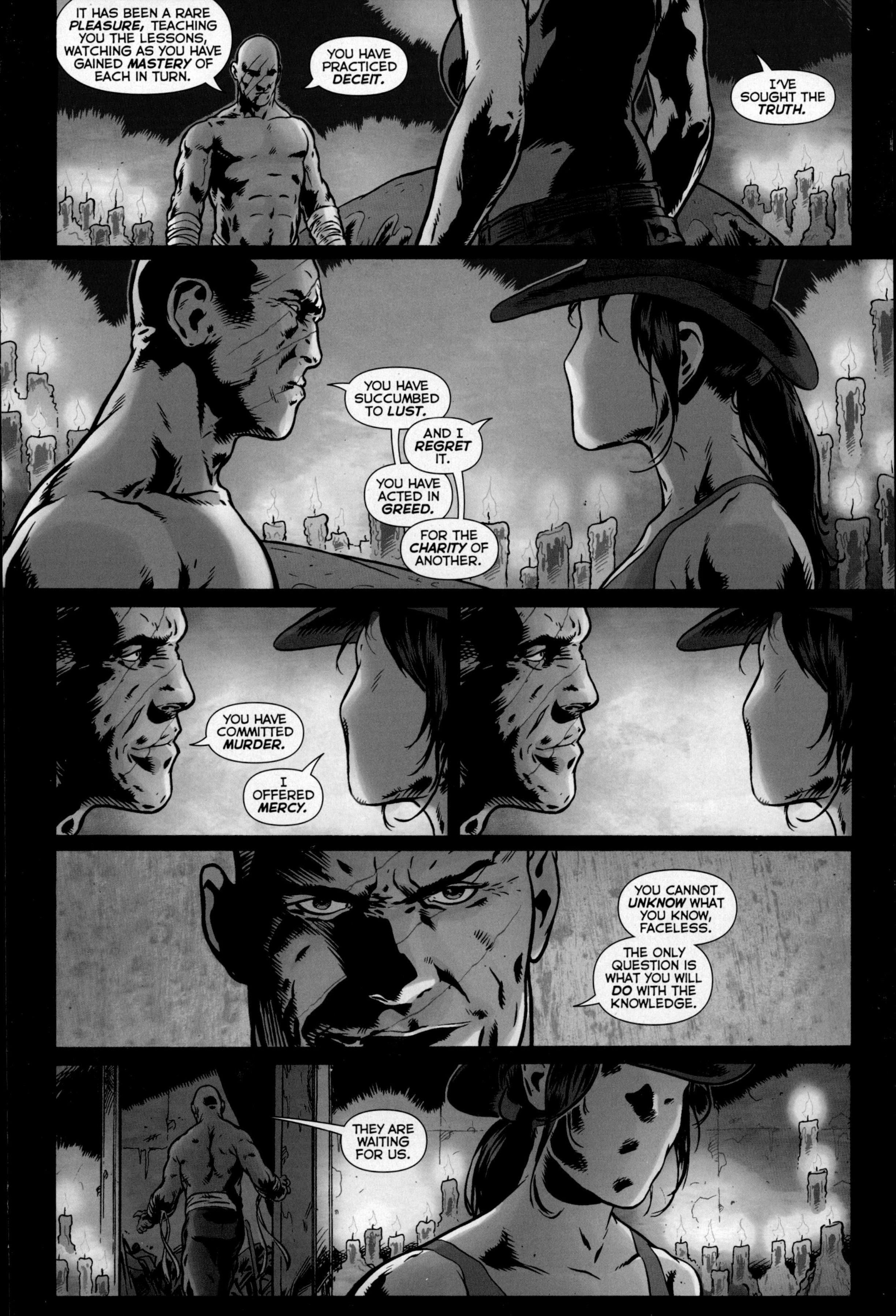

IT HAS BEEN A RARE PLEASURE, TEACHING YOU THE LESSONS, WATCHING AS YOU HAVE GAINED MASTERY OF EACH IN TURN.
YOU HAVE PRACTICED DECEIT.
I'VE SOUGHT THE TRUTH.
YOU HAVE SUCCUMBED TO LUST.
AND I REGRET IT.
YOU HAVE ACTED IN GREED.
FOR THE CHARITY OF ANOTHER.
YOU HAVE COMMITTED MURDER.
I OFFERED MERCY.
YOU CANNOT UNKNOW WHAT YOU KNOW, FACELESS.
THE ONLY QUESTION IS WHAT YOU WILL DO WITH THE KNOWLEDGE.
THEY ARE WAITING FOR US.

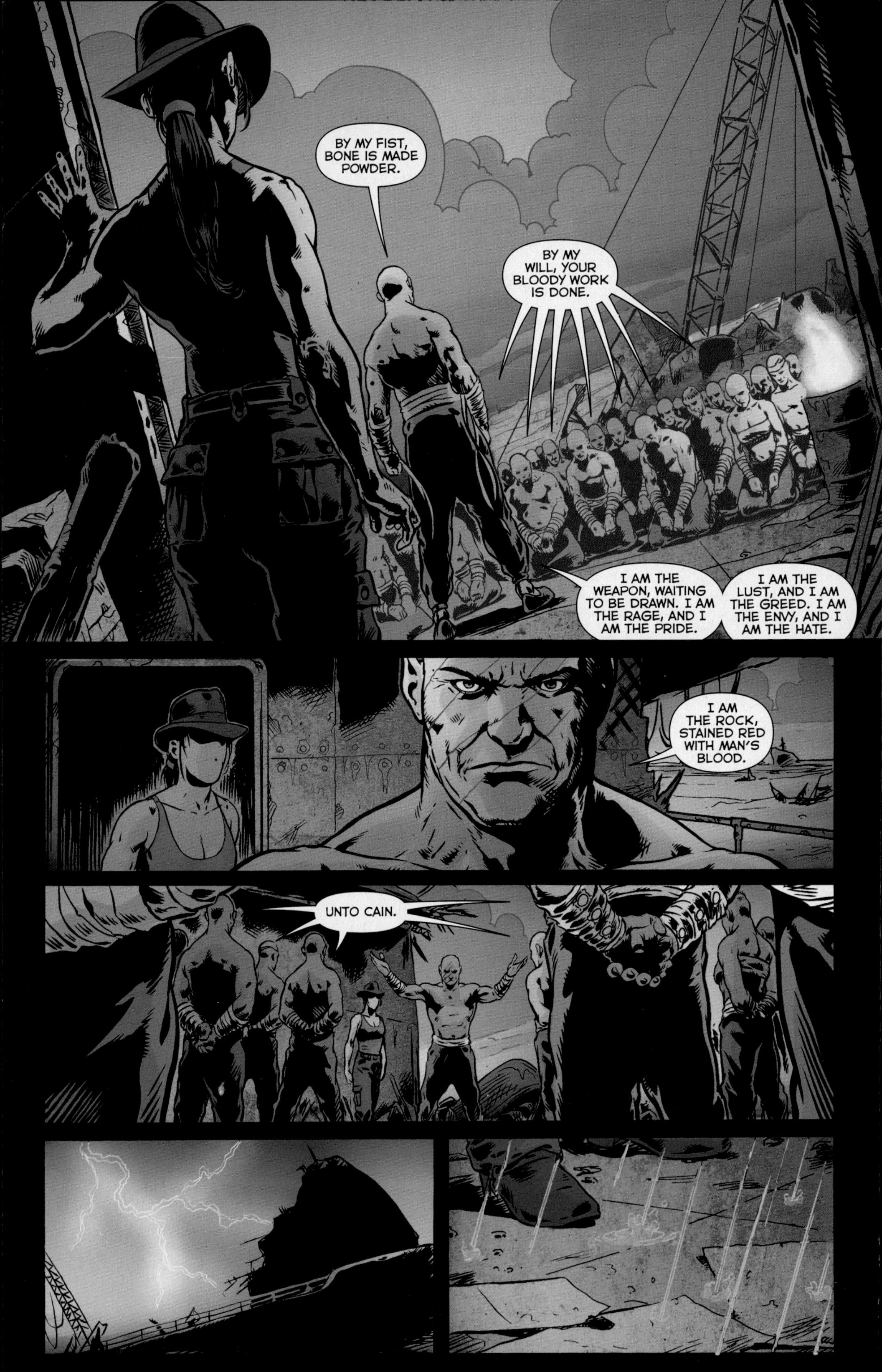
BY MY FIST, BONE IS MADE POWDER.
BY MY WILL, YOUR BLOODY WORK IS DONE.
I AM THE WEAPON, WAITING TO BE DRAWN. I AM THE RAGE, AND I AM THE PRIDE.
I AM THE LUST, AND I AM THE GREED. I AM THE ENVY, AND I AM THE HATE.
I AM THE ROCK, STAINED RED WITH MAN'S BLOOD.
UNTO CAIN.

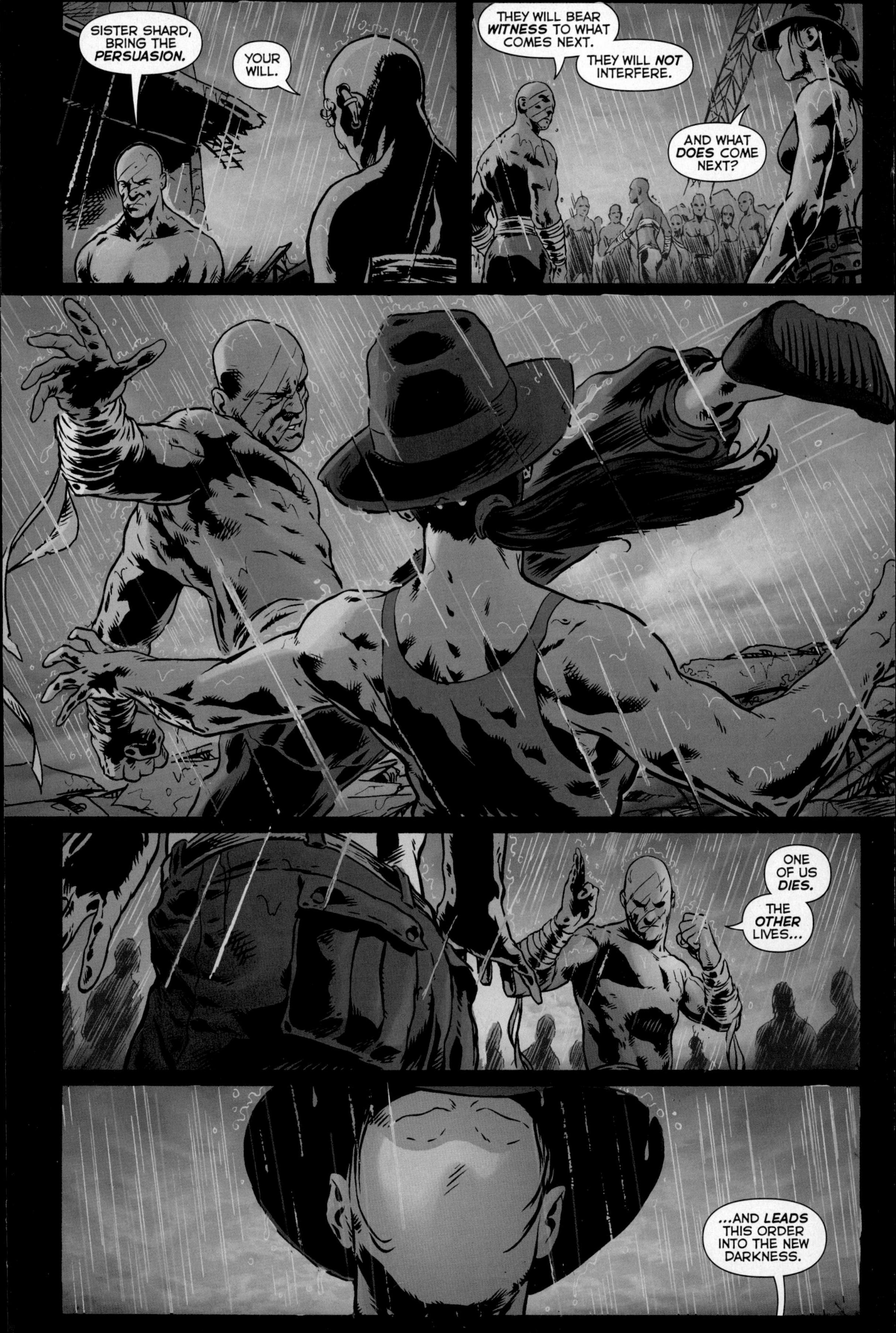
SISTER SHARD, BRING THE PERSUASION.
YOUR WILL.
THEY WILL BEAR WITNESS TO WHAT COMES NEXT.
THEY WILL NOT INTERFERE.
AND WHAT DOES COME NEXT?
ONE OF US DIES.
THE OTHER LIVES...
...AND LEADS THIS ORDER INTO THE NEW DARKNESS.

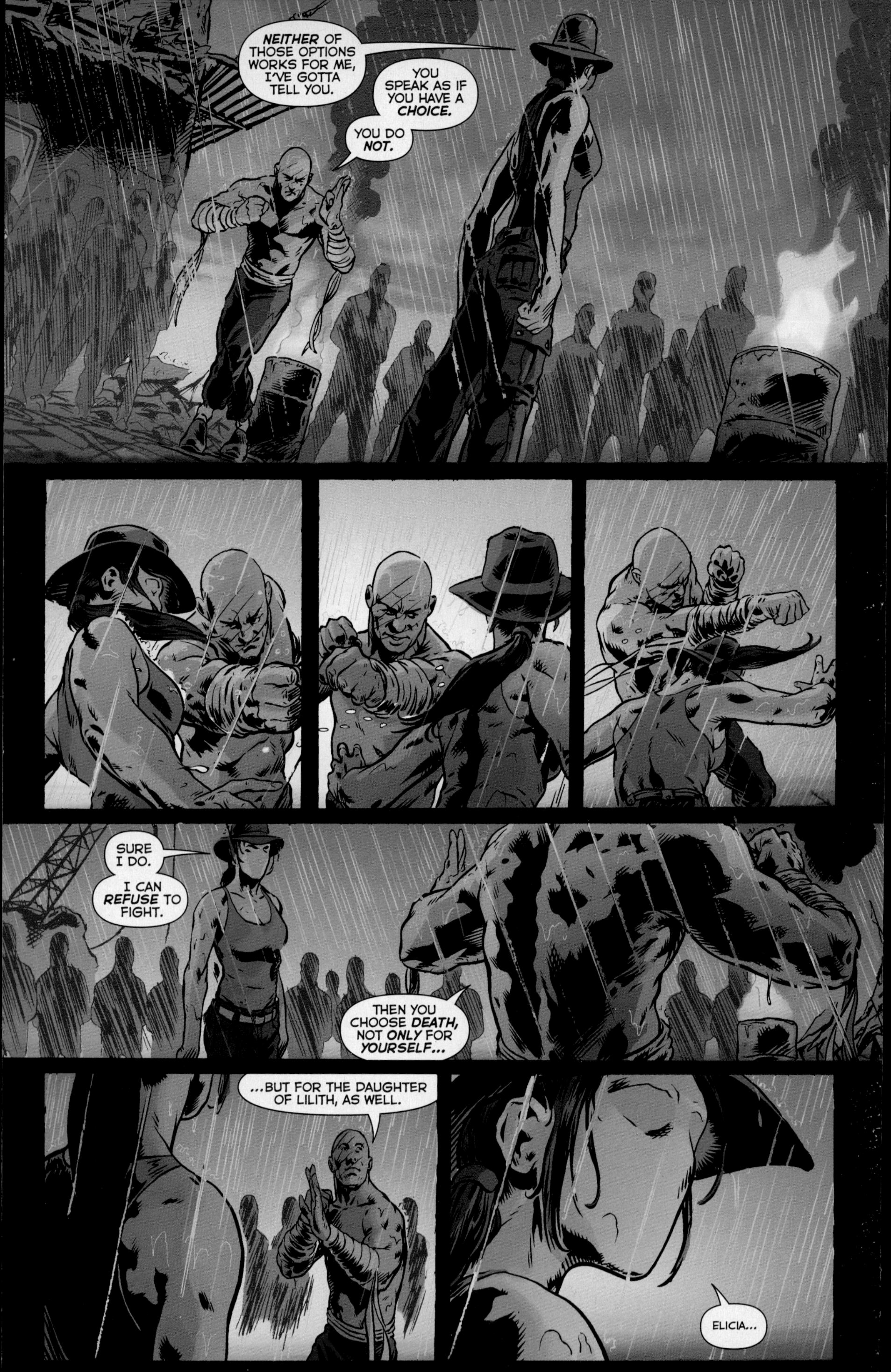
NEITHER OF THOSE OPTIONS WORKS FOR ME, I'VE GOTTA TELL YOU.
YOU SPEAK AS IF YOU HAVE A CHOICE.
YOU DO NOT.
SURE I DO.
I CAN REFUSE TO FIGHT.
THEN YOU CHOOSE DEATH, NOT ONLY FOR YOURSELF...
...BUT FOR THE DAUGHTER OF LILITH, AS WELL.
ELICIA...

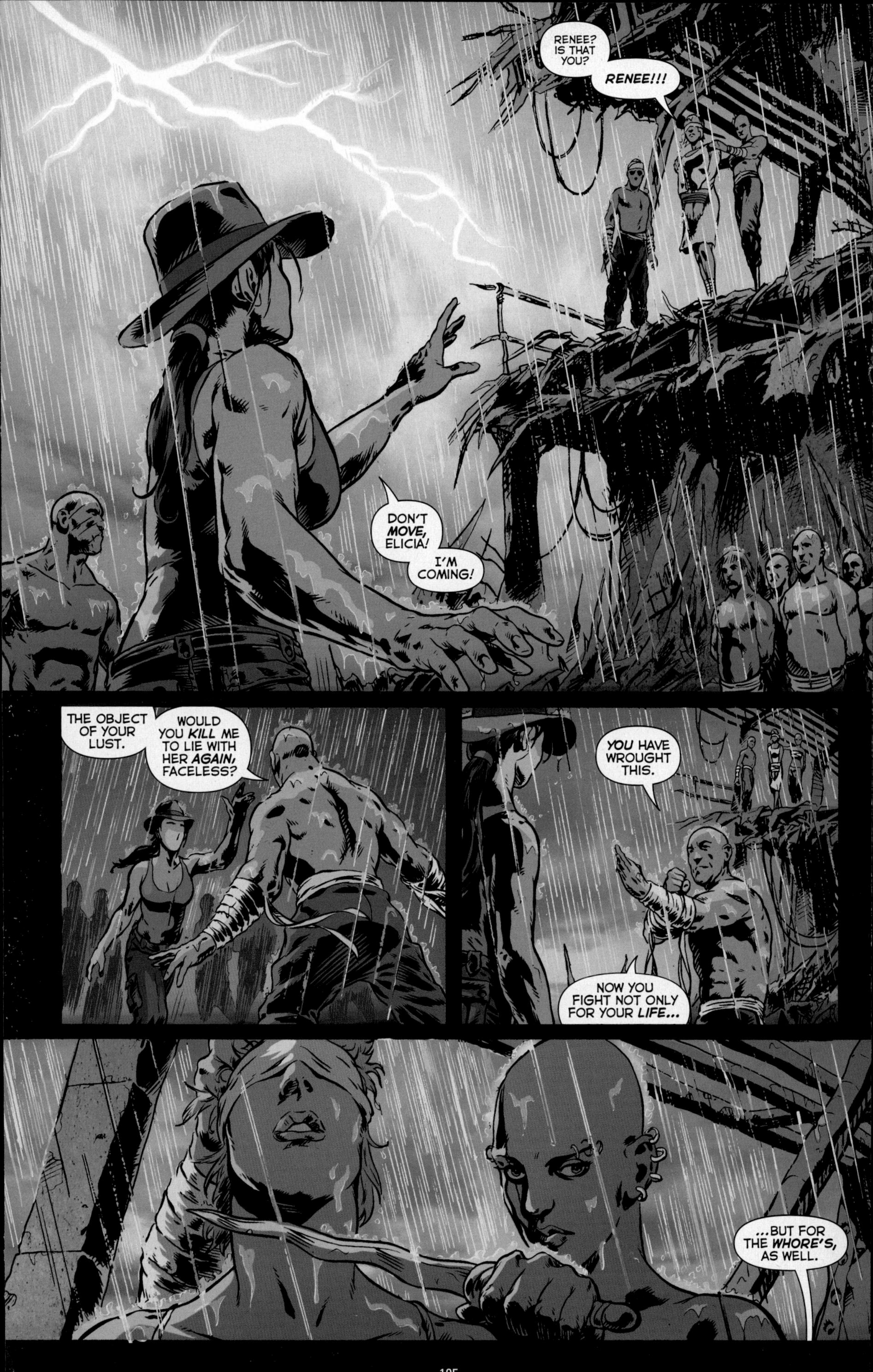
RENEE? IS THAT YOU?
RENEE!!!
DON'T MOVE, ELICIA!
I'M COMING!
THE OBJECT OF YOUR LUST.
WOULD YOU KILL ME TO LIE WITH HER AGAIN, FACELESS?
YOU HAVE WROUGHT THIS.
NOW YOU FIGHT NOT ONLY FOR YOUR LIFE...
...BUT FOR THE WHORE'S, AS WELL.

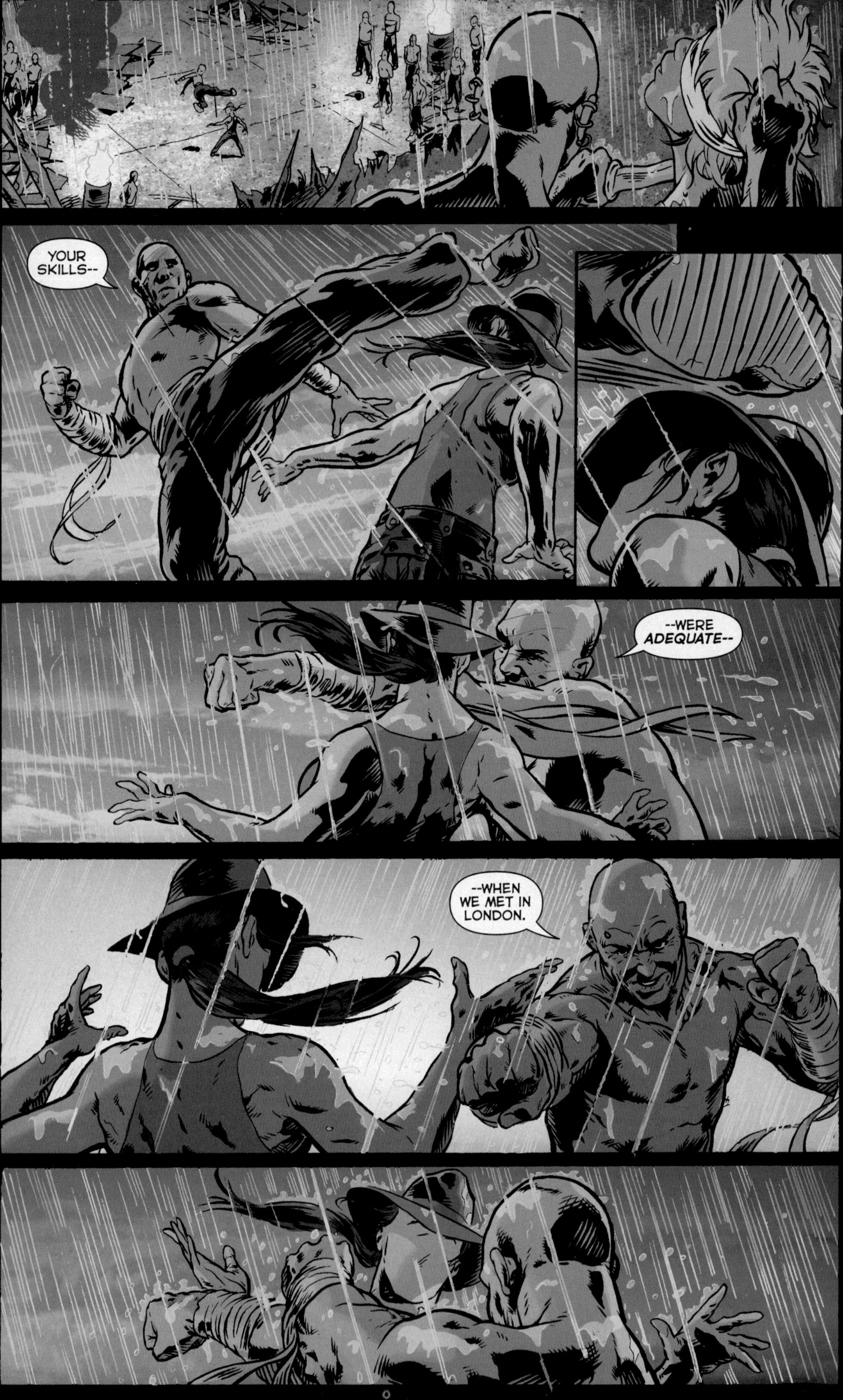
YOUR SKILLS--
--WERE ADEQUATE--
--WHEN WE MET IN LONDON.

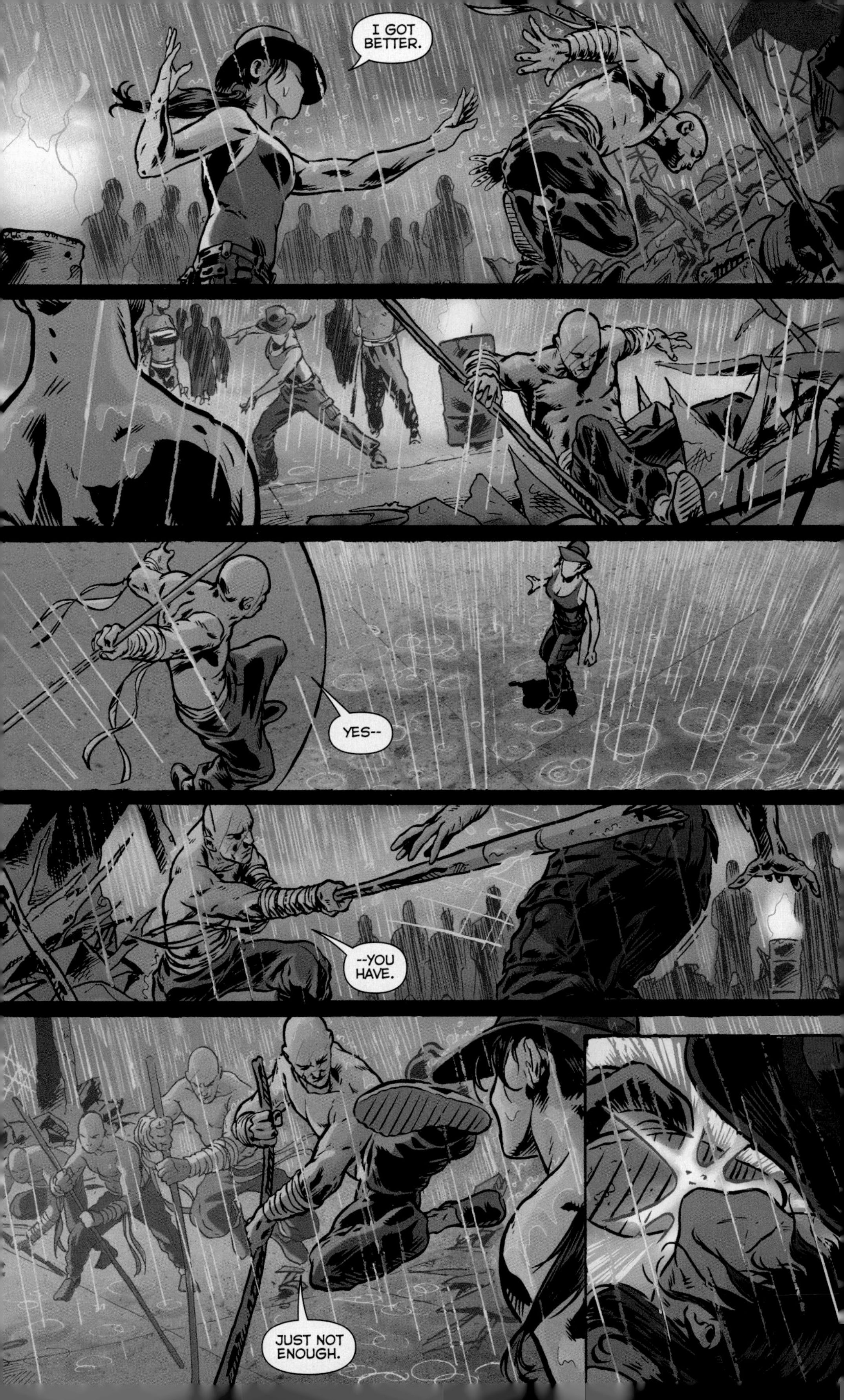
I GOT BETTER.
YES--
--YOU HAVE.
JUST NOT ENOUGH.

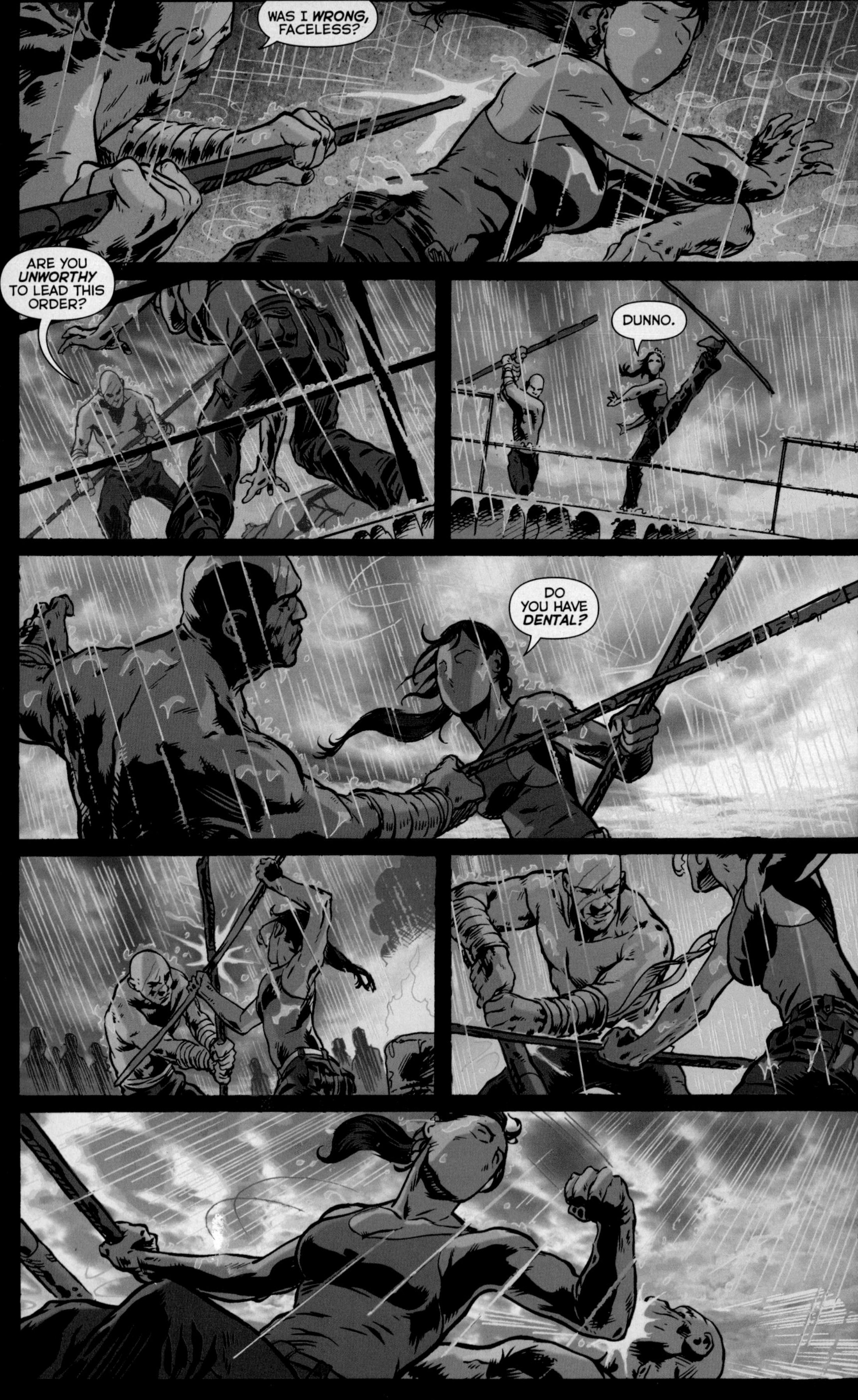
WAS I WRONG, FACELESS?
ARE YOU UNWORTHY TO LEAD THIS ORDER?
DUNNO.
DO YOU HAVE DENTAL?

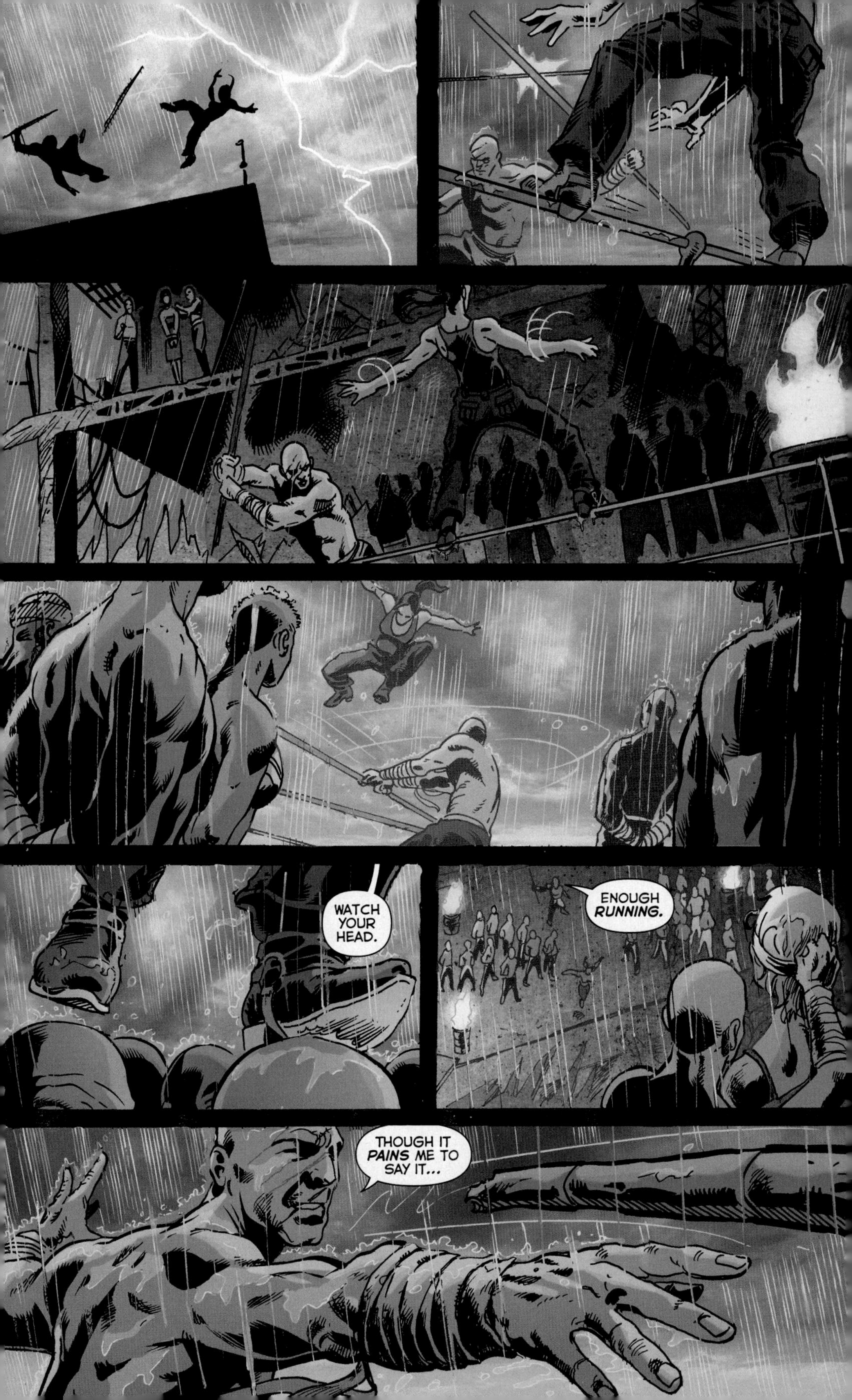
WATCH YOUR HEAD.
ENOUGH RUNNING.
THOUGH IT PAINS ME TO SAY IT...

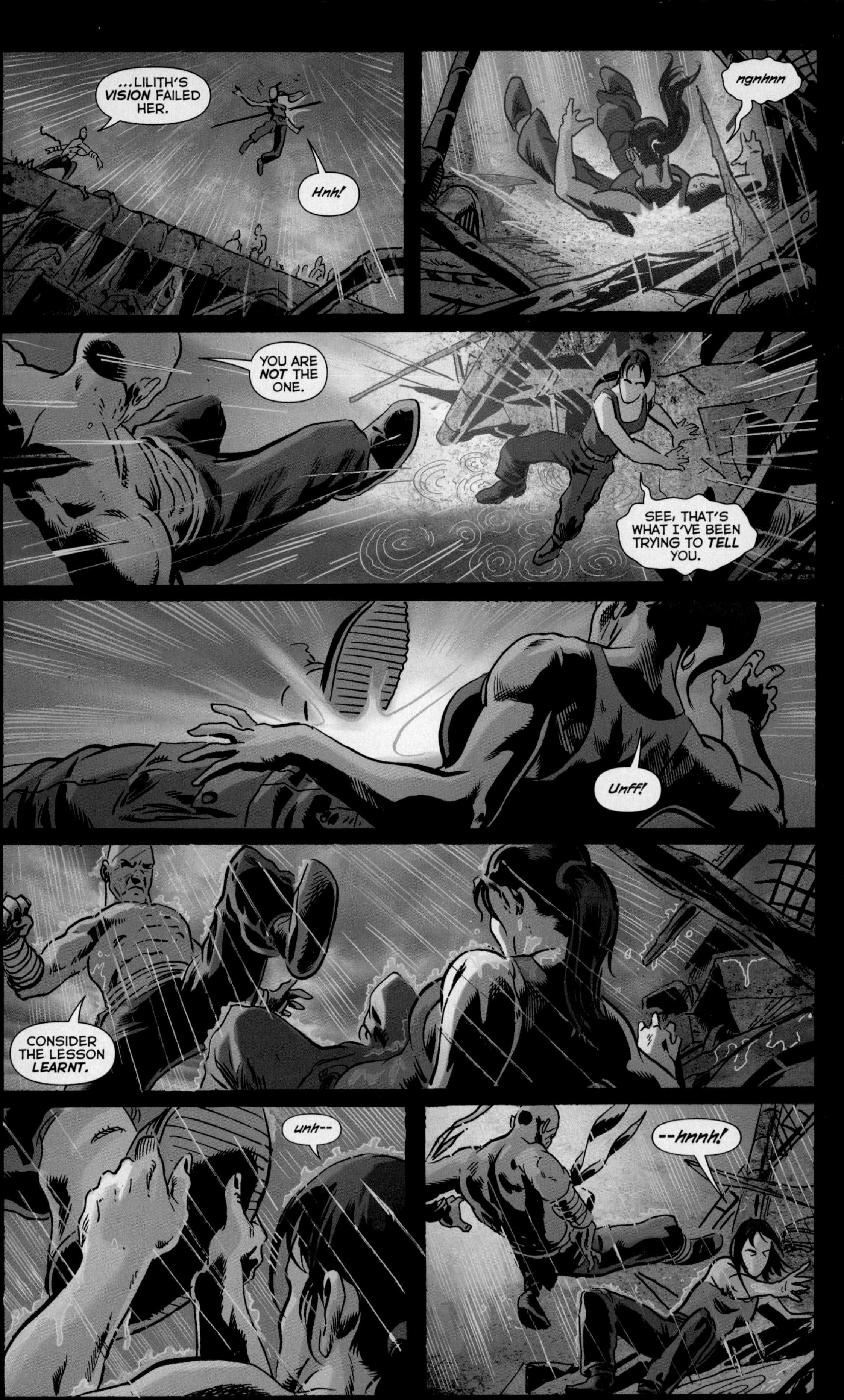
...LILITH'S VISION FAILED HER.
Hnh!
ngnhnn
YOU ARE NOT THE ONE.
SEE, THAT'S WHAT I'VE BEEN TRYING TO TELL YOU.
Unff!
CONSIDER THE LESSON LEARNT.
unh--
--hnnh!

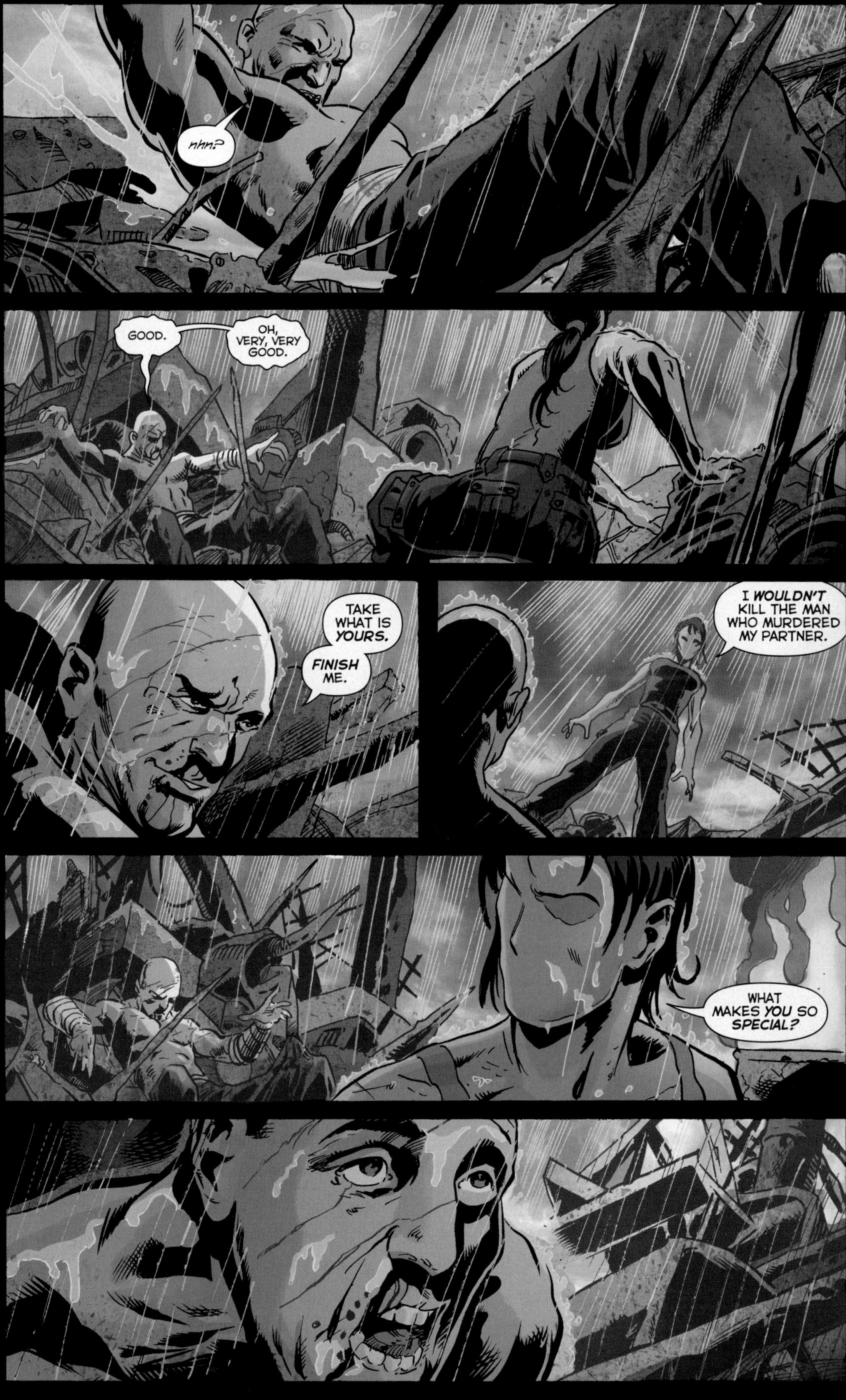
nhn?
GOOD.
OH, VERY, VERY GOOD.
TAKE WHAT IS YOURS.
FINISH ME.
I WOULDN'T KILL THE MAN WHO MURDERED MY PARTNER.
WHAT MAKES YOU SO SPECIAL?

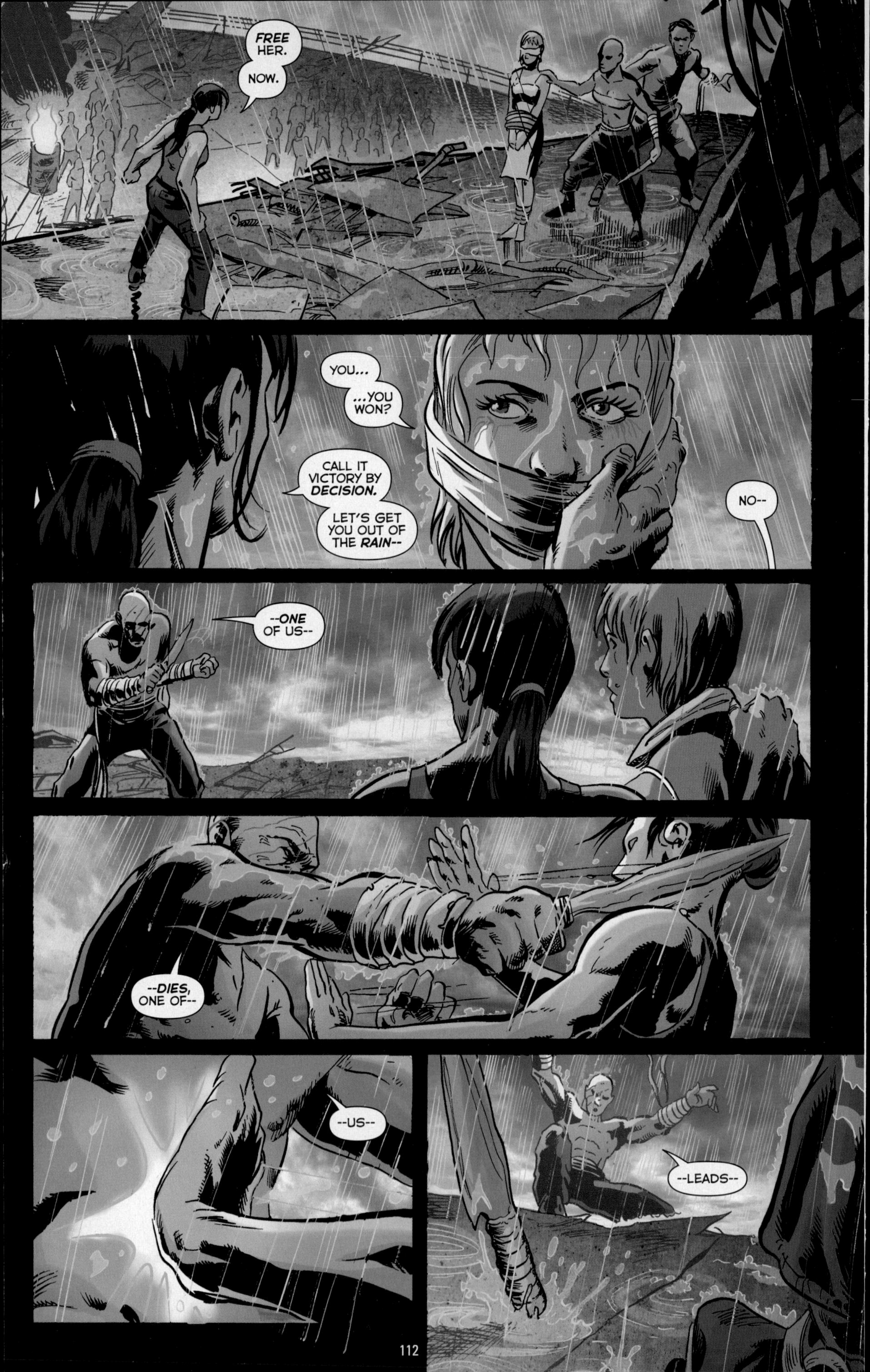
FREE HER.
NOW.
YOU...
...YOU WON?
CALL IT VICTORY BY DECISION.
LET'S GET YOU OUT OF THE RAIN--
NO--
--ONE OF US--
--DIES, ONE OF--
--US--
--LEADS--

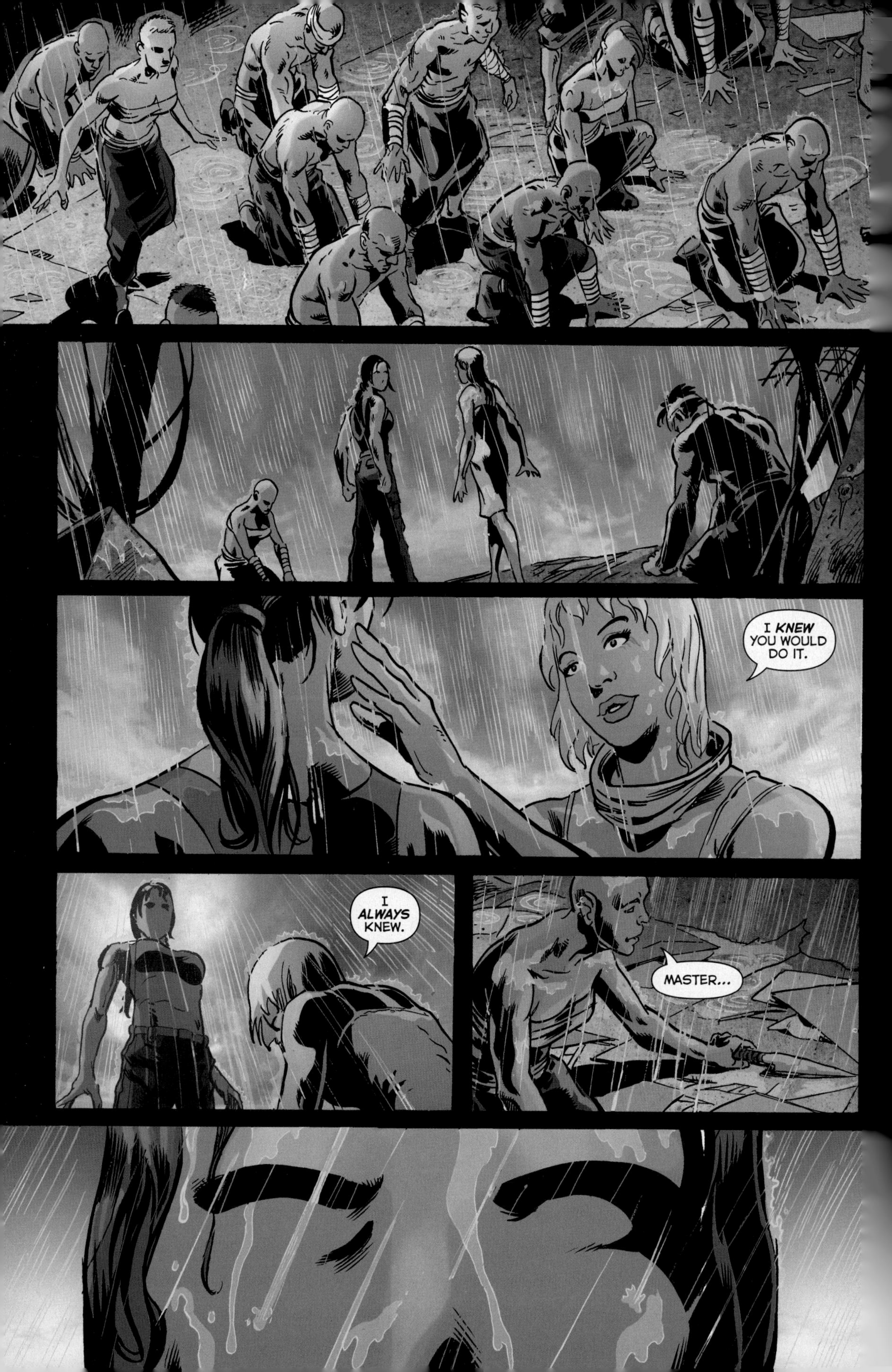
I KNEW YOU WOULD DO IT.
I ALWAYS KNEW.
MASTER...

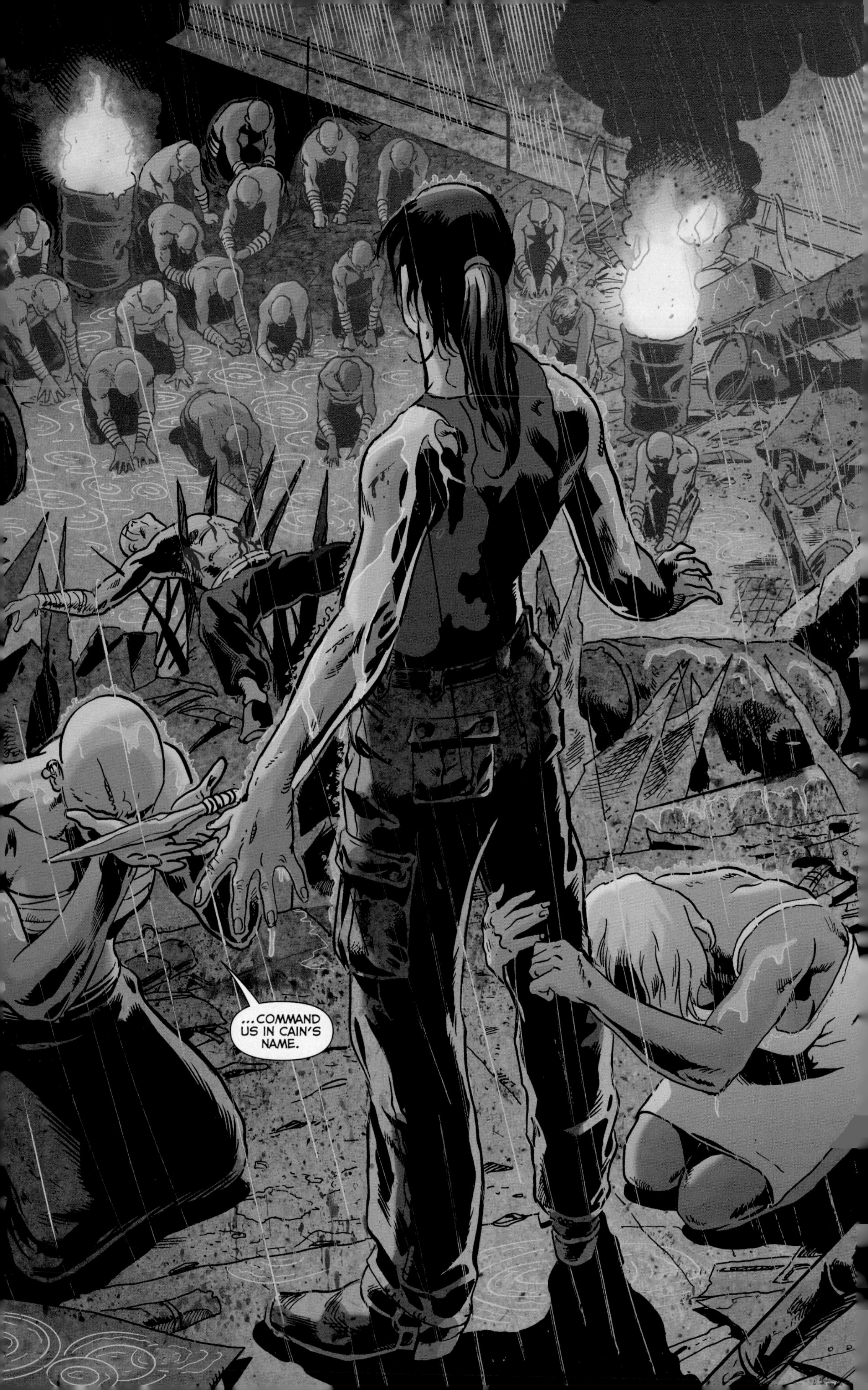
...COMMAND US IN CAIN'S NAME.

Cover Gallery
Art By John Van Fleet

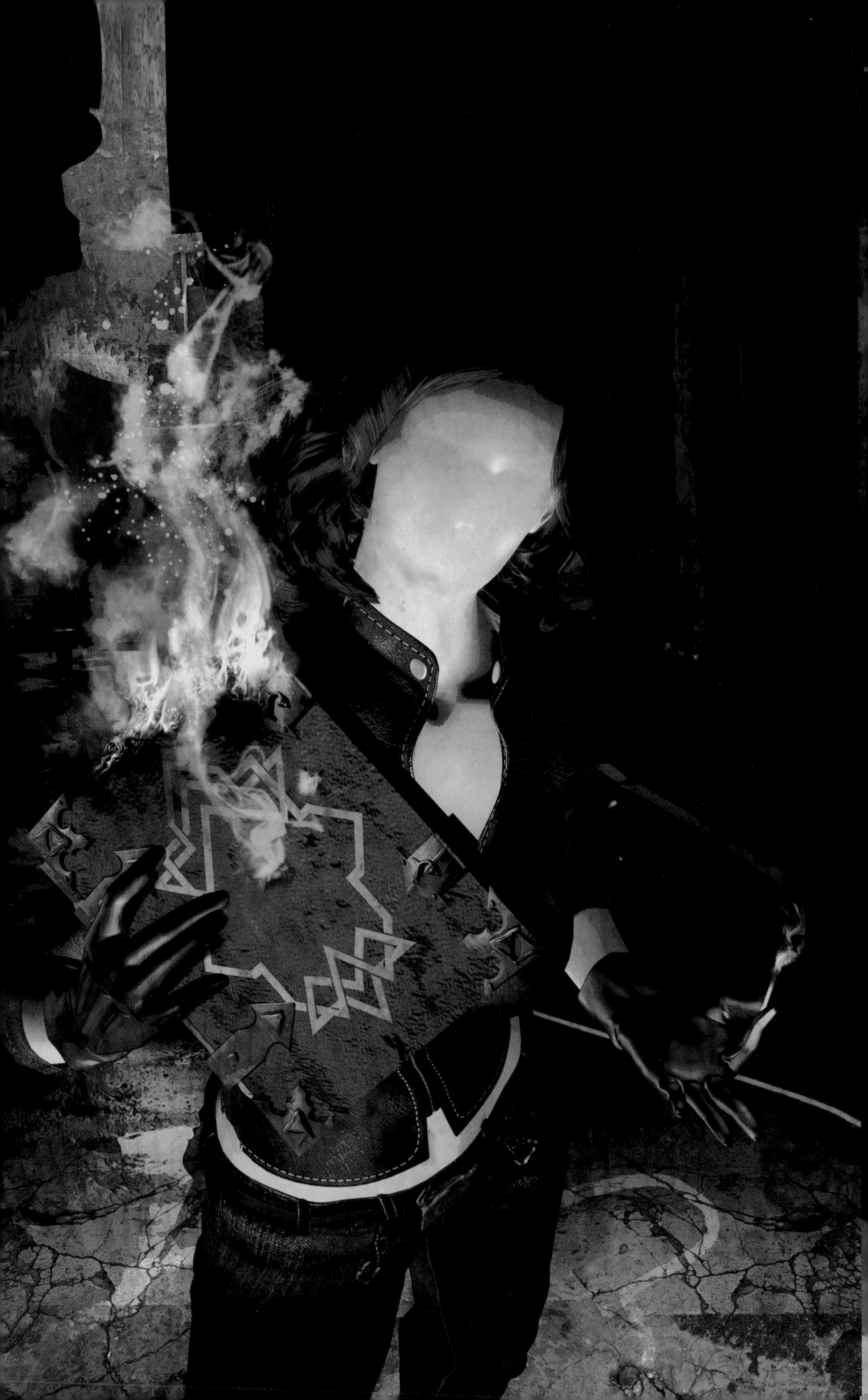

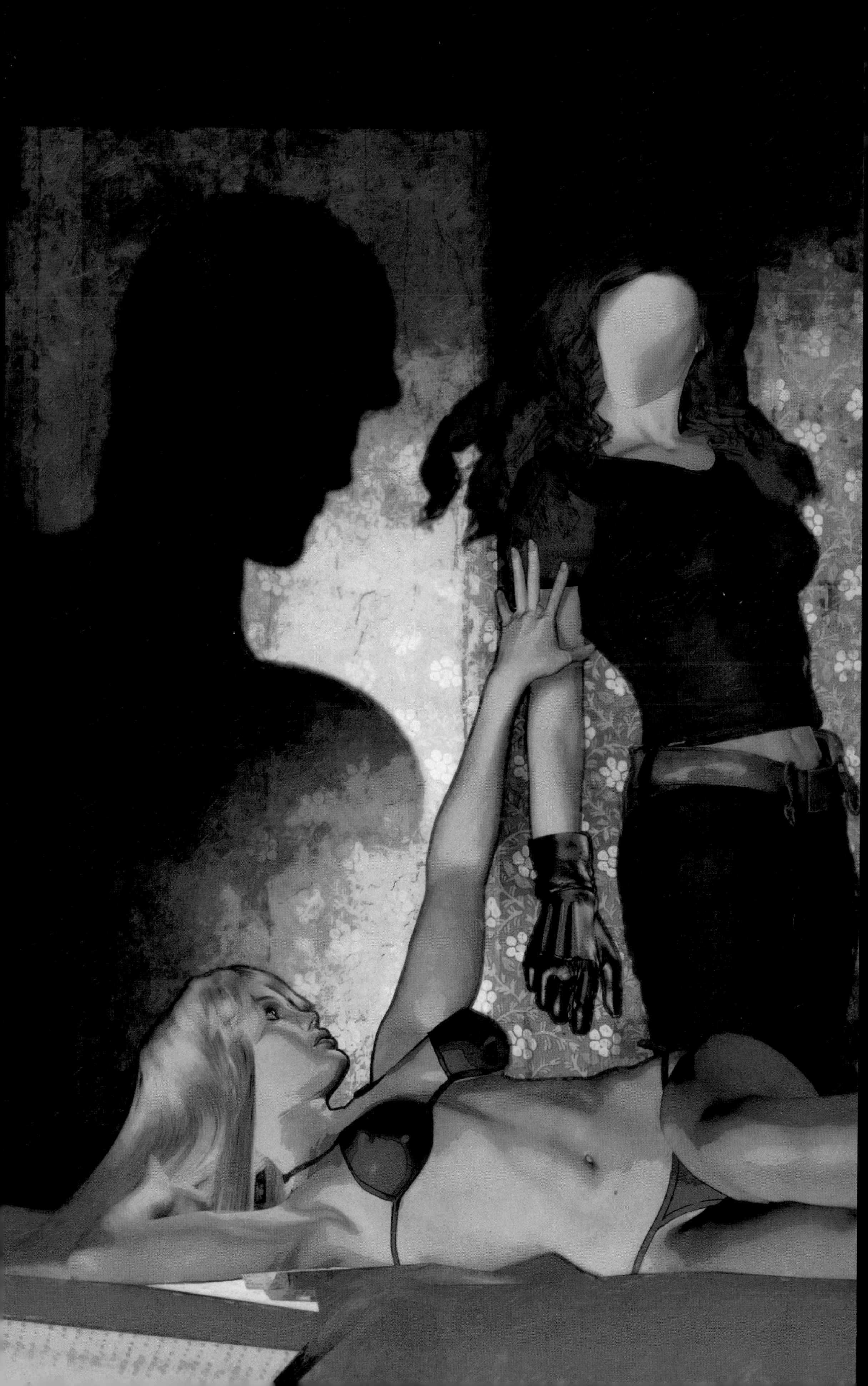

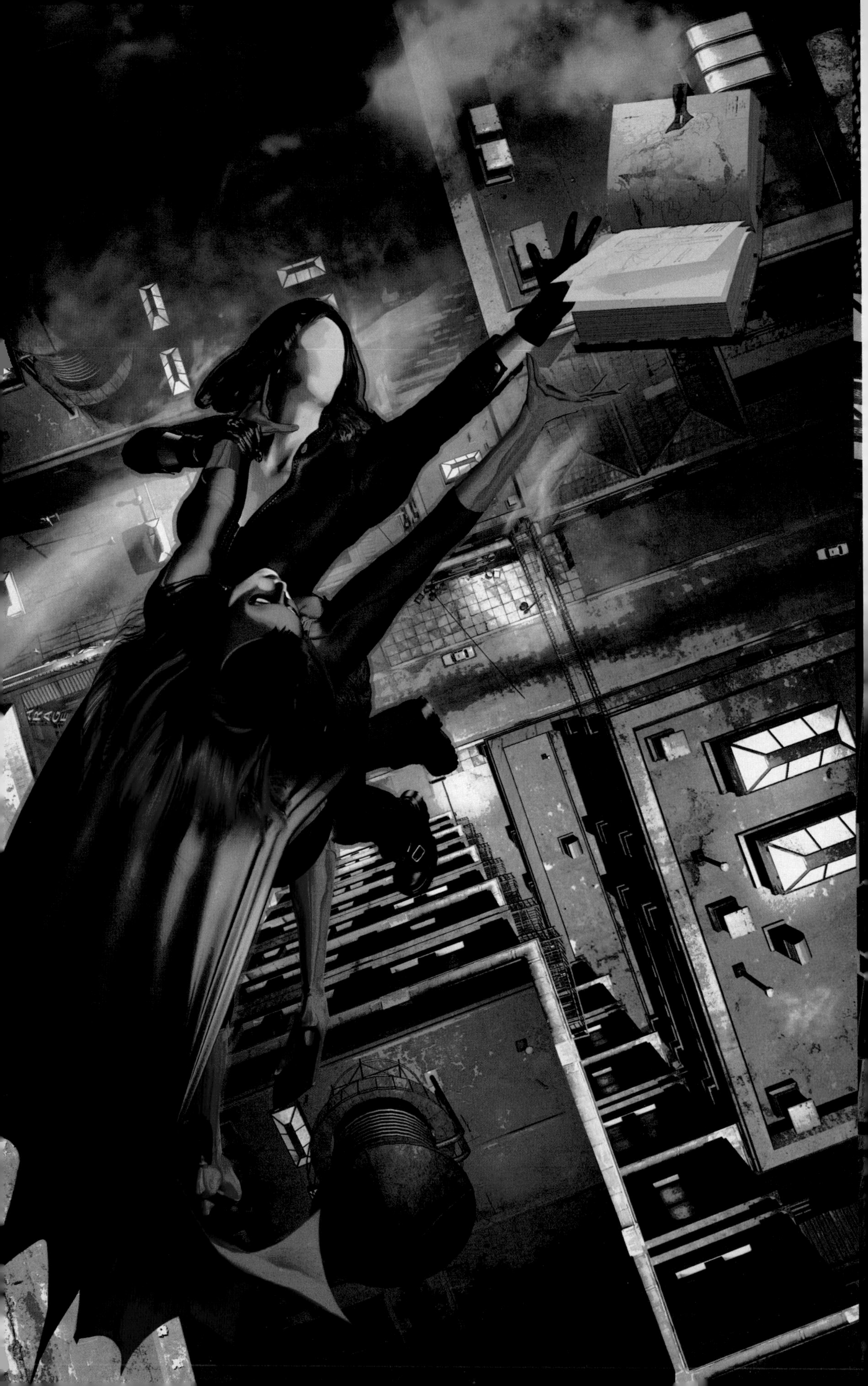

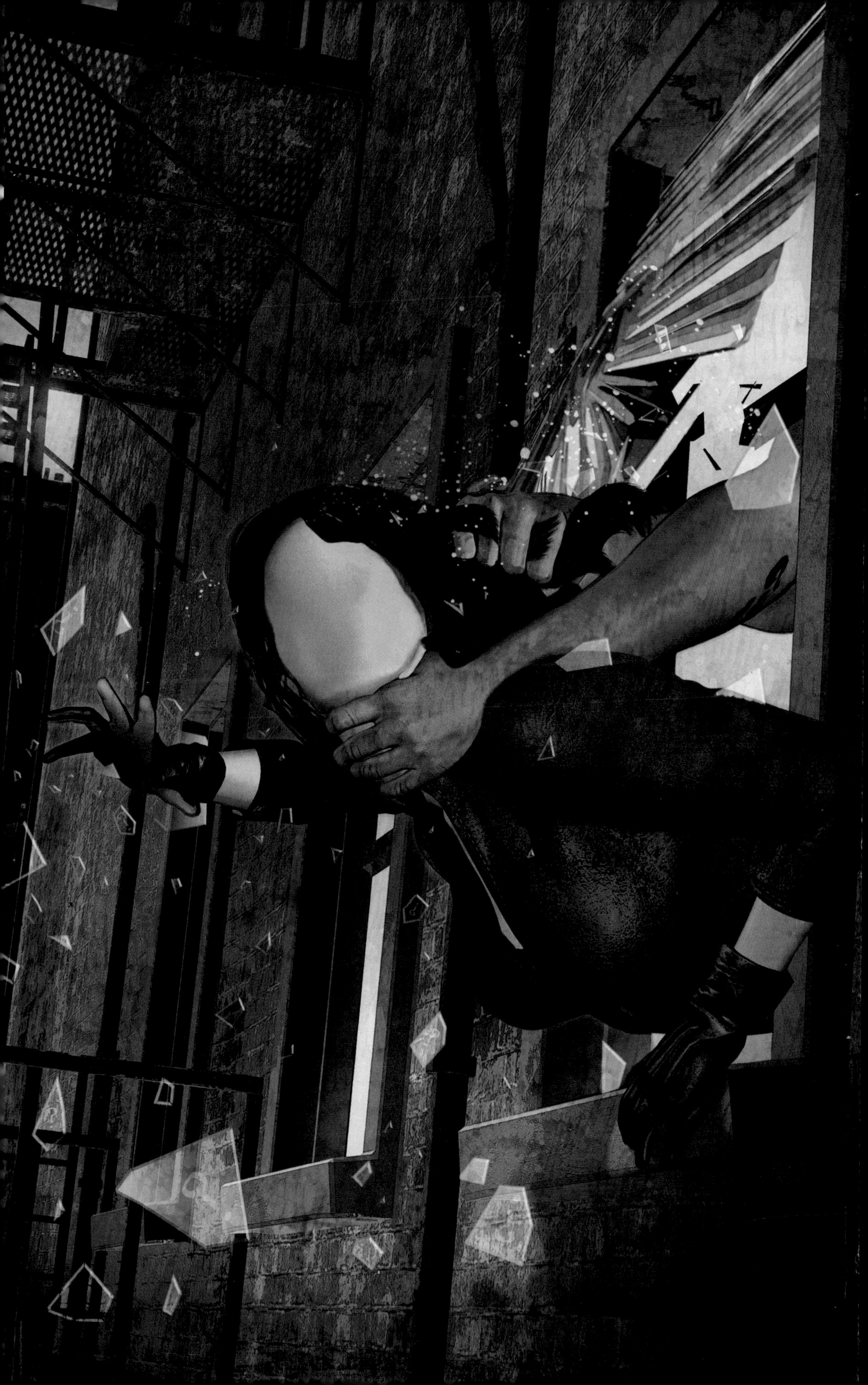

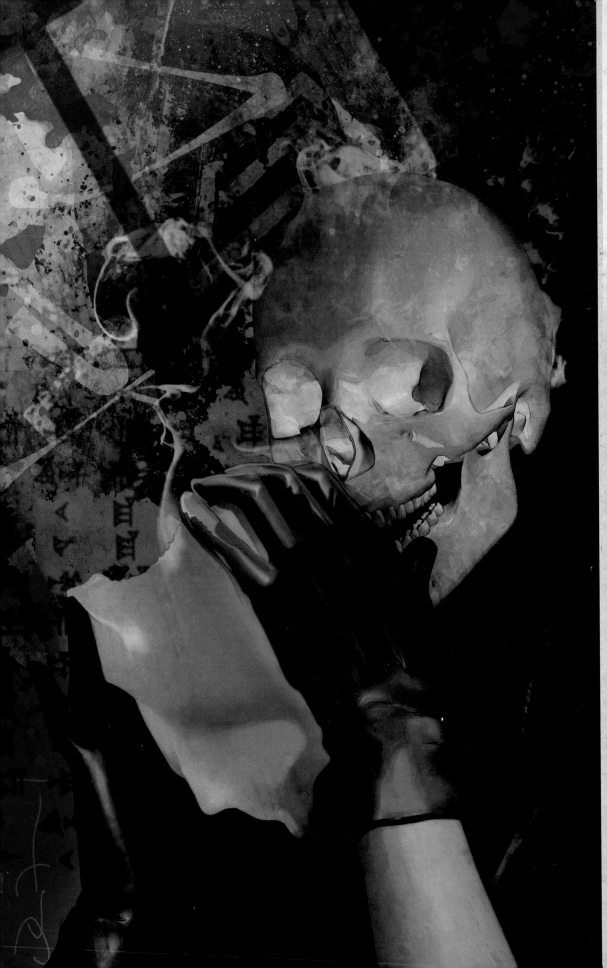

The Montoya Journal
An Explanation

Some ideas spring forth fully formed, or nearly so, and THE FIVE BOOKS OF BLOOD was one of those for me. From the moment editor Michael Siglain approached me about the project, I had a very clear vision of how I wanted the series to work, and the levels I wanted it to play on. Much of these ideas came from a long-running appreciation of the works of H.P. Lovecraft, and the idea that, in delving into the corrupting abyss of the unknown, the investigator is irreparably altered by the experience.

I had known that, coming out of the events of 52, Renee Montoya would take it upon herself to learn all she could of the Dark Faith — the religion of crime — in order to better combat it, a quest initially born out of concern for her estranged lover, Kate Kane. And I knew, as well, that the investigation would have a terrible price for Renee, and that the more she attempted to answer the Dark Faith's questions, the further into its web she would be drawn.

What follows here are excerpts from "The Montoya Journal" that was distributed to select retailers, reviewers, and comics professionals to coincide with the release of THE FIVE BOOKS OF BLOOD. Only sixteen of these journals were ever made, and of them, only thirteen were ever distributed (triskaidekaphobics can read into that however they like). The actual construction, design, and assembly took roughly as much time and effort as the writing of the series did, and is a prime example of an idea growing out of control.

Remember how I said that some ideas come fully formed? One of the first thoughts I had about THE FIVE BOOKS OF BLOOD was that each issue would begin with a piece of "scripture" pertaining to the "lesson" in question, and that in each piece would be embedded the elements of a rudimentary word-substitution code that would, in turn, reveal a "sixth scripture" that prophesized the Question's ultimate fate in the series. That's why there are those strange strings of numbers running around the borders of each piece — the numbers correspond to the book, chapter, verse, and word number of the hidden "sixth scripture."

Great idea. Murder to execute. And another example in my career of being far too subtle for my own damn good.

In consulting with the amazingly talented Eric Trautmann we hit upon the idea of the journals as a way to tip to fans that there was more to the scripture pieces than met the eye. It was Eric, in fact, who designed the code, and it was Eric, as well, who was the driving force behind the actual creation of the journal elements. While I wrote the actual text for the journal entries, it was Eric who created most of the "props."

One last note. While the journals were a hell of a lot of fun to make, they were also a hell of a lot of hard work, and the people who assisted in their construction and creation deserve, in my opinion, special mention. In particular, the afore-praised Eric Trautmann, as well as my wife, Jennifer Van Meter, who actually *sewed* the journals together. My son, Elliot, assisted in the collating; Steve Lieber, who took on art chores at a very late date and delivered more than I could've hoped for; and Eric Newsom, the brilliant webmaster of the pre-eminent Question website, not only posed for photos (unfortunately never used), but also created the only known recording of a Darkseid's Bitch song, "Ashes," which can be heard on the web.

So here you go: what was, until now, seen only by a select handful of fortunate (or unfortunate) folks — *The Montoya Journal*, in all its glory.

And if you, too, are drawn into the abyss by it, well...don't say I didn't warn you.

Greg Rucka
Portland, Oregon
April, 2008

High Madame's binding (unlikely)

Prophet's Codex

Sana'a Edition

bastard's Folio (unlikely)

Miser's Edition
(Check british Museum)

Fitzgerald's "modern"
Interpretation
(Tot says talk to
O'Neill at Metropolis U)

Koller Commentary (unconfirmed)

The first page of the journal, a list of "known" editions of the Black Book, or Crime Bible. In following the Lovecraft tradition, I wanted to establish that there were multiple editions of the Black Book, each with its own secrets. Note the reference to Tot about "Fitzgerald's Modern."

BOOK ONE CHAPTER VIII, VERSES XVI THROUGH XXVI

RUMINATIONS ON LIES AND DECEIT, AS TRANSLATED BY PROFESSOR MALCOLM FITZGERALD, UNIVERSITY OF METROPOLIS.

16 Then, the Caitiff raised the stone, high above his head, that those gathered could look upon it, and see the ichors that stained it.

17 'Behold,' he cried, 'The Crimson Rock, christened by my brother's blood! In my hand I hold Murder, and thus hold Murder over all who walk this Earth.'

18 And those foolish ones gathered, believing this, did as they were commanded by the Caitiff, falling to their knees, and in so doing, granted him great power.

19 Thus did the Caitiff descend into the Defile, walking amongst them, and the assembled hosts hid their eyes in darkness as he passed; and thus he took from them what service he pleased; and their cries and screams filled the depths of hell and shook the foundations of Heaven.

20 And soon, the First came to the defile, as part of his travels and wanderings, and was much amused by the villainy and blasphemy of the Caitiff.

21 And the First's laughter thundered through the gorge, and even the gathered host were fearful of His merriment, and their fear of the Caitiff fell away, replaced by terror of His presence; and they looked in awe and shame at Him.

22 And it was the Caitiff, believing his own deceptions, looked upon Him as well, but was blind to His presence; and besotted with arrogance and blinded with rage, the Caitiff demanded of the First, 'Wanderer, you mock the power that I hold, you make sport of Murder, and would draw its reckoning upon you.'

23 Then the First showed His palm to the Caitiff and all his followers; and upon His palm was the Stain, and he said, 'Through Deceit, you have liberated yourselves from the chains of illusory Truth. This is the First Lesson of Blood.'

24 'But you have also become prey to Deceit, and though there are many glories, there can be but one sin; you have believed so strongly in your deception that it as truth to you, and you are enslaved by it.'

25 And then the First withdrew the shard of Red Rock from His palm, and it shone with the blood of His brother; and laughing, he buried it in the Caitiff's eye.

26 And the Caitiff's followers were overcome with panic, and struggled to flee the Defile of Sem.

What is the code???

1:8:21:22 = "of"?
3:19:8:2 = ???

METROPOLIS UNIVERSITY SPECIAL COLLECTIONS

ARCHIVAL DOCUMENTS AND FOLKLORE, DEC. 1938

4:3:7:4 = ???
3:19:4:3 = ???

tear off above the blue line

Montoya's notes on the page — apparently torn from the copy of Fitzgerald — are the first mention of the code, and provide the key to its translation. The Fitzgerald, being a "modern" translation, doesn't work. These were printed on a heavy parchment stock, stained with a wash made from heavily over-steeped black tea, and then run through a clothes dryer in the company of 200 plastic poker chips — an old forger's trick, actually — to provide an authentic, "handled" feel.

This is the reverse of the previous piece. Trautmann searched up a variety of occult and arcane-looking images to further add to the ominous nature of the text. When printed, the page was folded and refolded, then inserted into the journal itself. The journals, it should be noted, were small Moleskines, chosen for their easy handling, and the fact that they were stitched together, and thus could be reassembled easily.

Signs, Characters, and Magical Knife.
A Type or Figure of the Circle for the Master and his Fellows to sit in shewing how, and after what fashion it should be made:
Whosoever beareth this Sign, all Spirits will do him homage.
Whosoever beareth this Sign need fear no Foe.
Agla
Tetragrammaton
Magister
Alpha
Omega
Emanuel
AGLA
This on the Other Side
A Great Character
The Greatest Character
The two Seals of the Earth without which no Spirits will appear

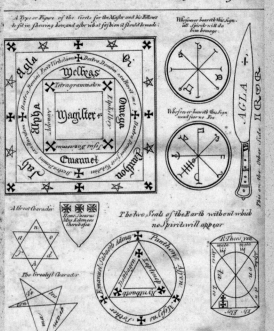

Notes on a Daughters of Lilith "convent" — read: whorehouse — outside of Barcelona. The address is a fake one, of course, though the street is real. She's still very much a cop at heart, keeping a log of her surveillance. The mentions of the security served a twofold purpose; first to reinforce what would be seen in the second issue of the series, but also to set up the inclusion of the next bit…

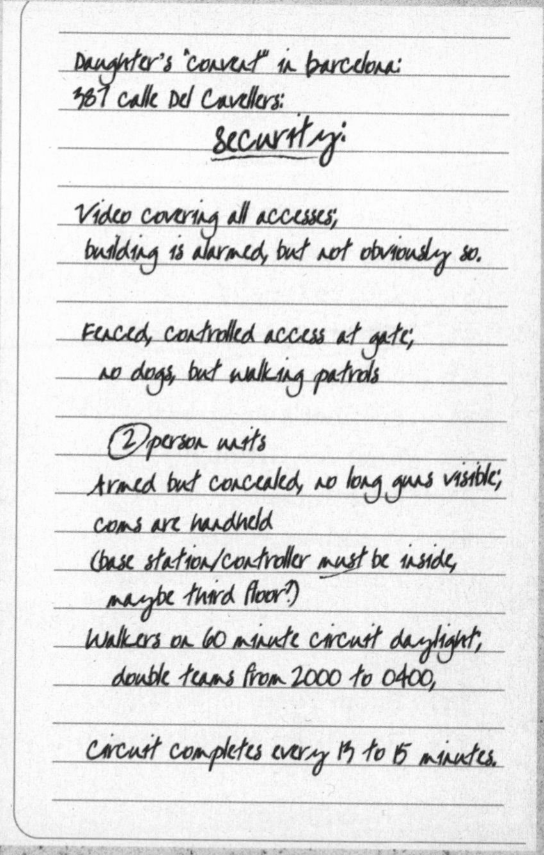
Daughter's "convent" in barcelona:
387 calle Del Cavellers:
Security:

Video covering all accesses;
building is alarmed, but not obviously so.

Fenced, controlled access at gate;
no dogs, but walking patrols

(2) person units
Armed but concealed, no long guns visible;
coms are handheld
(base station/controller must be inside,
maybe third floor?)
Walkers on 60 minute circuit daylight,
double teams from 2000 to 0400,

Circuit completes every 13 to 15 minutes.

…namely, these "nightvision" camera photos of the Question, apparently lurking around the outside of the aforementioned convent. To make these, Jen dressed up in a peacoat and fedora, and I took pictures of her lurking around our neighbor's yard. Trautmann, with the use of Photoshop, did the rest. We actually used three different photos, but including only one per journal, as a way to maintain variety amongst the journals.

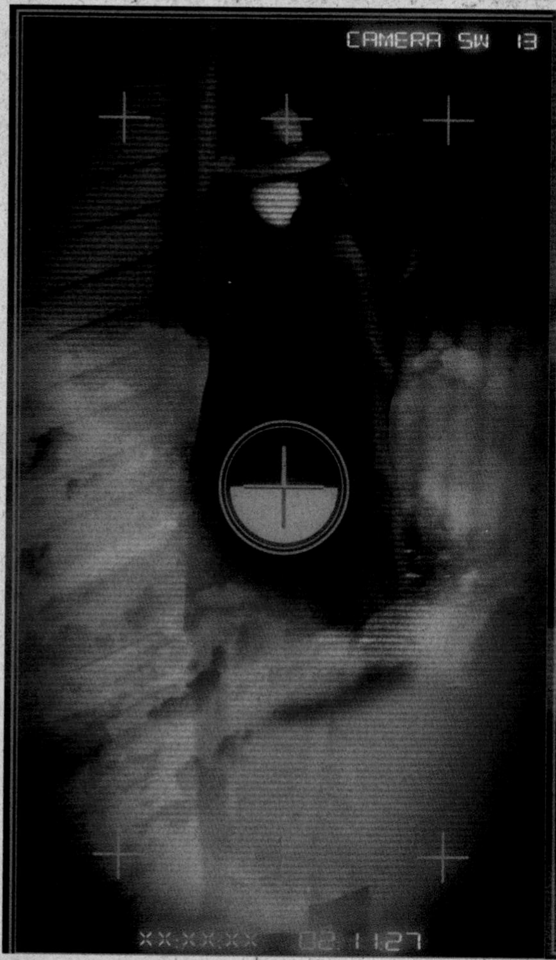
CAMERA SW 13
XXXXXX 02:11:27

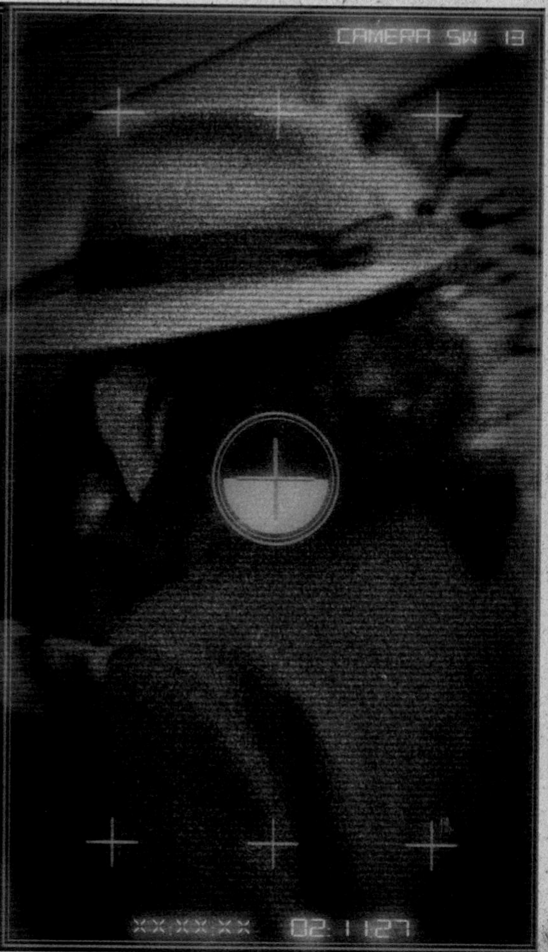
CAMERA SW 13
XXXXXX 02:11:27

CONFIDENTIAL

SET LIST

1) He's Coming, Look Busy
2) Hard as Stone
3) Zeta to Omega
4) Ashes All Fall Down
5) NullVoidFinalDemise
6) Prophet's Progress
7) Lust for Granny
8) Breath Last
9) Weakness Needs
10) Power Eats Its Young

ENCORE:

11) Boom Tube
12) Red Right Hand (Cover)

SECOND ENCORE:

13) High Madame's Slave

PROPERTY OF StarDoG Management, METROPOLIS.

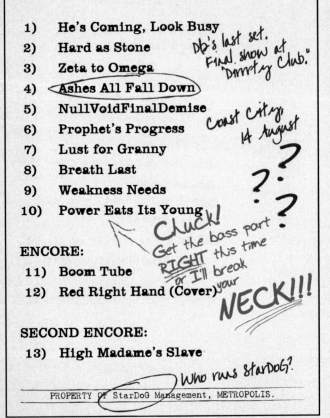

Db's last set. Final show at "Drrrty Club."

Coast City, 14 August

? ? ?

Chuck! Get the bass part RIGHT this time or I'll break your NECK!!!

Who runs StarDoG?

The investigation turns to a band called Darkseid's Bitch, a name, incidentally, I'd been dying to use for a band since I'd come up with it years ago. The band is a take on the death-metal rock-as-cult cliché. Renee, of course, begins following the band on their tour; in her journal, we mixed actual venues with fictional DCU ones. Here's the set list she cribs from their Coast City show, with notes by the bands lead singer, "serration," AKA Walter Minstassa. This was printed on just plain old printer paper, then crumpled, rumpled, and folded.

梶村古書・骨董店
完全予約制

店主　粢 武蔵野 & 本朝 吉祥寺

〒101-0021
東京都神田神保町5-6-1
電話: (03)5432-1098

KAJIMURA BOOKS AND ANTIQUES
By Appointment Only

KICHIJOJI HONCHO & MUSASHINO SHI
PROPRIETORS

5-6-1 KANDA-JINBOCHO, CHIYODA-KU
TOKYO
〒101-0021
JAPAN
TEL: (03) 5432-1098

The early pages of the journal consisted of Renee's notes regarding the differing editions of the "true" Black Book that she had either come across in research, or had been able to put her hands on during the course of *52*. In searching out other editions, she visited a bookseller in Tokyo, and our initial intent had been to include his business card, with some information scrawled on the back. The card itself was designed by Trautmann, of course, and the text on the "printed" face was provided by my brother, Nick, who — among his many skills — is fluent in both spoken Japanese and Kanji. Ultimately, the cards were excluded for a multitude of reasons, not the least of which being time and cost.

And suddenly Serration ends up dead. This is the coroner's report, or, actually, a photocopy of the coroner's report, our logic being that Renee wouldn't actually steal the real thing. Most of the work for this was done in Adobe Illustrator by Trautmann, including the stressing to the "paper" to give it the photocopied and smudged appearance. When included in the journal, there was an additional red stamp marking the page "Confidential."

Two different toe tags, taken from Serration's body. The discrepancy is deliberate, to imply that there's something suspicious about the cause of death, that, perhaps, a cover-up is taking place. Again, only one version was included in each journal, so, depending on which one you got, Serration either OD'ed or died from a GSW. These were printed on a cut-up manila file folder, then trimmed, punched, reinforced, and had a string added for easy toe-fitting.

What we can't show you here is that there were two small, glassine envelopes also stapled to the appropriate journal page. In one envelope were two small white "pills," potentially what Serration OD'ed on; in the other were two spent bullet cartridges, 9mm, though some people got .45s. The pills, incidentally, were candies.

COAST COUNTY
OFFICE OF THE SHERIFF—CORONER
CORONER'S REPORT

CLASSIFICATION: ACCIDENTAL DEATH / OVERDOSE CASE: 11-0815
DECENT: ___Mintassa___ ___Walter___ ___Philip___
                          LAST   FIRST   MIDDLE

DATE REPORTED: 08-15-06 TIME REPORTED: 0345 HOURS
DATE OF DEATH: 08-15-06 TIME OF DEATH: Approx. 0130 HOURS
AKA: "Serration" (Profes. Name) Other I.D.: DL#: 019MIN4122
DOB: 04-01-82 AGE: 24 YEARS (UNDER 1 YEAR: xxx MONTHS xxx DAYS)
SEX: Male RACE: Cauc. EST HGT: 5'10 EST WGT: 175 lbs.
HAIR: DK. BR. EYES: DK. BR. SOCIAL SEC#:
USUAL ADDRESS: SUITE A, MONARCH HOTEL
    COAST CITY
    CITY   STATE   ZIP: PHONE#:

IDENTIFIED BY: Reisch, Glenna DATE: 08-15-06 TIME: 0830 HOURS
ADDRESS and PHONE#: "StarDog Management", 14410 Avenue of Tomorrow
    Suite 44B, METROPOLIS, USA.
OTHER INVESTIGATING AGENCY: Coast City Metro PD, Narcotics Bureau Task Force
AGENCY FILE#: CCNA01991-29-B ASSIGNED OFFICER: Det. Srt. Gil Broome, CCPD

NEXT OF KIN

    NONE
  NAME OF LEGAL NEXT OF KIN   RELATIONSHIP TO THE DECEASED

ADDRESS:

RESIDENCE PHONE#:   BUSINESS PHONE#:

  Reisch, Glenna   Manager / Business Assoc.
  AUTHORIZED ALTERNATE NEXT OF KIN   RELATIONSHIP TO THE DECEASED
RESIDENCE PHONE#: (555) 421-0221 BUSINESS PHONE#: (555) 421-9549
LEGAL NOK NOTIFIED BY: Det. W. Lowry AGENCY: Coast City Metro PD.
NOTIFIED DATE: 08-15-06 TIME: 0630 HOURS HOW: IN PERSON.

REPORTED BY DEPUTY CORONER: R. Munoz.

COAST COUNTY SHERIFF CORONER'S REPORT

COAST COUNTY MEDICAL EXAMINER

NAME OF DECEASED CASE NO.: 11-0815
Walter Mintassa

AGE	SEX	RACE	WEIGHT	HEIGHT
24	Male	Caucasian.	175 Lbs.	5 Feet, 10 in.

PLACE OF DEATH Hotel Monarch, 1919 Front Street DATE OF DEATH Aug. 15, 2006
CAUSE OF DEATH Multiple Gunshot Wounds
PHYSICIAN Dr. V. Penrose
FUNERAL DIRECTOR Mr. L. Dent, Foster Mortuaries
COMMENTS Do not release; open investigation.

ATTACH TO TOE
CCME NO. TT-40001

COAST COUNTY MEDICAL EXAMINER

NAME OF DECEASED CASE NO.: 11-0815
Walter Philip Mintassa.

AGE	SEX	RACE	WEIGHT	HEIGHT
24.	Male.	Cauc.	175 lbs.	5' 10".

PLACE OF DEATH Monarch Hotel 1919 Front St. Coast City. DATE OF DEATH 15 August, 2006.
CAUSE OF DEATH Overdose.
PHYSICIAN Dr. Matthew Farrelly.
FUNERAL DIRECTOR Mr. Lawrence Dent, Foster Mortuaries.
COMMENTS Release to Next-of-Kin; Investigation closed.

ATTACH TO TOE
CCME NO. TT-40001

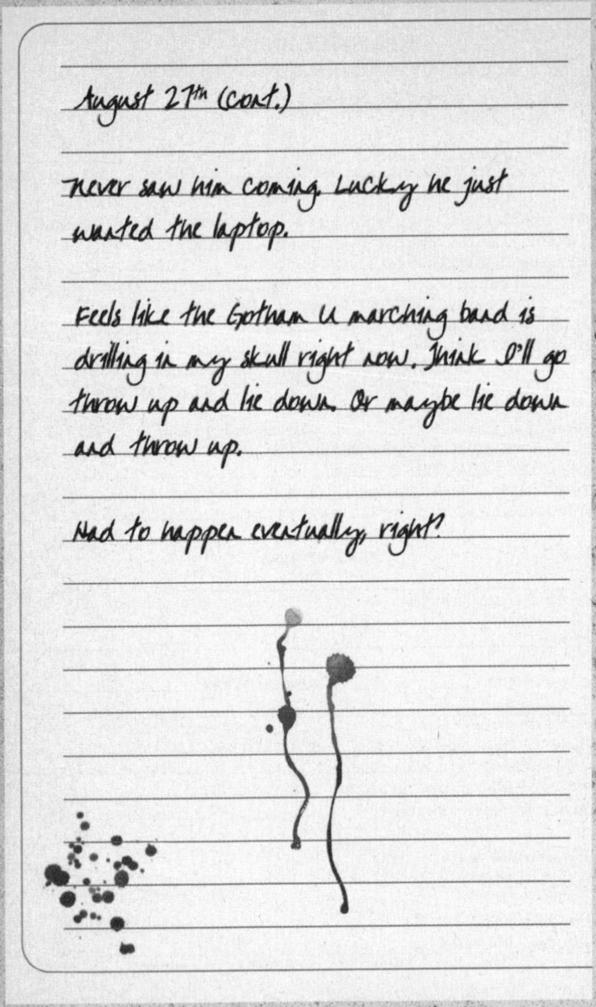

August 27th (cont.)

Never saw him coming. Lucky he just wanted the laptop.

Feels like the Gotham U marching band is drilling in my skull right now. Think I'll go throw up and lie down. Or maybe lie down and throw up.

Had to happen eventually, right?

Renee follows the trail back to Europe, investigating the band's manager. Then the manager dies mysteriously, and Montoya breaks into her hotel room to steal her laptop, presumably full of secrets. On this page, we learn that she's been mugged by a mystery thug — he's actually Flay, from the series, but she doesn't know that yet. I like this page not just because of what it reveals about Renee's sardonic sense of humor, but because Trautmann decided she was still bleeding when she wrote it, hence the blood-spatter. We thought about using real blood, but decided that was taking things too far. It's just ink.

GOTHAM GAZETTE

Your World. Your Way. On Your Doorstep.™

HOLY STRIKE OUT!

GOLIATHS STRIKE METRPOLIS
Fans, managemen
"Shuster Cur
SPORTS/B1

INTERNATIONAL EDITION — WED. ,SEPTEMBER 19, 2007

14 KILLED IN BARCELONA HOTEL BLAZE

FOUR AMERICAN TOURISTS AMONG THE DEAD

E. Roberts-Sanchez — Barcelona Correspondent

BARCELONA, Spain—FOURTEEN people, including four members of a tour group from Gotham City (US), are dead after a fire destroyed the St. Gervasi hotel on the Carrer De Vilarôs in the early hours this morning.

The cause of the blaze remains unknown, though investigators have not yet ruled out arson. "We are pursuing all active leads," according to Inspector Baldomero Marrero of the *Guardia Urbana Barcelona*.

Two responding firefighters, Ernesto Ruiz and Elian Ramírez de Arroyo died when part of the structure collapsed, trapping both men inside.

Officers from the Spanish Consulate in Gotham have notified the families of the victims, and have expressed deep regret for the incident.

The four American dead were part of an excursion group from the Gotham-based Far Ventures travel agency. "We're shocked to hear of the tragic events this morning," said Robert Nicols, Public Relations Manager for Far Ventures. "We've never, in over twenty years of arranging such excursions, had any kind of serious mishap. Tragic. Just terrible." ■

PHOTO: PAOLO ALVAREZ

Emergency response units attempt to put out the blaze. Firefighters Ernesto Ruiz and Elian Ramirez de Arroyo were killed in the conflagration, which claimed 14 lives.

KIDNAPPED IN BIALYA!

...is this a coincidence? Fire seems to be centered on my room. Who knew I was there?

DAUGHTER OF U.N. OFFICIAL CAPTURED BY INSURGENTS. PRIVATE MILITARY SECURITY FORCE MASSACRED.

R. al-Wazir — Middle East Correspondent

QADIYAH, BIALYA—MADELEINE Desmarais, the eight-year old daughter of the United Nations security attaché to Bialya, was seized by an insurgent faction in a bloody afternoon raid in Qadiyah, the southern capitol district of the ravaged nation, Bialya. The brutal attack cost the lives of an estimated 12 security troops, employed by Permanent Solutions, Inc., a Star City-based private military contractor.

Bialya, recently the site of a major metahuman conflict between the former ruler of Kahndaq, "Black Adam," and an international coalition of superheroes, has since been

And then the hotel she's staying in burns to the ground. This is, possibly, the one prop that took the most time, because the whole of the page had to be mocked up from scratch. The lead story, of course, is about the fire, but below the fold, the second story actually referenced the arc Trautmann and I were working on for CHECKMATE at the time (CHECKMATE #21 and #22, if you're interested).

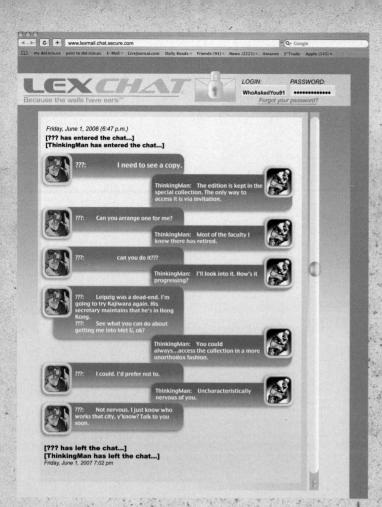

LEXCHAT
Because the walls have ears℠

LOGIN: PASSWORD:
WhoAskedYou91   ●●●●●●●●●●●●●●
Forgot your password?

Friday, June 1, 2006 (6:47 p.m.)
[??? has entered the chat...]
[ThinkingMan has entered the chat...]

???: I need to see a copy.

ThinkingMan: The edition is kept in the special collection. The only way to access it is via invitation.

???: Can you arrange one for me?

ThinkingMan: Most of the faculty I knew there has retired.

???: can you do it???

ThinkingMan: I'll look into it. How's it progressing?

???: Leipzig was a dead-end. I'm going to try Kajiwara again. His secretary maintains that he's in Hong Kong.
???: See what you can do about getting me into Met U, ok?

ThinkingMan: You could always...access the collection in a more unorthodox fashion.

???: I could. I'd prefer not to.

ThinkingMan: Uncharacteristically nervous of you.

???: Not nervous. I just know who works that city, y'know? Talk to you soon.

[??? has left the chat...]
[ThinkingMan has left the chat...]
Friday, June 1, 2007 7:02 pm

Chronologically, this comes at the start of the journal, but it was included in the "pocket" at the back. It's a transcript of a chat between Renee and Tot, each with their unique handles, using the DCU's AIM equivalent, LexChat (and you just *know* that's gonna be secure, right?). Again, the whole interface was created by Trautmann. The man verges on obsessive-compulsive when it comes to details.

This was in the "pocket" as well, a telegram sent to Renee in Leipzig, after the death of the manager, but before returning to Barcelona and the unfortunate hotel fire. I've always been a fan of the telegram, and lament its passing in the world of IM and email, and it seemed to me a telegram would be the best way to get information to and from Nanda Parbat, where Tot was at the time. The mentions of "Richard" — Richard Dragon — and the routing notes at the bottom are of particular delight to me. When printed, this had a "RECEIVED" stamp slapped on it, and then I added a date and signature as appropriate. The signature, incidentally, read — illegibly —."E. Newsom." Don't tell him I was using his name, okay?

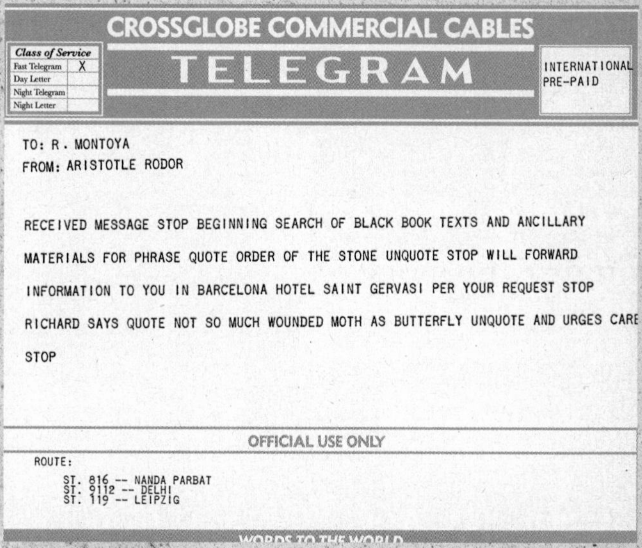

CROSSGLOBE COMMERCIAL CABLES

Class of Service	
Fast Telegram	X
Day Letter	
Night Telegram	
Night Letter	

TELEGRAM

INTERNATIONAL
PRE-PAID

TO: R. MONTOYA
FROM: ARISTOTLE RODOR

RECEIVED MESSAGE STOP BEGINNING SEARCH OF BLACK BOOK TEXTS AND ANCILLARY

MATERIALS FOR PHRASE QUOTE ORDER OF THE STONE UNQUOTE STOP WILL FORWARD

INFORMATION TO YOU IN BARCELONA HOTEL SAINT GERVASI PER YOUR REQUEST STOP

RICHARD SAYS QUOTE NOT SO MUCH WOUNDED MOTH AS BUTTERFLY UNQUOTE AND URGES CARE

STOP

OFFICIAL USE ONLY

ROUTE:
    ST. 816 -- NANDA PARBAT
    ST. 9112 -- DELHI
    ST. 119 -- LEIPZIG

WORDS TO THE WORLD

READ MORE OF THE DARK KNIGHT DETECTIVE'S ADVENTURES IN THESE COLLECTIONS FROM DC COMICS:

BATMAN

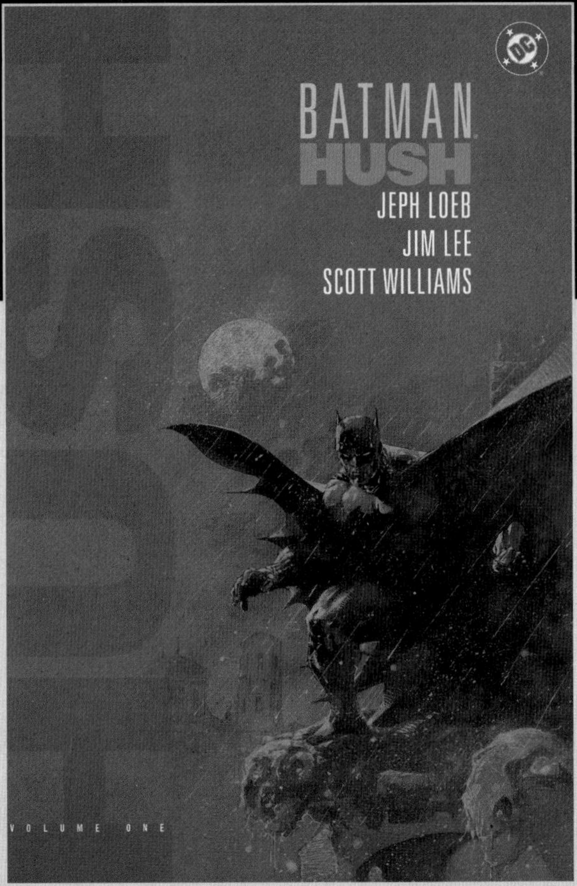
BATMAN
HUSH
JEPH LOEB
JIM LEE
SCOTT WILLIAMS
VOLUME ONE

BATMAN: HUSH VOLUME 1

Jeph Loeb, Jim Lee and **Scott Williams** tell an epic tale of friendship, trust and betrayal, in the first volume of a tale that spans a lifetime of the Dark Knight.

"THE ACTION IS EXCITING AND THE DETAIL IS METICULOUS."
— CRITIQUES ON INFINITE EARTHS

BATMAN:
THE DARK KNIGHT RETURNS

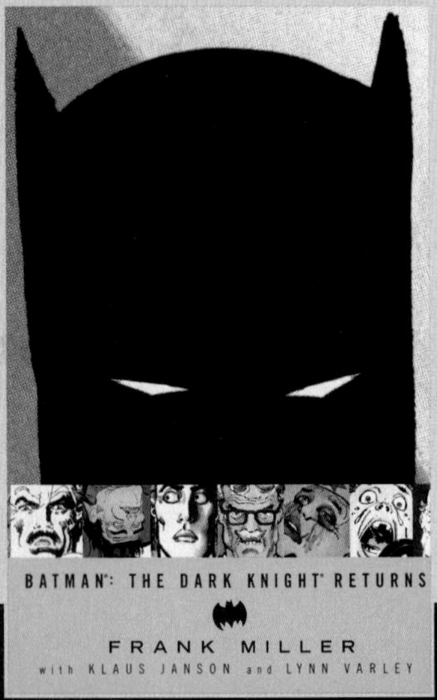
BATMAN: THE DARK KNIGHT RETURNS
FRANK MILLER
with KLAUS JANSON and LYNN VARLEY

FRANK MILLER
KLAUS JANSON
LYNN VARLEY

BATMAN:
THE LONG HALLOWEEN

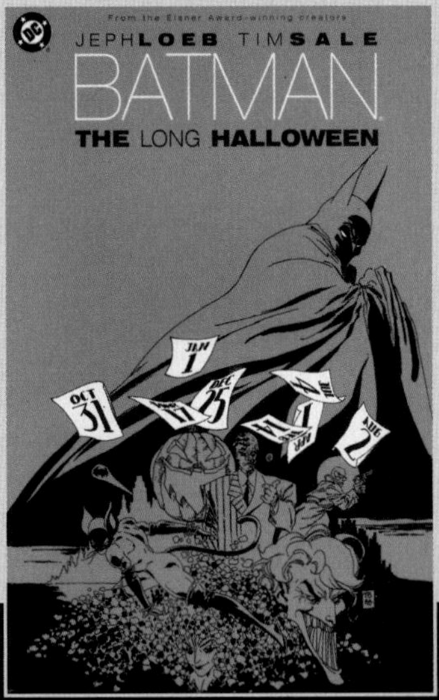
From the Eisner Award-winning creators
JEPH LOEB TIM SALE
BATMAN
THE LONG HALLOWEEN

JEPH LOEB
TIM SALE

BATMAN:
YEAR ONE

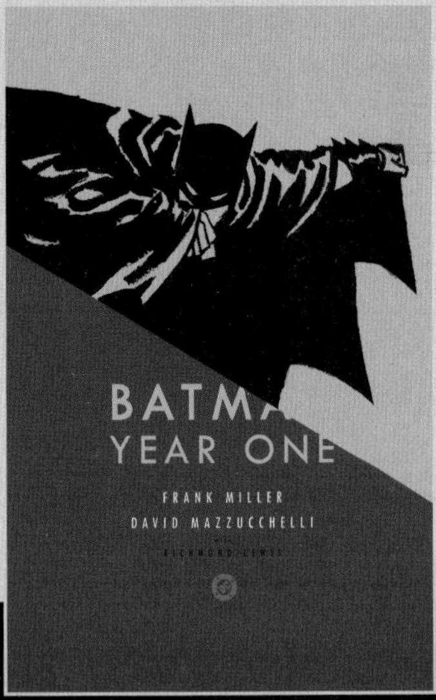
YEAR ONE
FRANK MILLER
DAVID MAZZUCCHELLI

FRANK MILLER
DAVID MAZZUCCHELLI

SEARCH THE GRAPHIC NOVELS SECTION OF
www.DCCOMICS.com
FOR ART AND INFORMATION ON ALL OF OUR BOOKS!